D0840741

# Essentials of Economic Evaluation in Healthcare

# Essentials of Economic Evaluation in Healthcare

## Rachel Elliott

BPharm, MRPharmS, PhD

Clinical Senior Lecturer
School of Pharmacy and Pharmaceutical Sciences
University of Manchester, UK

## Katherine Payne

BPharm, MRPharmS, MSc, PhD

Research Fellow in Health Economics
North West Genetics Knowledge Park (Nowgen)
Manchester, UK

London • Chicago  **Pharmaceutical Press**

**Published by the Pharmaceutical Press**

Publications division of the Royal Pharmaceutical Society of Great Britain

1 Lambeth High Street, London SE1 7JN, UK
100 South Atkinson Road, Suite 206, Grayslake, IL 60030-7820, USA

© Pharmaceutical Press 2005

(**PhP**) is a trade mark of Pharmaceutical Press

First published 2005

Text design by Barker/Hilsdon
Typeset by Gray Publishing, Tunbridge Wells, Kent
Printed in Great Britain by TJ International, Padstow, Cornwall

ISBN 0 85369 574 1

All rights reserved. No part of this publication may be
reproduced, stored in a retrieval system, or transmitted in any
form or by any means, without the prior written permission
of the copyright holder.
   The publisher makes no representation, express or implied,
with regard to the accuracy of the information contained in
this book and cannot accept any legal responsibility or
liability for any errors or omissions that may be made.

A catalogue record for this book is available from the British Library

# Contents

# Preface

This book was written primarily as an introduction to the use of economic evaluation of healthcare for undergraduate and postgraduate students of pharmacy, medicine, nursing and other healthcare professions. The level and presentation of material is designed for readers with little or no background in economics or health economics. Much of the material presented here is based on lectures and tutorials given by the authors to a range of students over the last 10 years.

Healthcare professionals require health economics to enable them to:

- Understand and critically appraise economic arguments proposed to support healthcare interventions, e.g. new drugs, or professional service development, e.g. screening services
- Participate in economic evaluations of treatments and services so that they are key players in national and local initiatives for resource allocation
- Initiate economic evaluations of services so that they direct the use of health economics in services provided by their profession
- Participate in the debate on and address wider policy issues, such as:
  - staff remuneration structures
  - need for, demand for and utilisation of services
  - reimbursement levels for healthcare.

The target audience for this book is students and qualified practitioners in pharmacy, medicine, dentistry, nursing and professions allied to medicine, health services researchers, and managers without a background in economics. It is not essential for all healthcare professionals to become health economists, and this is not the aim of this book. The level of complexity at which it is presented is based upon the following philosophy (Elliott and Noyce, 1998):

*Level 1*: All healthcare professionals should have an awareness and basic understanding of the following concepts:

- The finite nature of healthcare resources, leading to the need to make choices
- The economic impact of clinical policy decisions.

*Level 2*: All healthcare professionals should be able to evaluate an economic evaluation of a treatment with the aid of guidelines.

*Level 3*: A subset of healthcare professionals should have sufficient skills in health economics to enable them to:
- Use published economic evaluations in resource allocation and formulary decision-making
- Participate in the economic evaluation of treatments
- Produce information on the economic impact of healthcare services in bids for remuneration.

*Level 4*: A subset of healthcare professionals should have sufficient skills in health economics to enable them to:
- Work with health economists to develop more robust evaluation methodology
- Work with, and become, policy-makers on wider economic issues relating to health service provision.

A subset of people is required at Level 4. Individuals are encouraged to pursue these career paths, being made aware of training, research and employment opportunities.

If the reader works through the material in this introductory book, they will readily achieve Levels 1 and 2.

If the reader accesses the wide range of resources and further reading suggested throughout this book, they will be approaching the learning objectives at Level 3. Readers wishing to achieve competence in health economics above Levels 2 and 3 will find this book an essential introduction to the area, before moving on to more advanced texts that assume a higher level of knowledge.

We have assumed no previous knowledge in economics or health economics. If you work through the material in this book, our aim is that you will be able to:

1. Appreciate some of the theories of economics and their application to healthcare
2. Explain the concepts of scarcity and choice in healthcare
3. Understand why healthcare costs are rising

4. Examine ways of deciding how to allocate scarce resources based on efficiency
5. Discuss rationing
6. Demonstrate that costs extend beyond acquisition costs
7. Understand ways of measuring patient outcomes
8. Explain the different methods of economic evaluation and their application
9. Understand the process of economic evaluation and the use of decision analysis
10. Understand some key statistical methods used in the economic evaluation of treatments and services
11. Appreciate the use of discrete choice methods to value preferences for treatments and services.

If you are going to teach health economics and economic evaluation, familiarity with the key texts recommended in Chapter 12 is strongly advised. You may also consider attending a short introductory course in health economics. The contact addresses in Chapter 12 will provide you with places to start investigating these.

The worked examples and self-directed study exercises at the end of each chapter can be used and adapted for group work, written assignments and examination questions. We have tried to provide a wide range of published studies in each chapter. Students will benefit from reading some of these key texts and then assimilating the principles presented in them through group discussion or written essays.

The book is arranged in three sections. Chapter 1 provides an overview of economic theories that are relevant to healthcare, and upon which economic evaluation of healthcare is based. Chapter 2 discusses the phenomenon of healthcare rationing, which is the key economic issue in healthcare worldwide.

Chapters 3–9 take the reader through the various information and stages required to understand and use economic evaluations of healthcare. Chapters 3 and 4 describe in detail costs and outcomes, which are the main components of economic evaluation. These two chapters are a prerequisite for the remainder of the book. Chapters 5, 6 and 7 describe the main types of economic evaluation: cost-effectiveness, cost–utility and cost–benefit analysis. The use of decision analysis to design economic evaluations is described in Chapter 8. Chapter 9 completes this section by explaining how to assess the quality of economic evaluations and how they can be used in decision-making.

Chapters 10 and 11 present more advanced topics in economic evaluation. Chapter 10 explains the use of statistical methods in economic evaluations. Chapter 11 explains the use of discrete-choice experiments to measure preferences in economic evaluations.

Finally, this book is intended for teaching purposes and not as a reference work. It is presented as an introduction, although topics are covered extensively and sufficiently for the target audience. Each chapter is planned to be self-contained, with cross-referencing between chapters.

We are indebted to innumerable people in the writing of this book. Although the text here is ours, over the last 10 years we have both been fortunate to study under, or work with, a great number of bright, generous and supportive health economists. We have both learnt new information and skills within a paradigm very different from that of our early training. More importantly, experience with this group of people and their discipline has expanded our awareness and taught us both to question both our own and other healthcare systems.

We have made every effort to ensure that the information contained in each chapter was correct at the time of writing.

Rachel Elliott and Katherine Payne
Manchester, 2004

## Reference

Elliott R, Noyce P (1998). Health economics at the Manchester Pharmacy School. *Pharm J* 261: 579–581.

# About the authors

Rachel Elliott studied pharmacy at the University of Bath and qualified as a pharmacist in 1989. She was a resident pharmacist and an intensive care clinical specialist pharmacist at Charing Cross Hospital, London. She completed a Department of Health-funded PhD in the economics of intensive care with Professor Martin Buxton at Brunel University in 1995. She has been a clinical senior lecturer in the School of Pharmacy and Pharmaceutical Sciences, University of Manchester, since 1996. She has been teaching therapeutics and health economics to undergraduate and postgraduate pharmacists and doctors for 10 years. She has used a wide range of economic research methods, including primary RCTs, observational studies, meta-analysis, simulation, survey, interview, willingness-to-pay and discrete-choice in anaesthesia, rheumatology, surgery, emergency hormonal contraception and medication adherence. She is one of very few pharmacists in the UK with training and experience in health economics. She has recently obtained a Harkness Fellowship in Healthcare Policy.

Katherine Payne qualified as a pharmacist in 1990 and worked as a hospital pharmacist for 3 years. She has a Diploma in Clinical Pharmacy and a Department of Health-funded MSc in Health Economics (York University). Her Master's dissertation was completed at the Pharmacoeconomics Centre, South Carolina University. From 1994 to 2001 she worked as a researcher in the Academic Pharmacy Practice Unit, University of Manchester. In 2000, she completed a joint Medical Research Council/North West Region Special Training Fellowship PhD evaluating the managed entry of drugs. Since September 2003 she has been the health economist for the North West Genetics Knowledge Park (Nowgen). Her research areas include patients' preferences for equity in joint replacement surgery; economic evaluation of various health technologies including pharmacogenetics; designing outcome measures; and valuing preferences for genetic services. She teaches health economics to postgraduate pharmacists. Since 2003 she has been a member of a National Institute for Clinical Excellence Appraisal Committee.

# Abbreviations

| | |
|---|---|
| CA | conjoint analysis |
| CBA | cost–benefit analysis |
| CEA | cost-effectiveness analysis |
| CEAcc | cost-effectiveness acceptability curve |
| CMA | cost-minimisation analysis |
| CUA | cost–utility analysis |
| DCE | discrete choice experiment |
| ECT | electroconvulsive therapy |
| EQ-5D | Euroqol 5 Domains |
| $FEV_1$ | forced expiratory volume in 1 second |
| GP | general practitioner |
| HRQoL | health-related quality of life |
| HUI | Health Utilities Index |
| HYE | healthy year equivalents |
| ICER | incremental cost-effectiveness ratio |
| IHD | ischaemic heart disease |
| ISPOR | International Society of Pharmacoeconomic and Outcomes Research |
| MDD | major depressive disorder |
| MS | multiple sclerosis |
| NHP | Nottingham Health Profile |
| NHS | National Health Service |
| NHSEED | National Health Service Economic Evaluation Database |
| NICE | National Institute for Clinical Excellence |
| PCT | Primary Care Trust |
| QALY | quality adjusted life year |
| QoL | quality of life |
| QWB | quality of wellbeing |
| RAG | Rationing Advisory Group |
| RCT | randomised controlled trial |
| SD | standard deviation |
| SIP | Sickness Impact Profile |

SSRI        serotonin-specific receptor inhibitor
TCA         tricyclic antidepressant
WTP         willingness to pay

# 1

# Overview of health economics

## Introduction

Economics is a diverse discipline. Economics uses theories and methods to study the behaviour of people involved with allocating resources and aiming to reach some optimum situation. Health economics applies the same theories to health and healthcare.

In a similar manner to healthcare professionals, economists have their own language, using terms and concepts with specific meanings. '*Agent*' is the term economists use to describe people who may be *producers* (manufacturers, suppliers, hospitals, doctors) or *consumers* (general public, service users or patients) of goods or services. The producers are the people who manufacture and/or provide these goods and services. Consumers are people who want to buy or use (demand) goods (such as apples, cars or medicines) or services (such as a dry cleaning service or a cholesterol screening service). Both consumers and producers are viewed as trying to reach an optimum situation, such as 'maximising utility' or 'maximising profits'. Maximising utility can be described simply in terms of a person (consumer) getting the highest level of satisfaction (benefit) from a good (or service). Maximising profits usually involves a firm achieving the largest difference between the cost of making or providing a good (or service) compared with the market price of that product.

There are two main branches of economics: *macroeconomics* and *microeconomics*. Macroeconomics involves the study of entire economies in terms of the production (supply) and consumption (demand) of all goods and services, income earned, the use of resources, and the behaviour of market prices. These goods and services can involve anything, such as healthcare, education or defence. Macroeconomics covers economic concepts that look at issues on a large scale, such as gross national products and consumer price indices. Microeconomics is the study of the economic behaviour of individual consumers, firms and industries. It focuses on smaller-scale issues such as markets and the allocation of resources within, for example, a national health service.

Microeconomic theories exist that explore how the output of a firm relates to the inputs to that firm, such as items of capital and labour (production function).

Two theories used by microeconomists to describe human behaviour are the *theory of the firm* and the *theory of the consumer*. The *theory of the firm* aims to explain the behaviour of profit-maximising agents. The *theory of the consumer* looks at the behaviour of utility-maximising agents. A full description of theories and the difference between micro- and macro-economics is beyond the scope of this book. There are a number of useful economic texts where the interested reader can learn more about the basics of macro- and microeconomic theory (see Further reading, p. 23).

The overall aim of this book is to present an introduction to the methods of *economic evaluation*. This chapter is not intended to be a comprehensive description of all economic theories relevant to healthcare. It gives a brief introduction to some of the concepts relevant to microeconomics, but focuses on the main concepts that underpin the methods of economic evaluation. The interested reader will be directed to relevant further reading throughout.

## Healthcare economics or health economics?

There is an implicit assumption that healthcare services lead to changes in levels of health. If we are experiencing unwanted health-related symptoms, such as a painful knee, we may decide to go and see a doctor. The doctor may suggest an analgesic and is therefore providing a healthcare service. The aim of seeing the doctor is to remove the unwanted symptoms – the painful knee – and improve our health (health gain). The term 'health' itself is not easily defined. There is no universally agreed definition. Health itself is not just a product of healthcare interventions but may also be due to a person's social environment. Furthermore, there is no obvious and direct link between healthcare and resulting health status. Some economists have preferred to use the term 'healthcare economics'. McGuire *et al.* (1992) provide a useful discussion of the terms health and healthcare economics and the relationship between them.

## Why the interest in health economics?

In the UK, expenditure on the provision of a national health service is steadily increasing. Furthermore, there is the potential for expenditure on health service provision to rise in the future. A number of reasons have been suggested as to why expenditure has increased and may continue to do so.

The UK is experiencing changing demographic trends with respect to the age of the population. The average life expectancy is now 8 years longer than when the NHS was established in 1948, and mortality associated with birth and early childhood is also falling. The cost of treating the very young and the very old is proportionally much higher than that of providing healthcare to an individual of working age. Hence, as the percentage of very young and very old in the whole population increases, the cost of health service provision will increase disproportionately.

There have been many significant advances in the technologies used in the NHS since its inception. Generally, these newer modes of treatment are more expensive than existing methods. As new technologies are developed, the population expects that they should be made more freely available. One example is the advancement of joint replacement: this is now often considered a routine operation and is readily demanded by people with hip or knee pain.

Providing an NHS is labour intensive. As more advanced technologies are used it may be necessary to employ staff at higher grades to use these technologies and develop supportive training packages. To illustrate, the use of genetic information may have an effect on the knowledge base and skill mix of the NHS workforce, with increased requirements for general practitioners, pharmacists and nurses to understand and use new genetic-based tests and treatments. These trends all have potential cost implications for a future healthcare workforce.

Clinicians are now working in an environment with an increased threat of litigation. Consequently, they may be more likely to practise defensive medicine, possibly as a compensatory mechanism: they may intervene earlier in the disease process and do so more intensively. A practical example of where defensive medicine may be observed is with the increased rate of caesarian section births.

Generally, the UK population is taking less exercise, eating more food with low nutritional value, and consuming more alcohol and tobacco. This decline in 'healthy living habits' is matched by an increase in the incidence of heart, lung and peripheral vascular disease. These conditions all have resource implications for the NHS.

## Scarcity and choice and the NHS

The budget for healthcare is, and always will be, finite. The NHS is allocated a fixed budget and works within a 'closed system'. Resources – the inputs into providing a healthcare service – are in limited supply. They are scarce. In theory, all resources available for a particular financial year can have alternative uses within this system. When new health technologies or services are developed they will have to compete with existing technologies or services within the available healthcare budget. Given that the NHS is operating under a system with scarce resources, decision-makers involved with commissioning healthcare services and service providers must make choices and prioritise which treatments should be funded (Box 1.1).

'Prioritising' or 'rationing' healthcare resources may seem to be a modern development. However, the need to make choices about resource allocation has been with the NHS since its inception in 1948. Twenty-years ago, the Royal Commission on the NHS said that, 'the demand for healthcare is always likely to outstrip supply and ... the capacity of health services to absorb resources is almost unlimited. Choices have therefore to be made about the use of available funds and priorities have to be set. The more pressure there is on resources, the more important it is to

---

**Box 1.1**   Some choices that may be necessary when providing a national health service

**What?**
Should a hospital pharmacy department provide a ward service or expand the out-patient clinic?

**When?**
Should a population of people with asthma be treated with steroids at the first signs of worsening symptoms, or wait until they have experienced one acute attack?

**What level?**
Should everyone in the UK be given the influenza vaccine on the NHS?

**How and where to provide services**
**How?**
Should a consultant geneticist or a nurse trained in genetic counselling provide a genetic counselling service?

**Where?**
Should a genetic counselling service be provided in primary care or in a specialist centre in a hospital?

**Who should get the services?**
Should younger people (aged 50–75 years) or older people (over 75 years) be offered a total joint replacement?

get the priorities clear' (Royal Commission, 1979). However, it is clear that the methods decision-makers use to set priorities or 'ration' healthcare programmes are changing. Chapter 2 provides a more detailed account of rationing in the modern NHS.

## Rational decision-making

The term 'rational' is used throughout the economics and health services research literature. It may be viewed differently depending on the perspective taken. In 1994, *A prescription for improvement: towards more rational prescribing in general practice* referred to rational prescribing as that which 'takes account of efficiency, safety, appropriateness and economy – not cheaper prescribing' (Gilley, 1994).

The concepts of 'rational' and 'appropriate' prescribing were compared and contrasted by Buetow *et al.* (1997), who described how they view appropriateness as 'the outcome of a process of decision-making that maximises net individual health gains within society's available resources. This definition distinguishes between (in)appropriate prescribing, as an outcome, and (ir)rational prescribing as a process'. They described how 'prescribing is rational when prescribers logically process the information available to them, whereas erroneous reasoning describes irrational prescribing'.

### The theory of the consumer

The *theory of the consumer* (consumer behaviour) examines how rational individuals make consumption choices when faced with limited resources (Frank, 1997). Rational decision-making by consumers has been clearly defined in terms of four requirements:

- The decision-maker sets out all the feasible alternatives, rejecting any that are not feasible.
- S/he takes into account whatever information is readily available, or worth collecting, to assess the consequences of choosing each of the alternatives.
- In the light of their consequences s/he ranks the alternatives in order of preference, where this ordering satisfies certain assumptions of completeness and consistency.
- S/he chooses the alternative highest in this ordering, i.e. the alternative with the consequences s/he prefers over all others available to her/him.

Consumer theory states that consumers demand goods (or services) to maximise satisfaction (*utility*) given the available budget constraints. At the centre of consumer demand theory lie the basic principles of *expected utility theory*. This is the theory (developed by von Neumann and Morgenstern, 1944) of choice between alternatives that have an uncertain outcome. The theory says that people will choose an alternative with the highest expected utility. Expected utility is calculated from the product of the utility of an outcome times the probability of outcome occurring for all possible outcomes (utility of outcome × p [outcome]). The interested reader is directed to an introductory economic text which simply outlines the assumptions underpinning the theory of the consumer (Frank, 1997) (see Worked example 1.1).

**WORKED EXAMPLE 1.1** Requirements for the theory of the consumer

This example aims to illustrate how the 'requirements of rationality' seem to be fairly consistent with the decisions we all make on a day-to-day basis.

Imagine you have decided to replace your car. You are trying to decide which type, make and age of car to buy.

1. **What is the average amount of money available for you to spend each year?**
   Your annual salary will probably be the major source of your 'annual budget' for spending on goods, such as a car. We all have a limited amount of money and resources available to us. Some of us may be taking home £100,000 a year, but for others a more realistic income would be £15,000 a year.

2. **What types and makes of car are available to you, bearing in mind your annual salary?**
   Prepare a list of makes and types of cars that you would like to buy, no matter what the cost. Now add the market price for each car to this list. The price is guided by the market, which reflects the supply and demand for each make of car.

*Continued*

Now discard all the makes and types of car that, given your average income, you know you cannot afford.

The amount of resources available determines what options we can afford. If we were looking to buy a new car and earned £100,000 a year then we would probably be looking at different makes and types of car than if we earned £15,000 a year. An Aston Martin would not be a feasible option if we earned £15,000 a year.

3. **Which car would you choose from those that remain on your list?**
Given that we have identified the feasible set of alternatives (the cars we could afford to buy), we then attempt to pick the best car. We will base that decision on information about the cars available. To do this we need complete information on each car. This information may be about miles achieved per gallon of fuel, the type of fuel the car uses, the engine size, and perhaps the availability of different colours. We may use car brochures, experts, and our experience from test-driving the car to collect this information.

The final choice of car is guided by our preferences and probability or objectives for buying the car. Our preferences may be based on the top speed of the car, the colour, or the miles achieved per gallon of fuel. The objective of buying the car may simply be to get from A to B. We may also have more complex objectives, such as to get from A to B as safely as possible, or to get from A to B as safely as possible but also in style.

We use these preferences and objectives to place the cars in an order of preference. When doing this we must make sure we have completeness and consistency in our preferences. If we decide colour is the only important attribute, and we prefer a black car, then we must place all black cars ahead of other cars with different colours. We must also make sure that we rank all the options. We may decide that we are indifferent between two cars and cannot choose between them. This is fine, but we must be 'complete' in our preference ordering and be able to state a preference for all the cars from our list of feasible alternatives.

*Continued*

> The car at the top of this list will be the one we choose to buy. This car will have the majority of preferred attributes. It will be the best possible alternative given the amount of money we have to spend.

Aspects of the theory of the consumer may be applied to healthcare and the valuation of preferences. For example, the assumption of completeness in preferences forms the basis for valuation tools such as standard gamble, time trade-off, willingness to pay and discrete choice experiments (see Chapters 6, 7 and 11).

## The market for healthcare

The users (consumers) of the NHS and the service providers may be viewed as agents with a role in a (hypothetical) healthcare market. Primary Care Trusts, NHS Hospital Trusts, clinicians, allied healthcare professionals, and current and future patients act as economic agents within the market system. In the UK, the concept of healthcare being supplied in a market system was made explicit with the formation of the 'internal' market (McGuire, 1996). Health authorities and fund-holding general practitioners (GPs) were defined as healthcare purchasers who demanded drugs, services and treatments for their patient populations. NHS Trusts and GPs provided healthcare for patient populations. The 'internal' market was abolished in 1999, but the provision of healthcare in the UK may still be viewed as if it acts under market forces.

A market is made up of a system of suppliers and demanders. Box 1.2 illustrates some of the potential agents in a healthcare market. The careful reader will note that GPs have been placed as both suppliers and demanders. Doctors, acting as the patients' agents, may both 'supply' and 'demand' medicines (or services). They have what is termed 'a duality of roles'. A doctor will supply a drug, via an NHS prescription, to a patient who has presented him/herself to the surgery or hospital ward. The same doctor will demand a medicine from the health provider (in the UK a Health Authority or NHS Trust), who may use a committee, such as a Medicines Management Committee, to decide whether the medicine should be available for use in practice subject to the available budget.

Price is used as a reflection of consumer valuations of a good. The higher value a consumer attaches to a good, the higher its price will be. An Aston Martin car is marketed at a higher price than a Ford Escort.

---

**Box 1.2**  Supply and demand

Ideally:

*Providers supply*                    = *Purchasers demand*
Hospitals                             Health authorities
GPs                                   GPs
Community pharmacists                 *Consumers*

SUPPLY = DEMAND

Healthcare service providers perfectly meet the 'needs' of their local population.

In practice:

SUPPLY < **DEMAND**

---

Furthermore, consumers with the requisite amount of funds have purchased an Aston Martin rather than an Escort and indicated that there is some inherent value in doing so. Producers are therefore guided by consumers' valuations – the price signals. In an ideal world, consumer wants should be matched by producer demands (see Worked example 1.2).

---

**WORKED EXAMPLE 1.2**    The concept of supply and demand

Consider the example of a medicine for the management of mild to moderate Alzheimer's disease that was launched on to the market last year. There are 250 000 people in a local health authority. The Director of Public Health in that authority estimated that 1400 people have mild to moderate Alzheimer's disease. The pharmaceutical adviser estimated that 500 people were prescribed the new medicine in its first year on the market.

1.  **Who are the agents that will demand this medicine?**
    The agents demanding this medicine may be described at a number of levels. Each Primary Care Trust in the health authority will demand the medicine for its relevant patient population. Patients (or their carers) will demand the medicine for themselves (or the person they care for).

*Continued*

2.  **Who are the agents that will supply this drug?**
    Similarly, the agents supplying this medicine may be described at a number of levels. They could be thought of as the people who make this medicine – the pharmaceutical industry. At a local level, the suppliers may be the psychogeriatricians, old age psychiatrists, or general practitioners who will use an NHS prescription as a route of supply.

3.  **How many people are eligible for treatment with the new medicine?**
    A total of 1400 people are eligible for the new medicine for mild to moderate Alzheimer's disease. This is the number of people who could potentially demand this new medicine.

4.  **How many people were prescribed the new medicine?**
    Around 500 people were prescribed the new medicine.

5.  **Has supply matched demand in this example?**
    In this example, 500 people were supplied the new medicine and 1400 could demand it. Supply was less than demand. In a perfectly competitive and efficient healthcare market, the price mechanism will ensure that the level of demand for the medicine will match the level of supply.

### Market failure in healthcare

The market for healthcare provision and this perfect situation of supply matching demand is almost never reached. This is because the market for healthcare fails to meet some of the basic assumptions necessary for a perfectly competitive market. There are a number of reasons for market failure in relation to healthcare in the UK. This is not an exhaustive list but provides some of the key reasons why the market for healthcare fails:

- *Imperfect information* on the quality and price of the healthcare good (service)
- *Moral hazard*
- *Agency relationship* between patients and healthcare providers
- *Supplier-induced demand*
- The presence of *externalities*.

*Imperfect information*

Consumers require perfect information on the quality and price of the healthcare good being supplied and used. This is virtually never the case for healthcare interventions. The information may not be perfect because it does not exist, or because healthcare consumers:

- do not know they need the information
- do not know where to get the information
- do not know the information they require exists
- are not able to correctly interpret and use the available information in practice
- or because the available information is incomplete and uncertain.

If we assume that the aim is to achieve the efficient use of resources, then perfect clinical and economic data must be both available and used to guide the decision-making process. Consumers should question whether interventions show the potential to improve the health of the potential recipients of the therapy and at what total cost. Evaluation of the added clinical and economic consequences of an intervention requires comparison with the current therapy option. Information is therefore required on both the intervention and the current therapy option. According to economic theory, imperfect information is one barrier to the efficient use of healthcare interventions because it can result in market failure.

*Moral hazard*

*Moral hazard* is when having some form of insurance cover makes you less careful. Consider the situation of car insurance. If your car is insured against theft then you may be less careful about where you leave it parked overnight. This is because you will not bear the cost of replacing the car if it is stolen. The NHS is a public provided system and people may view it as a form of health insurance because they are aware that their taxes go towards paying for the service. This may mean people are more likely to go and see their GP even when they are only experiencing minor symptoms, because they feel they have paid for 'cover' from the NHS. Moral hazard means that a higher level of service is demanded than would have been without the 'insurance cover', and so inefficiency is the result.

*Asymmetry of information*

Healthcare providers, such as GPs, often act as 'agents' for their patients. Patients may have to rely on other parties to help them make decisions regarding the use of healthcare interventions. Healthcare providers tend to be 'the experts' on the service (intervention) they provide. Typically, providers know more about the intervention than the patient, but it may be possible for the reverse to be true, with an 'expert patient' knowing more than a doctor who has no expertise in a particular area. With respect to healthcare there is generally an *'asymmetry of information'*. This imbalance in the level of knowledge is unlike most other situations we find ourselves in when deciding whether to buy something on a day-to-day basis: we are all probably quite clear about the potential benefits of a certain brand of cornflakes when we visit the supermarket.

### Supplier-induced demand

Providers, with their superior knowledge about health and healthcare interventions, are therefore in a position to influence demand for them. This phenomenon is called *'supplier-induced demand'* (SID). SID is important in relation to healthcare because there is a potential for exploitation on the part of the 'supplier'. Doctors may bring about a level of service use different from that which would have occurred if a fully informed patient had been able to choose freely which service or intervention to use. SID could result in greater (or less) use of an intervention than would have been the case if the patient had had the necessary information to decide whether s/he required treatment with it rather than the existing treatment for their condition.

### Externalities

*Externalities* are prevalent in healthcare markets. Economists use the term to describe the situation when the actions of a person (consumer) or groups of people (such as a firm) affect the wellbeing, or production levels, of another person (or firm). An externality (external effect) occurs if someone external to a transaction is directly affected by it and not compensated. Externalities may be positive (good) or negative (bad). There are a number of different types of externality (see Frank, 1997 for detail). Pollution by a pharmaceutical company making medicines, which causes nuisance or harm to people or wildlife, is an example of a *negative externality*. An individual planting an attractive garden in front of his house may benefit others living in the area, and this is an example of a *positive externality*. The use of vaccination programmes is an example of positive externality associated with healthcare provision. If an NHS Trust chooses to vaccinate older patients against influenza, then individuals who are not currently receiving the drug, such as NHS staff, are affected by its availability because the persons treated are less likely to spread infection. This is assuming that the vaccine is effective in controlling the symptoms of influenza and prevents elderly people from requiring hospitalisation. Externalities are important in economics because they may lead to inefficiency. This is because the producers of externalities do not have an incentive to take into account the effect of their actions on others. Therefore, the outcome of producing the good or service will be inefficient. There may be too much activity that causes negative externalities such as pollution, and not enough activity that creates positive externalities, relative to an optimal outcome.

Imperfect information, moral hazard, agency relationship, SID and externalities are just five examples why market failure is a potential problem in relation to healthcare provision and the introduction of drugs in the UK. The automatic outcome of a perfect market is efficiency. Market failure is important because it may lead to inefficiency in the healthcare market.

## Efficiency

*Efficiency* as a term is widely misused, particularly when referring to aspects of prescribing in the NHS. Its antonym *'inefficiency'* is often not clearly defined and may be considered synonymous with the term 'waste' (Rittenhouse, 1994). The concept of efficiency is core to many economic theories and methods of evaluation.

Welfare economics views efficiency in terms of achieving Pareto optimality (Pareto efficiency): 'A project is unequivocally desirable only if there are some gains and no one is made worse off' (Sloman, 1999).

A related concept presenting an alternative theory is the idea of a compensation test described by Hicks (1939) and Kaldor (1939). An intervention should be used if those who gain from the intervention can compensate (pay) the losers but still be better off. The compensation test forms one underlying rationale for cost–benefit analysis (see Chapter 7). An intervention should be used if the benefits exceed the costs. Using economics terms, these concepts involve consideration of value judgements or normative statements, which offer suggestions about how things ought to be. This is in contrast to positive statements, which describe how things are. Dolan and Abel Olsen (2002) provide a good basic introduction to some of these principles. The dedicated reader is directed towards Frank (1997), Sloman (1999) or Gravelle and Rees (1992) for an overview of the basic concepts of welfare economics.

Achieving efficiency in the NHS is about comparing the relative costs and benefits of competing healthcare programmes. Decision-makers who use this information can work towards ensuring that resources are allocated in such a way as to maximise health gains to society. Health economics in general, but more specifically economic evaluation, aims to provide decision-makers with a theoretical framework with which to inform resource allocation. Resources are the inputs into a good or service, and are valued in terms of costs. Economic theory suggests that costs should be valued in terms of opportunity cost.

## Opportunity cost

Choices have to be made about allocation of resources from a limited budget. One approach suggested by economists is to minimise 'opportunity cost'. All 'costs' in economics are valued in terms of their opportunity cost. Opportunity cost has been defined as the benefit that would be derived from using a resource in its best alternative use. Decisions made in the NHS have an opportunity cost attached to them. If a choice is made to use one medicine or service over an alternative, then there will be benefits forgone. Economists argue that the ideal way to prioritise treatments or programmes is to aim to minimise opportunity cost for a given level of benefit (see Worked example 1.3).

---

**WORKED EXAMPLE 1.3**   The concept of opportunity cost

Imagine you have just won £15,000. You are given three options to spend this money.

1.   **Which of the following three options would you choose?**
     (a)   Holiday
     (b)   Car
     (c)   Donate it to charity.

2.   **What were the benefits you identified with your choice?**
     If you selected the holiday you may have done this because you would benefit from time away from work and enjoying yourself with friends or family.

*Continued*

You may have selected a car because your current mode of transport is not satisfactory.

You may have decided to donate the money to charity because you feel there will be some benefit from being altruistic.

Here you are making choices about how to spend your money by attaching some measure of satisfaction, or *utility*, to each option. You are weighing up the benefits, given your preferences for each option.

3.   **What were the costs identified with your choice?**
If you selected the holiday you will not receive the potential benefits from the car or donating to charity. This is viewed as a cost or a lost opportunity.

Similarly, there are opportunity costs with not choosing whichever options you did not select.

Similarly, you could think about opportunity cost from the perspective of the NHS spending £15,000. Should it select:
(a)   five hip replacements
(b)   one heart transplant
(c)   a 1-year smoking cessation programme?

The main implication for using opportunity cost to inform the choice between competing health services is that any evaluation used to inform the decision should involve a comparison between at least two alternatives.

The 'efficient' ideal would be achieved if maximum health gain in a defined patient population were attained at the lowest opportunity cost. This may also be viewed as getting the most out of an intervention, given a defined budget. The relevant opportunity cost is defined by the perspective and time horizon (see Chapter 5).

## Allocative efficiency and technical efficiency

Economists further divide efficiency into two types: allocative and technical. These represent different breadths of perspective to society.

*Allocative efficiency* judges whether an activity is worth doing. In the case of a new service for cholesterol screening, allocative efficiency would address the question of whether it is worth having cholesterol screening as a policy compared to alternative uses of those resources in the provision of healthcare or other publicly funded goods or services. Cost–benefit analysis (see Chapter 7) is suggested as the appropriate method of economic evaluation to look at issues of allocative efficiency. *Technical efficiency* is relevant when the assumption that an activity is worth doing has been made, and judges the best way of providing it. For cholesterol screening, technical efficiency would assume that it is worthwhile in terms of a policy and then evaluate what is the best approach to use. Cost-effectiveness (utility) analysis is suggested as the relevant framework to use for questions of technical efficiency.

Application of the concept of efficiency to the NHS (or other organisations) implies that decision-makers are striving to reach an optimal situation. A key question is whether decision-makers are health maximisers. What output do decision-makers wish to achieve when using or recommending a healthcare intervention? Clinicians may be entirely concerned with maximising the health of their patient population. Finance managers may want to focus on cost minimisation to control their budget. Patients may want to maximise their satisfaction from the NHS given their budget constraint, which will be a different budget from that of the finance manager. It is important to be aware of the incentives driving decision-makers and their desired objectives in the context of health service provision. In using the methods of economic evaluation, health economists assume that the main objective of the NHS is to maximise health gain.

A more 'efficient' intervention may not necessarily be the cheaper one for the NHS to provide. The results of clinical studies may indicate that a new medicine or treatment regimen offers the potential to increase the health of a defined patient population, compared to current practice. However, the new medicine may be more expensive, in terms of acquisition price, than the existing therapy. Decision-makers must then, taking the societal perspective, evaluate the total incremental cost and benefit associated with using the new medicine. Furthermore, the impact on the drug budget must then be considered. This is where the value of a decision-maker's 'willingness to pay' for a given cost over unit of health gain (incremental cost-effectiveness ratio) must be defined. Chapter 6 describes this in more detail.

## Achieving efficiency and the role of economic evaluation

Economic evaluations can be used to determine whether efficiency has been achieved. They provide a framework for measuring efficiency. Economic evaluation involves comparison of the costs and benefits associated with alternative programmes or treatments. There are four methods of economic evaluation: cost-minimisation analysis; cost-effectiveness analysis; cost–utility analysis; and cost–benefit analysis. These are described in the relevant following chapters. Each of these methods may be used to quantify the costs and benefits attached to a programme or service. The role of economic evaluation is to aid the decision-making process, not replace it. Economic evaluations provide another type of information to guide the decision-making process. In general, decisions that compare the costs and consequences of an action should not be made on an individual basis, but rather when policies for populations of individuals are being formulated. These decisions need to be based on accurate, reliable and generalisable effectiveness and economic evidence.

## Efficiency and equity

Efficiency may not be the only endpoint decision-makers want to achieve. An efficient level of health service provision may leave many people in society dissatisfied with the outcome. There may be distributional or *equity* issues which have not been answered regarding who receives the benefits and who bears the cost. Efficiency looks at maximising benefit in one set of individuals; *equity* or fairness looks at interpersonal comparisons. An efficient option will not necessarily be equitable or fair.

Equity is a complex concept and comes in a number of guises. Several theories of social justice have been used to define equity. The interested reader is directed towards Dolan and Abel Olsen (2002) for a good introduction. Put simply, equity can be viewed as one of two types. *Horizontal equity* deals with the equal treatment of equals; *vertical equity* deals with unequal treatment of unequals (Box 1.3).

Methods of economic evaluation in general, and cost-effectiveness analysis in particular, provide information about technical efficiency. Currently, methods of economic evaluation provide information on how we should provide treatment, but do not allow us to incorporate

---

**Box 1.3** Illustration of vertical and horizontal equity

*Horizontal equity*: People who can be viewed as 'EQUAL' in terms of their need are able to access and gain benefit from healthcare for a particular treatment.

- Ivan has had arthritis in his hip for 5 years and is in moderate pain.
- Frank has had arthritis in his hip for 5 years and is in moderate pain.
- Ivan and Frank are viewed as EQUAL in terms of their need for treatment.
- Horizontal equity will occur when Ivan and Frank are both able to visit their GP. At the GP they are offered the treatment that will work best for their level of pain.
- Ivan and Frank should both achieve the same benefit from their treatment, measured in terms of improved pain levels.

*Vertical equity*: The overall level of health, or improvement in health as a result of a treatment, is equally distributed throughout a population. The population could be everyone in Great Britain.

This will mean that people who are viewed as 'UNEQUAL' in terms of their need may be offered different types of treatment.

For example:

- Sharon has had arthritis in her knee for 1 year and is in mild pain.
- Tracey has had arthritis in her knee for 5 years and is in severe pain.
- Vertical equity will occur when Sharon is offered a different treatment (painkillers) from Tracey (a new knee joint).
- The health of both Sharon and Tracey will be improved by the treatment and they will then be at the same level of overall health.
- Tracey may have experienced more improvement in her health, measured in terms of the level of pain avoided, than Sharon.

---

information on preferences for who should get that treatment. An economic evaluation provides information to decision-makers about the additional costs and benefits associated with one intervention compared to another in the form of the incremental cost-effectiveness ratio. This provides information about the overall increase in incremental costs given the incremental benefits for a population of patients eligible for treatment. This population is not likely to be a homogeneous group and is likely to contain people of different ages, with different disease severities and from different social backgrounds.

Cost-effectiveness analysis values health gain using non-preference based natural units, such as improved levels of pain and mobility. Economic evaluation favours those with the greatest capacity to benefit, such as patients more severely affected by osteoarthritis. Using this method of evaluation may systematically discriminate to the advantage of certain groups against others. Inequalities in health between individuals and/or groups may increase as a result of seeking to maximise health gain.

Equity incorporates distributional issues into the decision-making process. Economic evaluations do not currently incorporate distributional concerns (Gafni and Birch, 1991). A recent review of the literature on equity argued that in order to take distributional concerns into account with regard to healthcare, both individual and societal utilities should be reflected more fully in economic evaluations (Sassi *et al.*, 2001). It is possible to incorporate concern for equality into cost-effectiveness analysis by using *equity weights*. These express the relative importance of equity concepts. The greater the equity weight, the more society is willing to sacrifice a unit of health gain in pursuit of fairness. To do this we must first decide what attributes, or factors, are encompassed in the nebulous term 'equity'. There are no UK-based studies that have conducted the necessary empirical work to support equity weighting of this type (Sassi *et al.*, 2001).

Imagine a situation in which people think the age of the person should be considered in the decision about who is treated, but this does not accord with the decision rule in an economic evaluation of achieving the maximum increase in health gain for a given set of resources. Consider a hypothetical situation where the results of a cost-effectiveness study have shown total hip replacement to be more cost-effective than managing patients with anti-inflammatory drugs, using improvement in pain levels as the primary outcome measure. The study will have been conducted in a sample of patients with hip disease. The sample will probably contain people of different ages, for example between 55 and 85 years. If we incorporated a measure of preference – equity weight – that reflected the desire for younger people to be treated, this would change the decision rule of the study. It would no longer be sufficient to consider improved pain levels for a given cost, and it would be necessary to adjust the incremental cost-effectiveness ratio. First, we would have to define 'younger' and the age threshold. This could be based on Williams' (1997) recommendation of 70 years of age – 'three score years and 10' – as the 'normal span of life', and beyond this point we should be classified as 'older'. Second, we would have to consider whether the general view was indeed to treat the younger rather than the older person. If the overall preference of the general public were to treat the younger person, then we would have to produce two incremental cost-effectiveness ratios, each weighted appropriately. The result would show a preferential cost-effectiveness ratio for a younger population of people with hip disease.

No-one has looked specifically at equity associated with different health states. It is likely that people's perceptions of equity will differ between health states. Before equity weights can be incorporated into the decision-making process guiding the use of NHS interventions, it will be necessary to conduct robust research to identify clearly what people – members of the public, patients and clinicians – think equity is, and begin to describe the key attributes that make up the equity weights.

• • • • • • • • • • • • • • • • • • • • • • • • • • • • • • • • • • • • • • • • • • • • • • • • • • • • • • • • • • • • • • • • • • • • • •

### SELF-DIRECTED STUDY EXERCISES

### EXERCISE 1: Moral hazard

Read the paper Lundin D. Moral hazard in physician prescription behavior. *Journal of Health Economics* 2000; 19: 639–662.

1.   **What is the example of *moral hazard* described in this paper?**

The paper aims to explore why trade-name (branded) drugs have a large share of the Swedish medicine market even though generic versions of the same medicine with identical therapeutic effects are available.

In Sweden, patients do not always bear the full cost of a medicine supplied on prescription because the healthcare system is supported by a third-party payer (insurance). This is not the case for all patients, and different levels of insurance cover exist in Sweden. Doctors may therefore act more in the interest of certain patients rather than the third-party payer, and provide the more expensive brand of medicine. There are no incentives for the doctor to keep medicine costs down, and prescribing decisions will probably be made on factors other than price, such as perceived (rather than actual) differences in quality between medicines, or brand loyalty.

2.   **What information does the author use to illustrate this example?**

The author uses prescribing data from the records of medicines dispensed from two pharmacies in a small area of Sweden. The data contain information on the following variables:

*   The identity of the doctor
*   The identity of the patient

- The medicine prescribed
- The price paid
- The patient's insurance status.

The author analyses the decision to prescribe a branded or a generic version based on these variables.

**3.   What other reasons does the author suggest for the high proportion of high-cost branded medicines being prescribed in Sweden?**

The author discounts doctors' ignorance about medicine prices as one reason for the continued use of branded medicines.

The results of this paper suggest that even when doctors know the difference in price between branded and generic medicines they do not act on this information.

Doctors make decisions on a patient-by-patient basis, which requires knowledge about how much each patient pays.

Doctors could be uncertain about the equivalency in therapeutic effect of the generic medicine compared to the brand version.

Doctors could have divided loyalties between the pharmaceutical company that researched and developed the branded medicine and the patient.

Doctors may also have divided loyalties between the patient who pays for medicines out of pocket and the third-party payer who pays for medicines on their behalf.

**EXERCISE 2:** Decision-making behaviour and the role of completeness in preferences

Read the article by Ryan M and San Miguel F. Revisiting the axiom of completeness in health care. *Health Economics* 2003; 12: 295–307.

**1.   What theory of decision-making behaviour is referred to in this article?**

This article looks at the application of the theory of the consumer and the assumption that people are utility maximisers. The preferences of people for goods and services are driven by the desire to maximise utility, and these preferences are based on certain assumptions (axioms).

**2.   Which assumption from the theory of the consumer does this paper question?**

This paper explores the reliability of the assumption that people have complete preferences when making choices between pairs of goods or services.

Consider two services, A and B. Both may be described by a list of attributes (factors). The axiom of completeness assumes that preferences do exist. That is, people can state a preference and think A is at least as good B, or that B is at least as good as A. It has been suggested that this may not always be the case for healthcare services. People may not always have well-developed preferences for any type of service or good they are asked about, especially if the goods or services are unfamiliar to them.

3.    **Which methods have been used to elicit people's preferences?**

Standard gamble, time trade-off, contingent valuation and discrete choice experiments are four methods that have been used to elicit people's preferences for goods or services. They all rely on the axiom of completeness.

This study used a discrete choice experiment (see Chapter 11) to test the axiom of completeness.

4.    **Which goods were used to test preferences for healthcare interventions rather than 'common' or familiar goods?**

The study compared people's preferences for three different goods using a discrete choice experiment. The goods were a supermarket, a dental practice, and tests screening for bowel (colorectal) cancer.

5.    **What were the conclusions of this study in terms of healthcare interventions satisfying the completeness axiom?**

The authors concluded that people had clear and complete preferences for all three goods, including the healthcare interventions. This is despite some of the people in the sample having different levels of experience and knowledge of cancer screening. This suggests that healthcare interventions, which may represent unfamiliar goods, conform just as well as common goods to the axiom of completeness.

The robustness of the axiom of completeness is important when using valuation tools to elicit preferences for healthcare interventions.

## References

Buetow SA, Sibbald B, Cantrill JA, Halliwell S (1997). Appropriateness in health care: application to prescribing. *Soc Sci Med* 45: 261–271.

Frank RH (1997). *Microeconomics and Behaviour*, 3rd edn. New York: Irvin/McGraw Hill.

Gafni A, Birch S (1991). Equity considerations in utility-based measures of health outcomes in economic appraisals: an adjustment algorithm. *J Health Econ* 10: 329–342.

Gilley J (1994). Towards rational prescribing. *Br Med J* 308: 731–732.

Gravelle H, Rees R (1992). *Microeconomics,* 2nd edn. Harlow: Longman.

Hicks JR (1939). The foundations of welfare economics. *Econ J* 49: 696–712.

Kaldor N (1939). Welfare propositions in economics and inter-personal comparisons of utility. *Econ J* 49: 549–552.

Lundin D (2000). Moral hazard in physician prescription behavior. *J Health Econ* 19: 639–662.

McGuire A (1996). Where do internal markets come from and can they work? *J Health Serv Res Policy* 191: 56–59.

McGuire A, Henderson J, Mooney G (1992). *The Economics of Health Care,* 2nd edn. London: Routledge.

Rittenhouse BE (1994). Economic incentives and disincentives for efficient prescribing. *PharmacoEconomics* 6: 222–232.

Royal Commission on the NHS (1979). London: HMSO.

Ryan M, San Miguel F (2003). Revisiting the axiom of completeness in health care. *Health Econ* 12: 295–307.

Sassi F, Archard L, Le Grand J (2001). Equity and the economic evaluation of healthcare. *Health Technol Assessment* 5(3): 1–130.

Sloman J (1999). *Economics,* 3rd edn. London: Prentice Hall.

von Neumann J, Morgenstern O (1944). *Theory of Games and Economic Behavior.* Princeton, NJ: Princeton University Press.

Williams A (1997). Intergenerational equity: an exploration of the 'fair innings argument'. *Health Econ* 6: 117–132.

## Further reading

Dolan P, Abel Olsen J (2002). *Distributing Health Care.* Oxford: Oxford University Press.

Folland S, Goodman AC, Stano M (1997). *The Economics of Health and Health Care.* New Jersey: Prentice Hall.

Frank RH (1997). *Microeconomics and Behaviour,* 3rd edn. USA: Irvin/McGraw Hill.

Gravelle H, Rees R (1992). *Microeconomics,* 2nd edn. Harlow: Longman.

McGuire A, Henderson J, Mooney G (1992). *The Economics of Health Care,* 2nd edn. London: Routledge.

Sloman J (1999). *Economics,* 3rd edn. London: Prentice Hall.

# 2

# Rationing healthcare

## Introduction

Much recent discussion in the medical literature and the media at large has revolved around whether or not the rationing of healthcare is inevitable. It has been said that rationing, resource allocation, prioritising and choices can all be used to describe the same task: that of making choices between competing priorities when resources are scarce. Rationing is not a simple issue: in fact, defining the boundaries of healthcare leads to questions about the limits of a public institution's responsibilities. In the UK NHS there is a growing sense of confusion and uncertainty about what is reasonable to expect from a publicly funded healthcare provider.

In the UK, you may hear the following questions being debated:

- Is it the NHS's job to provide fertility treatment, physiotherapy for sports injuries, long-term nursing care, gender reassignment, adult dentistry and cosmetic surgery?
- Should the NHS be defining a package of healthcare services that it is responsible for?
- Why is it that where one lives in the UK appears to have an effect on whether or not NHS treatment is available (sometimes called 'postcode prescribing')?

This chapter examines why rationing exists; various mechanisms tried to ration healthcare; the difference between implicit and explicit rationing; how some countries have tried to deal with healthcare rationing; and key issues on the rationing agenda. This is a very large and important topic and there are many excellent discussions and arguments from a range of commentators. They cannot all be covered here, and so further reading is recommended throughout.

## Is rationing inevitable?

The cost of healthcare in all developed countries is rising at an alarming rate (see Chapter 1, p. 2, Why the interest in health economics?).

Healthcare providers such as the UK NHS attempt to provide a comprehensive service in a world where expectations are continually changing and rising, where the boundaries of what is medically possible are continually expanding. It is unlikely that the dilemmas associated with healthcare resource allocation will diminish, as there are likely to be demographic shifts, potentially increasing costs, and no real prospect of unlimited resources being available for healthcare.

Many people would argue that rationing is inevitable. Rationing has been around in some form ever since free healthcare has been provided. The limits of a finite budget for healthcare mean that not everything that is demanded will be supplied. In the UK, the NHS is frequently accused of rationing healthcare. However, rationing is not a new phenomenon, as discussed in Chapter 1 (p. 3, Scarcity and choice and the NHS), and is not limited to the UK. If rationing is inevitable, then healthcare budgets should be used wisely, such that priority services are funded. In the UK, many medical opinion leaders and policy makers have admitted that priority setting will form the future framework of clinical practice in the NHS. Health professionals, the public and the government need to accept that boundaries for medical treatment must be set, and there needs to be a discussion about establishing a prioritised service. Some mechanisms that may reduce the need for rationing are to improve the efficiency of existing healthcare services, to stop offering services that are of no proven benefit, redeploy resources from lower-priority public services, and to reduce or eliminate waste in the system.

The dilemmas concerning the allocation of scarce resources have been referred to as the *inconsistent triad* (Weale, 1998). This phrase refers to the inability of any healthcare system to provide care that is comprehensive (i.e. provides all services), of high quality, and available to everyone. In the UK, healthcare is available to all, and some suggest that the comprehensive nature of the NHS is bought by the sacrifice of quality. In the USA, comprehensive high-quality healthcare is available, but only to those who can afford it. This inconsistent triad means that there is always a tension between conflicting values about healthcare provision.

## Implicit or explicit rationing?

Implicit rationing occurs when care is limited and where neither decisions about which forms of care are provided, nor the bases for those decisions, are expressed clearly (and often the decision-maker is not apparent).

Currently, healthcare rationing in the UK and most other countries is generally implicit. Thus the limitation of healthcare is not obvious to the users of the service. Explicit rationing is the opposite of this. The availability of healthcare services is transparent, as is the process by which the decisions on healthcare availability are made.

Explicit rationing occurs when care is limited and where decisions about the provision of healthcare are clear, as are the reasons for those decisions. There is growing support for the idea of making rationing within healthcare more explicit (Doyal, 1997). The assumption seems to be that explicit rationing is a wholly good thing – implying openness and honesty, and consequently paving the way to a more equitable and efficient service in which people can democratically influence the process and outcome of rationing. However, explicit rationing may cause distress to both providers and users of healthcare, as well as to other members of society, as illustrated in Case study 2.1.

## Some reasons to support the implicit rationing of healthcare

### Disutility

Utility is a term used in economics to describe satisfaction or preference. For example, a patient is likely to have a greater preference for a more effective drug with fewer side effects. Such a treatment would be said to provide higher utility. *Disutility* is the opposite of utility.

It is argued that explicit rationing is associated with a higher level of disutility than implicit rationing (Mechanic, 1995; Coast, 1997). For example, under the current system in the UK, where the majority of rationing is implicit, society as a whole is unaware of the extent to which rationing takes place. Whereas most of society may be aware that there are restrictions placed on what are viewed as lifestyle drugs and treatments, for example impotence and fertility treatment, most people will be unaware that there is rationed access to potentially life-saving treatments such as renal dialysis.

Implicit rationing means that only the healthcare professional (HCP) or the deliverer of healthcare is aware that treatment is denied to patients who are sick and who die or suffer years of disability. Rationing such treatment would naturally cause those responsible disutility. HCPs have to rationalise such decisions by giving clinical justifications. Thus the '*denial disutility*' associated with implicit rationing is experienced primarily by HCPs, who have to justify such decisions to themselves and to the patient on medical grounds. The patient's alternative courses of treatment can be explained in such a way as to exclude certain treatment

**CASE STUDY 2.1**

**The case of Child B**

In the UK, the case of Child B became a focus for discussion about explicit rationing and the ethical dilemmas associated with distributing limited resources. Child B suffered from non-Hodgkin's lymphoma with common acute lymphoblastic leukaemia. At the age of 9 she suffered a relapse after her bone marrow transplant. Her doctors advised against a second transplant as they felt she had a less than 10% chance of recovery. Her family did not accept this decision and obtained a second opinion from a specialist in the USA, who suggested she had a 60% chance of recovery with a second transplant. The original UK clinicians did not support this opinion because the US estimate was based on adult evidence, but they still referred Child B for a second transplant. The local health authority refused to fund this treatment on the basis of limited effectiveness. The also refused to pay £75,000 for an experimental treatment, donor lymphocyte infusion, because the potential donor, Child B's sister, would have been exposed to risks from this dangerous intervention. At this point, Child B's family took the health authority to judicial review. The High Court examined the health authority's decision on two principles: the nature of the right to life and the principle of acting in the patient's best interests. The High Court ruled that the health authority had assaulted Child B's right to life and that they must reconsider their decision. However, the same afternoon, the Appeal Court revoked this ruling. Not surprisingly, the media's attention was caught by this case and a wide-ranging debate began. Ultimately, Child B's treatment was paid for by a private donor, she went into remission, but then died a year later.

One of the key issues that arises again and again when discussing this case, and other similar cases, is the lack of an agreed set of criteria upon which to base these types of decisions.

There are many discussions about this case, and it is quite difficult to get behind the real facts of this difficult and painful event to see whether what happened was rationing or not. Pickard *et al.* (1999) provide a detailed discussion of what probably happened. For an examination of the media involvement in this case, read Entwistle *et al.* (1996).

possibilities, or certain treatment options can be made to seem unattractive for specific reasons.

Explicit rationing would involve a more informed patient being fully aware of all treatment options and the rationales behind possible denial of treatment. Society as a whole would effectively be denying the patient treatment, causing people to experience disutility. Callahan (1992) states: 'this disutility will be greater when the victims are visible and when accountability for their condition can not be evaded'. Furthermore, by increasing the visibility of the decision process, the potential for conflict among decision makers is likely to increase.

It would be expected that the increase in disutility experienced by society as a whole would be offset by the decreased disutility experienced by the HCP. However, this is not the case, because as things stand the HCP can ration treatment without the service user's awareness, and rationalise the decision-making process in clinical terms. It is much harder for an HCP to deny individual patients care explicitly on a day-to-day basis.

*Deprivation disutility* is also experienced as a consequence of explicit rationing. This occurs as the patient is better informed about treatment options, and is aware of why treatment may be denied. For example, where treatments are rationed, two individuals, X and Y, may both be eligible for a certain treatment. If this treatment is only made available for X, and the situation is explained to Y in terms of the treatment only being beneficial for X for medical reasons, it is likely that Y will accept this. However, if the explanation to Y were in explicit terms, for example 'both of you would benefit from this treatment, however you (Y), will not be treated for reasons of rationing', this would cause Y to feel deprivation disutility.

The essence of deprivation disutility derives from knowing, or believing, that something could have been done but was not. Deprivation disutility can also be extended to society as a whole. Individuals may experience deprivation disutility on behalf of others, such as family or friends. Altruistic deprivation disutility may also extend to patients not known personally, but where publicity has been generated. For example, in the case of Child B (Pickard and Sheaff, 1999), when the national press reported that the reason for denying treatment was resource limitation, ultimately a charitable donation funded the denied treatment.

### Lack of evidence

It is also argued that the evidence relating to the clinical and cost-effectiveness of treatments is poor and in many cases unavailable, making it difficult to assess the merits of various treatment options.

### Lack of clear guidelines

Explicit rationing relies heavily on guidance about effective and cost-effective treatments being clear and unequivocal. Usually, guidance is open to interpretation and therefore is not applied uniformly by all health service providers.

### Insensitivity to individuals

Explicit rationing can be perceived to be a strict list of rules about allocating treatments and therefore not taking into account individuals and differing circumstances. This can lead to not only disutility but also protracted legal challenges, as was the case with Child B.

So, in summary, implicit rationing is supported by the following arguments:

- It is evitable, as there are no clear criteria on which to base explicit rationing.
- Patients and providers would be happier.
- Administrative and political processes run much more smoothly.
- Members of the public are shielded from the 'disutility' that explicit denials of treatment would create.

## Some reasons to support the explicit rationing of healthcare

### Moral responsibility

Prioritising healthcare services presents moral dilemmas certainly, but if society fails to attempt to prioritise, it is accepted that healthcare resources may well be distributed unfairly. The moral foundation of publicly funded healthcare providers such as the UK NHS is that there is equal access to healthcare based on equal need (see Chapter 1, p. 17, Efficiency and equity). It is difficult to evaluate which healthcare interventions and which illnesses should be allocated resources. This does not mean, however, that it cannot, or should not, be done. Fair allocation of resources depending on need and capacity to benefit is essential, or consistent patterns of practice will not be achieved.

### Public accountability

Until rationing is explicit, decision-makers will not have to publicly defend the criteria for rationing. This disempowers the consumers of healthcare because it prevents debate. More informed public understanding and participation should aid the efficacy, accuracy and equity of healthcare rationing by enabling more accurate needs assessments and more representative research.

*Increase in evidence-based medicine*

Also, the argument that it is too difficult to prioritise services because of the unavailability of effectiveness data is progressively being eroded. In these days of evidence-based medicine, authoritative guidance relating to treatment options is being produced and updated as never before.

*Patient empowerment*

Patients now have greater access to information via the Internet, and the UK government is encouraging the educated, self-caring patient. Patients now question clinicians, so they will not remain oblivious to rationing. It was undoubtedly easier for healthcare workers when patients unquestioningly accepted what they were told.

*Openness between patients and HCPs*

It is argued that explicit rationing will ultimately lead to less utility for both patients and doctors. It is suggested that it is not in the patient's interest to give them information that would cause distress. In a number of cases the deception relating to rationing has been uncovered; stories of this kind receive extensive press coverage, and this undermines the doctor–patient relationship. Explicit priority setting involving societal consultation may well lead to a lower level of disutility. Individuals will be aware of how difficult the prioritisation of resources is, and consequently accept that everything that can be done may not be done in every case.

So, in summary, explicit rationing is supported by the following arguments:

- Clear, precise policies and guidelines could be defended publicly.
- Rationing decisions would be open and transparent.
- Patients are more informed and will no longer tolerate implicit rationing.

## Rationing in the UK

One of the key issues to cause controversy in rationing healthcare is how to prioritise services, and who should prioritise them. There does not appear to be an obvious set of ethical principles or methodologies on which to base rationing, given the large number of objectives that healthcare is required to pursue. Terms such as 'pragmatic incrementalism' (Klein, 1995) and 'muddling through elegantly' (Robinson, 1999) have been used when describing the way in which the UK deals with the need for priority setting in healthcare.

In the UK there is a move towards involving the public in developing priorities for healthcare. Bowling (1996) surveyed a large nationally representative sample of adults on priorities in healthcare. This was in response to a 1995 House of Commons Report which identified a higher priority for acute interventions that were perceived as being life saving (HMSO, 1995). The people in the survey ranked 'treatments for children with life-threatening diseases' and 'special care and pain relief for people who are dying' highest. They ranked 'treatment for infertility' and 'treatment for people aged 75 and over with life-threatening diseases' much lower (Bowling, 1996). Preventative measures and chronic illnesses and disabilities were also given lower rankings. This survey showed that the public felt that self-inflicted diseases (such as tobacco-mediated) and older people should have a lower priority. Most respondents thought that surveys like this one should be used in the planning of health services. Some commentators question the value of involving the public in healthcare priority setting, because of concerns with lack of knowledge about healthcare (Torgerson and Gosden, 2000). A study by Dolan *et al.* (1999) showed that members of the public were keen to be involved in priority setting, but after an opportunity for discussion and deliberation on the issues and decisions involved they became less keen and were more sympathetic to the role healthcare managers play. Interestingly, they also became less likely to discriminate against smokers, heavy drinkers and illegal drug users.

The Rationing Agenda Group (RAG) was founded in 1996 in order to contribute to the British debate on the rationing of healthcare (New, 1997). RAG believes that rationing in healthcare is inevitable and that the public needs to be involved in the debate about related issues. The group comprises people from all parts of healthcare, none of whom represents either their group or their institution.

## Questions raised by the Rationing Agenda Group

1.   What is the range of services relevant to healthcare rationing?
2.   What are the objectives of the NHS, and what is the range of ethically defensible criteria for discriminating between claims for resources?
3.   Whose values should be taken into account?
4.   Who should undertake rationing?
5.   What accountability mechanisms are appropriate?
6.   How explicit should be the principles by which rationing is conducted?

7.   What additional information would be required to make rationing more explicit and those responsible more accountable?
8.   Is there enough knowledge to implement particular rationing strategies successfully?

Suggested RAG answers to these questions can be found in: New B. The rationing agenda in the NHS. *Br Med J* 1996; 312: 1593–1601.

### Rationing, ethics and responsibility

Many ethical dilemmas arise from rationing, leading to moral arguments, discussions about accountability, the responsibility of the professions and the application of the legal process. For a detailed discussion of this complex area the reader is directed to Newdick (1996).

## Rationing lessons from abroad

The UK is not alone in trying to develop explicit rationing processes. It is possible that lessons can be learnt from the processes carried out in other countries.

### The Netherlands

In 1992, a priority-setting debate was carried out by a government-appointed committee, the Committee on Choices in Healthcare, which produced what has since become known as the Dunning Report, named after its chairman. They set out to advise their government on a basic package of healthcare to which everyone would be entitled. The Dunning Report recommended that all competing claims on healthcare resources should have to pass four tests (van der Grinten and Kasdorp, 1999):

1.   Is treatment necessary to allow individuals to function in society?
2.   Is treatment effective?
3.   Is the treatment efficient?
4.   Could the treatment be considered a matter of individual responsibility?

By indicating that individuals have a responsibility for their own health the Report acknowledged that the healthcare service does not have an obligation to provide a comprehensive healthcare system. The committee reached the following conclusions:

1.   It is fairer to provide 'necessary' healthcare for everyone, than to provide all healthcare for some.

2.   Explicit rationing was publicly accountable and preferable to 'covert rationing'.

3.   'Social values' must be combined with medical and expert opinion when prioritising health care.

They devised a system whereby a mix of strategies for rationing was implemented at different levels (national to local). Responsibility for decision-making was also mixed between the Dutch government and the civil service. They also wanted to limit the introduction of new technologies to slow down spending on new, unproven treatments.

Criticisms at the time included concerns about the utilitarian nature (greatest good for the greatest number) of the proposals, such that the individual would suffer for the sake of society. However, the reforms became politically 'stuck' in the 1990s and current commentators consider that decision-making concerning rationing in The Netherlands is actually carried out at the individual HCP level. For a more detailed discussion of the Dutch experience, read van der Grinten and Kasdorp (1999).

## New Zealand

In New Zealand a similar approach was taken and in 1992 a government committee was set up to define more explicitly a set of core services to ensure that the services people believed most important would be provided. This process would acknowledge more honestly what the health service could afford. The committee set out to advise the government on a basic package of healthcare to which all members of the population would be entitled. In the end they came up with a set of criteria for assessing competing claims on resources (Devlin *et al.*, 2001).

The committee decided that the exclusion of whole healthcare programmes, services or patient groups would be too arbitrary and would not have the capacity to tailor services according to the needs of individuals in society. It proposed the use of the following criteria for making decisions about the allocation of healthcare resources:

1.   A treatment or service should provide benefit and value for money.

2.   A treatment should represent a fair use of resources.

3.   A treatment should be consistent with community values.

The committee's main work was to try to generate consensus about clinical protocol among the medical profession and to gather public opinion on whether social as well as clinical factors should be used to determine priorities in healthcare.

This committee, however, failed to produce an explicit list of core services, leaving the situation much as it was. However, this process seems to have persuaded the public in New Zealand to accept that rationing is inevitable (Feek *et al.*, 1999).

## Oregon

The Oregon experience is perhaps the most widely publicised priority-setting exercise in the USA. Oregon wanted to extend the number of people covered on the Medicaid programme for healthcare provision to the poor. This required the number of services provided by this programme to be limited. The concept was to rank in order of priority what services would be provided by Medicaid. Those proposing the scheme wished to offer a basic health service package that covered services with the highest priority, by drawing a cut-off at a particular point on the list and funding all services that lay on or above this line and refusing funding for all services below it. In 1989 Oregon began devising a list of conditions and treatments, with those having the highest priority at the top and those with the lowest priority at the bottom (Blumstein, 1997).

The task of determining what should be on the permitted list of services was entrusted to a health services commission whose 11 members comprised professional and lay people. They ranked 714 'condition–treatment pairs' in order of priority. The state legislature decided how much money to give to healthcare, and low-priority services were not funded (Blumstein, 1997).

The decision principles used intended to take into account:

- How much a treatment costs
- What improvement in a person's quality of life it is likely to produce
- How many years that improvement will probably last.

The list was finalised in 1991.

All pairs were subdivided into 17 categories, for example:

- Maternity care, e.g. medical therapy for low birthweight (750–999 g)
- Chronic fatal conditions (treatment improves lifespan and quality of wellbeing), e.g. medical therapy for HIV disease
- Chronic non-fatal conditions (one-time treatment improves quality of wellbeing), e.g. cataract removal for adults

- Fatal or non-fatal conditions (treatment produces little or no improvement in quality of wellbeing), e.g. life support for extremely low birthweight (<500 g).

Some examples of final ranking are shown in Table 2.1.

### Criticisms of the Oregon experiment at the time

During its development the Oregon health plan attracted a range of criticisms. One of the main concerns was that by concentrating on Medicaid, Oregon was rationing services only for the poor (most of whom were women and children), and thereby accentuating the inequalities in the US healthcare system. Other concerns were:

- Rationing should not only be based on a cost–benefit approach: there should be an ethical input as well.
- Effectiveness data were seriously inadequate.
- The formulae used were not sensitive to individual patients.

After a number of false starts the Oregon scheme was implemented in 1994, but priority setting did not end then. There is a legal requirement to keep the basic healthcare package under review; this continues to be the responsibility of the healthcare commission. One of the major changes in the years since its introduction has been the full integration of mental

**Table 2.1** Examples of final ranking

| Rank | Condition | Treatment |
|------|-----------|-----------|
| 123 | Low birthweight (750–999 g) | Medical therapy |
| 158 | HIV disease | Medical therapy |
| 243 | Leukaemia | Bone marrow transplant |
| 337 | Adult cataract | Cataract removal |
| 364 | Cirrhosis of liver (non-alcoholic) | Liver transplant |
| 600 | Infertility | Medical therapy |
| 695 | Cirrhosis of liver (alcoholic) | Liver transplant |
| 707 | Terminal HIV disease (<10% survival at 5 yrs) | Medical therapy |
| 713 | Extremely low birthweight (<500 g) | Life support |

health and chemical dependency services into the basic healthcare package.

For a more detailed discussion of the Oregon experience, read Blumstein (1997) and Marmor and Boyum (1999).

## What are the different approaches to explicit rationing?

There appear to be two main approaches to the explicit allocation of scarce resources: pluralistic bargaining and technical.

### Pluralistic bargaining approaches

These occur when limited public healthcare resources are rationed through the designation of core or essential health services based on widespread consultation with healthcare professionals and the general public. This is said to be the approach in The Netherlands and New Zealand.

### Technical approaches

Limited public healthcare resources are rationed through the use of technical formulae that attempt to measure the cost-effectiveness of different healthcare interventions, sometimes moderated to reflect the value judgement of healthcare planners, professionals and the public, as in the Oregon Health Plan.

Klein (1995) argues that The Netherlands and New Zealand have in common a rejection of this purist economic approach to priority setting, in which services are ranked in order of their relative cost-effectiveness. This purely utilitarian approach can be said to put the overall health of the population before the health of individuals. Also, there is evidence that people value treatments that save lives over treatments that improve quality of life (Bowling, 1996). This is termed the 'rule of rescue' (Robinson, 1999) and means that purely technical approaches using decision rules based on cost-effectiveness may never be acceptable to populations.

One common theme of all the approaches described seems to be that they are promoting healthcare coverage for everyone, rather than attempting to provide all possible treatments. This approach is in agreement with the concept of 'universalism' promoted by the World Health Organization (Brown, 1999). They suggest that priorities should be set on the basis of resources available, and priority should be given to immunisation, tobacco control, antibiotic resistance and 'safe motherhood'.

## The 'fair innings' argument

There is plenty of evidence to suggest that elderly patients are less likely to be referred for interventional treatment (Hamel *et al.*, 1999; Dey and Fraser, 2000). Age-based rationing of healthcare is a particularly sensitive and complex issue. There is an ongoing lively debate about the ethical arguments in this area, and the interested reader is directed to Dey and Fraser (2000), Williams (1997) and Grimley Evans (1997).

### The argument for rationing by age

Those in favour of prioritising treatments for younger people argue that the elderly have already had their life – a 'fair innings' – whereas the young have not (Williams, 1997). They also argue that treating the young is more efficient, because treating the elderly secures smaller increases in life-years than does treating the young (Dey and Fraser, 2000).

### The argument against rationing by age

Arguments against the 'fair innings' approach have three main themes. The first is that the elderly may be considered to have earned their healthcare, either through payments or through contributing to society throughout their working lives (even contributing to current peace by fighting in wars). The second theme is need: a compassionate society should provide healthcare where it is needed (Grimley Evans, 1997). The third theme is that age does not determine ill health or capacity to benefit, and so choosing to treat on the basis of age is meaningless.

When unfairness is uncovered in the distribution of healthcare resources in relation to age there is public outrage. However, ironically, when the public is consulted and involved in priority-setting exercises, the prioritisation mirrors that currently applied implicitly. Bowling (1996) determined that one of the lowest priority treatment areas was 'treatment for people aged 75 and over with life-threatening illness'.

## Conclusion

Rationing is likely to remain a fact of life in healthcare, owing to the rising cost of treatment due to technological advances and demographic change. Pressure is being exerted to move from the current system of implicit to explicit rationing. A number of other countries have already moved to a more explicit approach. This has not proved either easy or popular.

Implicit rationing has worked in the UK to date, mainly because of consumer ignorance. However, as the public becomes better informed and expectations rise it is probable that patients will be more questioning. Healthcare also excites much media attention and is a major political issue, raising public awareness of resource restrictions.

Implicit rationing is more flexible than explicit rationing and can be said to work better for individuals, as well as leading to lower levels of conflict. However, it can result in unfair allocation of resources. Patient groups with good advocacy skills tend to benefit more than poor advocates when resources are allocated. Also, at times of financial shortage, such as the end of the financial year, patients may receive suboptimal treatment: had they had the same condition at a different time of the year, better treatment would have been available. Explicit rationing would hopefully lead to uniformity of treatment within disease states.

It seems that although implicit rationing has historically had many advantages, it will be progressively less acceptable to patients. Implementing explicit rationing will not, however, be easy. It has been suggested that the informed patient will be more accepting of an evidence-based, democratically decided system of explicit rationing for more expensive and newer treatments. However, for current effectiveness and cost-effectiveness evidence to be used more effectively in explicit rationing, it needs to have a broader focus in public sector decision-making, looking at incentives and constraints governing the use of economic data. Finally, making painful, difficult decisions about healthcare rationing and acting upon those decisions are two very different things.

• • • • • • • • • • • • • • • • • • • • • • • • • • • • • • • • • • • • • • • • • • • • • • • • • • • • • • • • • • • • •

**SELF-DIRECTED STUDY EXERCISES**

**EXERCISE 1:** Rationing in healthcare

In this exercise, you are going to make some decisions about how to allocate healthcare resources.

Imagine that you are an adviser for Welltown Health Commission. At the last financial meeting of the Commission you were informed that the funding had not increased by £2m as expected, but only by £1.5m. This has implications for what the Commission has the power to fund over the following year. It has implications for the amount of money available to fund initiatives coming from the budget. The Commission has approached you, as the adviser, with four areas that they were considering expanding with the extra funds that have now been reduced. They want you to advise them on which of these areas they should withdraw their funding from for the following year:

- Smoking cessation counselling
- Quadruple therapy in HIV
- Lipid-lowering drugs in all people with cholesterol levels over 6.5 mmol/l
- Depression.

The evidence available for each area is detailed below. Your task is to recommend to the Commission which of these areas they should drop from this year's funding programme.

**What you need to do:**
1. Read the details of each healthcare programme and make sure you understand the costs and benefits associated with each.
2. Rank the programmes from 1 to 4 in order of importance. Bear in mind that the programme ranked fourth will not be funded. Give each programme a score of 1 to 4 as appropriate.
3. Have you considered equity issues?

NB: The scenarios described below are based on data taken from real statistics as far as possible. However, the scenarios are fictitious and any resemblance to reality is entirely coincidental.

## Healthcare Programme 1: Smoking cessation counselling

### Costs and benefits
The smoking cessation programme to be funded is to be run in conjunction with local community pharmacists, consisting of a combination of advice giving and use of over-the-counter (OTC) antismoking products. This programme will target pharmacies in North Welltown, where smoking rates are highest. It is expected to cost £500,000 per year. The impact on health outcomes is expected to be gradual and spread over a long period of time. The only data available are an expected reduction in deaths from lung cancer of 1 per year, rising to 5 per year in 10 years' time, and in deaths from heart disease of 0.5 per year, rising to 4 per year in 10 years' time.

## Healthcare Programme 2: Quadruple therapy in HIV

### Information about quadruple therapy in HIV
There have been over 650 positive test results for HIV infection in Welltown. There are probably about 500 people living in Welltown who are HIV positive. Over 50 people in Welltown are living with AIDS. It has been proved that the use of quadruple therapy in patients who are HIV positive can delay the progression to end-stage AIDS for longer than with triple therapy. The exact delay is not known. Once the patient has AIDS their average lifespan is 5 years. Mortality is 100%. There has

been a lot of publicity in the Welltown press, as these patients are aware of the possible benefits of this therapy and are demanding it from their GPs.

### Costs and benefits
This programme is intended to fund the use of quadruple therapy in these 500 patients. It costs about £1,000 per year extra to treat someone with quadruple therapy, but it is not known exactly how much extra lifespan will be achieved by these patients.

## Healthcare Programme 3: Lipid-lowering drugs in all people with cholesterol levels over 6.5 mmol/l

### Information about coronary heart disease in Welltown
Last year there were 1338 deaths from coronary heart disease. This was a quarter of all deaths in the city. In the same year 513 people died of stroke. One of the risk factors for heart disease is a raised cholesterol level.

### Costs and benefits of treating high cholesterol levels with lipid-lowering drugs
It is estimated that 30 000 people in Welltown have cholesterol levels higher than 6.5 mmol/l. The current annual cost of treatment with lipid-lowering drugs is about £540. To treat all these patients would cost £16.2 m. It is not known how many are already being treated. However, screening programmes would probably pick up less than 10% of these people. £500,000 will be made available to GPs and will be allocated to those practices that apply for funds for *new* patients. This will provide treatment for about 1000 people and is expected to prevent about four deaths from coronary heart disease over the next 10 years.

## Healthcare Programme 4: Depression

### Information about depression
In the Welltown Health Needs Survey 2004, one-third of people in Welltown reported 'psychological stress' (slightly more women than men, 36.2% vs 29.0%); 69 deaths were officially reported as suicide or self-inflicted injury.

A government target is to reduce suicides by 15% by 2020 (from 11.0 per 100 000 to 9.4 per 100 000). The current rate in Welltown is 15.9 per 100 000, and 90% of those who commit suicide have some form of mental illness.

It is estimated that 37.4% of people with mental health problems in Welltown have depression which is not being treated. This is equivalent to about 14 700 people.

### Costs and benefits of treating depression
The Commission intends to mount an awareness campaign in Welltown about depression, targeting local newspapers, GPs, pharmacies, women's groups, social services

and pubs. They expect to pick up about 5000 extra cases by doing this. As far as drug costs are concerned, it costs the Commission about £100 per year to treat one patient.

**What to do now:**
For each treatment programme answer the following questions:

1.    What are the costs?
2.    What are the benefits?
3.    Who are the people that get the benefits?
4.    How many people get the benefits?

Rank the treatment programmes detailed above from 1 to 4, remembering that the fourth programme will not be funded. Now think about the following questions:

1.    What type of rationing is this?
2.    What factors did you find yourself taking into consideration when making your decision?
3.    What other mechanisms could have been used to decide which treatments to fund?

## EXERCISE 2: Discussing key issues in healthcare rationing

In this chapter you have read many different approaches to, and opinions of, rationing. Try to answer the following questions:

1.    Do you think that the rationing of healthcare is inevitable in the NHS?
2.    Would you prefer an implicit or an explicit approach to the setting of priorities in the NHS?
3.    Which non-UK approach to rationing do you most agree with?
4.    Do you think the media influences the general public's attitude to the rationing of healthcare in the NHS?

## EXERCISE 3: Rationing by age in healthcare

Read Williams A. Rationing healthcare by age: the case for. *Br Med J* 1997; 314: 820–823, and Grimley Evans J. Rationing healthcare by age: the case against. *Br Med J* 1997; 314: 820–825. Also read Dey *et al.* (2000).

Present a synopsis of these articles, outlining the principal arguments for each side, and briefly discuss which argument comes out more strongly and why.

## EXERCISE 4: Rationing or social responsibility: defining the boundaries of healthcare

1.    List all the healthcare services you can think of that are provided, both publicly and privately.
2.    Rank them in the order of priority in which you believe they should be provided by the NHS.

3.    Draw a line between the services you think should (your 'service package')
      and should not be funded by the NHS.


Imagine that you now had to save money. Would you: a) move the line of your
'service package' up (i.e. provide fewer services of low priority): indicate which
services you would get rid of; or b) leave the line where it is and provide less funding
for each service in the package? Indicate which services you would reduce, and in
what ways.


Imagine now that you are given extra funds. Would you: a) move the line of your
service package down (i.e. provide services originally excluded from the package):
indicate which services you would include; or b) leave the line where it is and
provide more funding for each service in the package? Indicate which services you
would expand, and in what ways.

..................................................................................

## References

Blumstein JF (1997). The Oregon experiment: the role of cost benefit analysis in the
      allocation of Medicaid funds. *Soc Sci Med* 45: 545–554.
Bowling A (1996). Healthcare rationing: the public's debate. *Br Med J* 312:
      670–674.
Brown P (1999). WHO urges 'coverage for all, not coverage of everything'. *Br Med
      J* 318: 1305.
Callahan D (1992). Symbols, rationality and justice: rationing health care. *Am J
      Law Med* 18: 1–14.
Coast J (1997). Rationing within the NHS should be explicit: the case against. *Br
      Med J* 314: 1118–1122.
Devlin N, Maynard A, Mays N (2001). New Zealand's new health sector reforms:
      back to the future? *Br Med J* 322: 1171–1174.
Dey I, Fraser N (2000). Age-based rationing in the allocation of health care. *J Aging
      Health* 12: 511–537.
Dolan P, Cookson R, Ferguson B (1999). Effect of discussion and deliberation on the
      public's views of priority setting in health care: focus group study. *Br Med J*
      318: 1346–1348.
Doyal L (1997). Rationing within the NHS should be explicit: the case for. *Br Med J*
      314: 916–919.
Entwistle VA, Watt IS, Bradbury R, Pehl LJ (1996). Media coverage of the Child B
      case. *Br Med J* 312: 1587–1591.
Feek CM, McKean W, Henneveld L, *et al*. (1999). Experience with rationing health-
      care in New Zealand. *Br Med J* 318: 1346–1348.
Grimley Evans J (1997). Rationing healthcare by age: the case against. *Br Med J* 314:
      824–825.

Hamel MB, Teno JM, Goldman L, *et al.* (1999). Patient age and decisions to with-hold life-sustaining treatments from seriously ill hospitalized adults. *Ann Intern Med* 130: 116–125.

Health Committee (1995). *Report on Priority Setting in the NHS: Purchasing.* House of Commons, Session 1994–95. Vol 1. (HC 134-1.) London: HMSO.

Klein R (1995). Priorities and rationing: pragmatism or principles? *Br Med J* 311: 761–762.

Marmor TR, Boyum D (1999). Medical care and public policy: the benefits and burdens of asking fundamental questions. *Health Policy* 49: 27–43.

Mechanic D (1995). Dilemmas in rationing healthcare services: the case for implicit rationing. *Br Med J* 310: 1655–1659.

New B (1996). The rationing agenda in the NHS. *Br Med J* 312: 1593–1601.

New B (1997). Defining a package of healthcare services the NHS is responsible for: the case for. *Br Med J* 314: 503–505.

Newdick C (1996). *Who Should we Treat? Law, Patients and Resources in the NHS.* Oxford: Oxford University Press.

Pickard S, Sheaff R (1999). Primary care groups and NHS rationing: implications of the Child B case. *Healthcare Anal* 7: 37–56.

Robinson R (1999). Limits to rationality: economics, economists and priority setting. *Health Policy* 49: 13–26.

Torgerson DJ, Gosden TB (2000). Priority setting in health care: should we ask the tax payer? *Br Med J* 320: 1679.

van der Grinten TED, Kasdorp JP (1999). Choices in Dutch health care: mixing strategies and responsibilities. *Health Policy* 50: 105–122.

Weale A (1998). Rationing health care. *Br Med J* 316: 410.

Williams A (1997). Rationing healthcare by age: the case for. *Br Med J* 314: 820–823.

## Further reading

Beecham L, Dorozynski A, Sheldon T, *et al.* (1998). Viagra falls: the debate over rationing continues. *Br Med J* 317: 836–838.

Brooks A (1998). Viagra is licensed in Europe but rationed in Britain. *Br Med J* 317: 765.

Fears R, Roberts I, Poste G (2000). Rational or rationed medicine? The promise of genetics for improved general practice. *Br Med J* 320: 933–935.

Frankel S, Ebrahim S, Davey Smith G (2000). The limits to demand for health care. *Br Med J* 321: 40–45.

Klein R (1997). Defining a package of healthcare services the NHS is responsible for: the case against. *Br Med J* 314: 506–509.

Richards C, Dingwall R, Watson A (2001). Should NHS patients be allowed to contribute extra money to their care? *Br Med J* 323: 563–565.

# 3

# The nature and assessment of costs in healthcare

## Introduction

An economic evaluation is a study that compares the costs and benefits of two or more alternative interventions or services. Therefore, it is clear that the two major components of an economic evaluation are costs and benefits. It is important to know how costs and benefits should be presented correctly in the economic evaluation of a healthcare intervention, such as a medicine or a service.

The resources consumed in the process of healthcare mean that there is a cost associated with any intervention. Correct identification, measurement and valuation of costs is essential in health economics. This chapter defines and describes the different types of costs used in economic evaluation, and appraises the importance of perspective when assessing cost. A published study is examined and the quality of cost reporting assessed.

The methods used to incorporate cost data into economic evaluations are described in Chapters 4–7. More detailed discussion on the statistical analysis of cost data is provided in Chapter 10.

## Identifying costs

In economic analysis we are looking at the costs associated with a process. True economic cost is concerned with the *opportunity cost* of that process or intervention (Palmer and Raftery, 1999). Ideally, resources used in economic studies should be valued at their opportunity cost, but doing this is difficult, so unit costs tend to be used instead, based on the costs of the various inputs (Raftery, 2000) (see also Chapter 1, p. 14, Opportunity cost) Some of these costs are very obvious, but some are not quite so obvious.

It is important to take into account all the costs associated with an intervention, not just acquisition market prices. Calculation of true economic cost is difficult, but it is essential to make sure that cost information reflects true economic cost as closely as possible. This is not usually straightforward in healthcare because normal markets and pricing mechanisms are not necessarily operating. For example, prescribing the highly effective antipsychotic drug clozapine for a person with schizophrenia does not just incur the costs of buying the drug. Clozapine can have serious side effects, and so regular blood monitoring tests have to be carried out in all patients. Therefore, these monitoring costs must be taken into account when the economic implications of using clozapine are being assessed. A very small number of patients go on to experience serious side effects that require hospitalisation and treatment, and these costs must also be identified and measured.

## Types of costs

Economic studies use a range of costs. It is important to be able to distinguish between the different types of costs that are used. Costs are usually divided into direct, indirect and intangible (Figure 3.1).

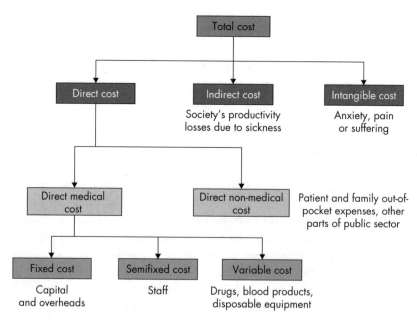

**Figure 3.1** Types of costs.

## Direct costs

Direct costs are those costs associated directly with a healthcare intervention. *Direct medical costs* are the costs incurred by the health service and are split into fixed, semifixed and variable (see p. 48, Fixed, semifixed and variable costs). These costs include staff time, medical supplies, hotel costs, capital costs and overhead costs. Also, there may be direct costs not incurred by the health service (*direct non-medical costs*). These can include:

- Patients' out-of-pocket expenses (such as travelling or child care costs)
- Costs falling on other parts of the public sector, such as social services (this would include the provision of domestic help, or disability pension payments).

## Indirect costs

Indirect costs are incurred by the reduced productivity of a patient and their family, resulting from illness, death or treatment. They may include time off work or housekeeping; time spent going to healthcare providers; time spent caring for the patient by relatives or paid carers; time forgone from leisure; and other non-market activities (Hodgeson, 1994). Only the following indirect costs can be calculated reliably from data:

- Time off work due to sick leave
- Early retirement
- Reduced productivity at work.

The significance of indirect costs depends upon the particular illness and treatments involved. Diseases such as asthma, migraine and depression affect working age groups, whereas other diseases, such as Alzheimer's, do not.

Indirect costs are difficult to measure. Also, there are unresolved issues about including indirect costs because this would tend to favour interventions where the individuals are in employment (i.e. not children, housewives, the unemployed and the elderly). The alternative to this is to attach a value to unpaid activities, such as attending school or carrying out housework. Indirect costs play an important role if the intervention produces benefits that enable the target group to return to work or their normal daily activity. For example, this could include management of depressive illness, asthma or rheumatoid arthritis.

Because of the difficulties concerning indirect costs, they are not often included in economic studies. However, it is likely that most interventions

**Table 3.1** Example of direct, indirect and intangible costs in a pharmacy based cholesterol screening service taking a health authority's perspective

---

**Direct medical costs**
Refurbishment of screening area
Screening machine
Training
Pharmacist's time spent screening
Reagents
Disposable equipment
Increased lipid-lowering drug prescribing
Changes in GP visits

**Direct non-medical costs**
Time spent travelling to pharmacy and GP surgery
Patient's travel costs

**Indirect costs**
Reduced time off work due to reduced cardiac morbidity

**Intangible costs**
Worry associated with a high-level fear of screening process

---

will affect indirect costs, so they should always be considered, if not measured. When indirect costs are included, they can have a dramatic effect on the results of the analysis.

## Intangible costs

Intangible costs are difficult or impossible to measure, but they still occur and it is of value to identify them. They can include anxiety, pain or suffering from an illness or treatment.

An example of a service that would incur direct, indirect and intangible costs would be a community pharmacy-based cholesterol screening service. Table 3.1 lists the types of costs that would be included.

## Fixed, semifixed and variable costs

The costs of healthcare can be split into *fixed costs* and *variable costs*. There is an intermediate category called *semifixed* costs.

### Fixed costs

Fixed costs are those incurred whether patients are treated or not. The two major components of fixed costs are overhead and capital costs.

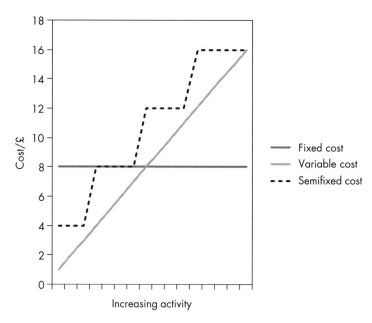

**Figure 3.2** The relationship of fixed, semifixed and variable costs with patient activity.

Capital costs are incurred when major capital assets such as counselling rooms are built, or equipment is purchased. Overheads are those incurred by the running of the service, such as lighting, heating and cleaning costs.

### Variable costs

Variable costs are incurred from a patient's treatment. They include disposable equipment, drugs, blood products, investigations and so on. Drugs and other consumables may have prices that vary between purchasers owing to the influence of buying groups, contractual agreements, quantity discounts and competitive bidding.

### Semifixed costs

Semifixed costs tend to increase only when there is a large increase in activity. This virtually always refers to staffing costs. Staff costs may vary directly with activity, and then they can be treated as variable costs. However, staff costs may only increase when there is a large increase in activity, when they are referred to as semifixed costs.

Figure 3.2 illustrates the relationships between activity (number of patients treated) and fixed, semifixed and variable costs.

**Table 3.2** Example of fixed and variable costs in a pharmacy-based cholesterol screening service

---

**Fixed costs**
Refurbishment of screening area
Screening machine
Training costs

**Variable costs**
Pharmacist's time spent screening
Reagents
Disposable equipment

---

The community pharmacy-based cholesterol screening service introduced in the section above would incur both fixed and variable costs. These are outlined in Table 3.2.

## What costs need to be included in an economic evaluation?

When a medicine is prescribed or a service used, some costs are incurred by some people and not by others. For example, when a person goes to their local pharmacy for a cholesterol test the pharmacist does not bear the cost of their travel. In an economic evaluation, the costs included depend on the *perspective* of the evaluation. It is necessary to state the perspective of the study, as this determines which costs are included.

Health economics is based on welfare economics, and so it is concerned with society's welfare, not just the welfare of individual patient groups or healthcare providers. Therefore, the ideal perspective is considered to be the *societal perspective* (Byford and Raftery, 1998). This is the widest perspective because it looks at the costs from the viewpoint of society as a whole. The societal perspective includes direct, indirect and intangible costs. Owing to the difficulties described above, most economic studies concentrate on costs from the perspective of the healthcare provider only. This means that only direct medical costs are included. However, it is necessary to be clear which healthcare provider's perspective is being used. An economic evaluation carried out from the perspective of the UK NHS could determine the resources used for interventions within the limited NHS budget. However, other sectors could incur costs or benefits as a result of that intervention. Figure 3.3 illustrates the three possible perspectives that could be used to assess the costs associated with a patient having a total hip replacement in a UK NHS hospital.

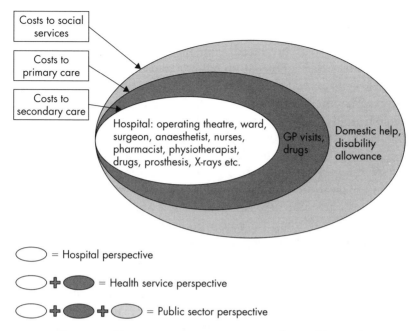

**Figure 3.3** Three possible perspectives to assess costs of a total hip replacement.

Figure 3.3 shows that the costs will increase as the perspective widens. It also shows that using narrower perspectives allows *cost shifting* to take place, from secondary care to primary care, or from the healthcare provider to other public sector services.

This can also be illustrated by the example of the cholesterol screening service used earlier. If this service were to be funded by the local health authority, the authority would also be incurring the costs of any increased prescribing of lipid-lowering agents as a result of use of the service. So, if the economic evaluation took their perspective, it would need to include the changes in prescribing costs. If the pharmacist was providing this service independently, they would not incur the changes in prescribing costs and so would not need to include these costs in their economic evaluation. However, the local health authority would still incur those prescribing costs.

## How are costs valued?

The two ways of collecting costs are either 'top down' or 'bottom up' (also called microcosting). Top-down studies use the total budget to produce average costs per patient. This method is the quicker one, but assumes that all patients have the same diagnosis, severity of illness and treatment. The costs produced from this method are not sensitive to changes in treatment. Bottom-up studies measure resource use by individual patients and so are able to detect treatment differences between patients. This method produces much better quality costs, but can be time-consuming and expensive. Also, top-down costs are often available from healthcare accounting systems, whereas bottom-up costs may need to be collected especially for that economic evaluation.

So, resource use associated with an intervention is best identified through observational studies of practice. For example, to find out how much it costs to treat depression, it is necessary to ask the following questions: When treating a person with depression, how many GP visits do they have in the first year, how long is each appointment, and what treatment does the patient receive? These data can be collected by following a patient (or group of patients) over a year as they are treated, and recording all the treatments they have for depression.

Resource use is measured in physical units, such as hours of staff time, or quantities of drugs given. The next step is to attach costs to that resource use. Most resource use has an associated unit cost, such as cost per hour for staff, or cost per dose for drugs. Overheads such as heating and lighting will also have a unit cost, sometimes per hour, or maybe per unit area per year. Market prices for resources are used to approximate to the opportunity cost of that resource. Some resources may not have easily accessible market prices, or may not have market prices at all. Indirect costs are a good example of this. Attaching values to resources for which no market (and therefore no prices) exists, such as patient time and informal care, means that economists must attach 'shadow prices'. This is where the true social value (or the opportunity cost) of non-marketed resources is estimated.

## Costs vs charges

It is important to understand the distinction between real cost of a healthcare intervention and the charges that may be used to generate a price for that intervention. The real cost is a reflection of the resources consumed during the intervention, and thus approximates to their opportunity cost. Charges used by healthcare providers often do not reflect true costs. This is because healthcare providers may cross-subsidise losses on some services with profits from others, at the same time running an overall surplus on services to finance new growth (Feldstein, 1981). These charges do not reflect the true economic cost of the service, although they have an obvious operational function, and are not recommended for economic evaluation.

## When to stop collecting costs

It is important to carry on collecting information about resource use until it is clear that no more events are likely to occur related to the original intervention. These events may be further interventions, such as follow-up outpatient appointments or treatment, or they can be side effects of the intervention, consequences of failed treatment, and changes in rates of negative outcomes requiring treatment. The study must carry on collecting cost information until all these events have stopped occurring. This may be a month, a year, or longer, depending on the type of intervention or illness being treated. The time when costs are no longer collected should coincide with when outcomes are also no longer going to be collected (see Chapter 8) and is called the *time horizon*.

Many interventions are designed to prevent further illness, or premature death, later in life. One example is the use of lipid-lowering agents to reduce cholesterol levels and hence the risk of stroke and myocardial infarction later in life. Ideally, an economic evaluation should continue until all the patients in the study have lived out their lives to see whether the use of these drugs reduced the negative outcomes, and hence the costs associated with treating them (termed 'downstream medical costs'). Often, trials do not continue with such a long-term follow-up period because of expense, and a shorter time horizon will be employed.

## Incremental costs and marginal costs

The terms *incremental cost* and *marginal cost* are often used in economic evaluations. An incremental cost is the difference in overall costs between two alternatives. A marginal cost is the cost of carrying out one more intervention. In the example of the pharmacy-based cholesterol screening service, the marginal cost would be the cost of doing one more test. This is likely to be only the added variable cost of the reagents and disposables needed for that one test. This is usually less than the *average cost*, which will incorporate all the fixed costs of the service as well (Torgerson and Spencer, 1996).

## Short-term *vs* long-term costs

It is necessary to define which costs are being considered in an economic study. The *total cost* of an intervention, for a given unit of time, is the whole cost of producing a particular quantity of output in that period. This may be the number of patients treated per year, for example. In the short term, total cost is made up of *fixed* and *variable* costs. Fixed costs do not vary with the quantity of output in the short term. In fact, the short term is usually defined as the time over which fixed costs do not vary. These costs have either been incurred at the beginning of the short-term period and so are 'sunk costs' (capital), or they are incurred independently of activity levels (overheads). In both cases they are unaffected by activity. Short-term variable costs do vary with activity (for example drugs). The short-term total cost for a patient's treatment includes both fixed and variable costs. However, treating one more patient increases the total variable cost to the healthcare provider but has no effect on the fixed cost. Therefore, the variable cost of that extra patient is the *short-term marginal cost* to the healthcare provider of treating one more patient.

In the long term there are no fixed costs. This period is considered to be long enough for all the inputs to the process to be varied. In the long term the healthcare provider can make the decision to change its activity level to treat more or fewer patients. This may mean building a new operating theatre or a new primary care clinic. This spending will lead to changes in the *short-term fixed costs* to accommodate this change. So, in the long term, short-term fixed costs can be treated as variable costs. So, the *long-term marginal cost* of treating one more patient includes the short-term fixed cost. Therefore, the *short-term total cost* of a patient is equivalent to the *long-term marginal cost* of that patient. See Worked example 3.1.

---

**WORKED EXAMPLE 3.1** Costing a service

This example illustrates the cost principles covered so far. Table 3.3 provides some theoretical cost information on providing a pharmacy-based cholesterol screening service.

Using this information we can answer the following questions:

1. **What are the fixed costs for setting up the screening service?**

    Fixed costs = refurbishment of screening area (£5,000)
    + screening machine (£1,200)
    + training costs (£1,500)
    = £7,700

*Continued*

**Table 3.3** Fixed and variable costs in a pharmacy-based cholesterol screening service

| | |
|---|---|
| **Fixed costs** | |
| Refurbishment of screening area | £5,000 |
| Screening machine | £1,200 |
| Training costs | £1,500 |
| **Variable costs** | |
| Pharmacist's time spent screening | £2 per patient |
| Reagents | £0.50 per patient |
| Disposable equipment | £0.50 per patient |

2.  **What are the variable costs for screening 1000 patients over a year?**

Variable cost for one patient
= pharmacist's time spent screening (£2 per patient)
+ reagents (£0.50 per patient)
+ disposable equipment (£0.50 per patient)
= £3.00

Variable cost for 1000 patients = £3,000

3.  **What are the total costs to the pharmacist of setting up and running the service for 1 year (assuming 1000 patients are screened)?**

Total cost for 1 year = fixed cost
+ variable cost for 1000 patients
= £7,700 + £3,000
= £10,700

4.  **What is the average cost of screening a patient over this first year?**

$$\text{Average cost} = \frac{\text{total cost}}{\text{number of patients treated}}$$
$$= \frac{£10,700}{1000}$$
$$= £10.70$$

5.  **What is the marginal cost of screening the 1001st patient?**

Marginal cost = variable cost
= pharmacist's time spent screening
(£2 per patient)
+ reagents (£0.50 per patient)
+ disposable equipment (£0.50 per patient)
= £3.00

*Continued*

This illustrates that the marginal cost is usually lower than the average cost.

Suppose that 250 of the screened patients have a high plasma cholesterol level and are sent to the GP by the pharmacist. Of these 250 patients, 200 are then prescribed lipid-lowering agents, which costs the local health authority £100 per year per patient.

If the health authority funds the service, what are the total costs to the authority of paying the pharmacist to set up and run the service for 1 year (assuming 1000 patients are screened)?

Total cost to health authority
= total cost of screening service
  + total lipid-lowering drug prescribing costs
= £10,700 + (200 patients × £100)
= £30,700.

## Discounting

The final requirement when determining true economic cost is consideration of adjustment of costs for differential timing (Drummond *et al.*, 1997; Smith and Gravelle, 2001). Discounting makes current costs worth more than those that occur in the future because individuals would rather spend money later than in the present. This is because any capital held now can be invested, yielding a real rate of return – that is, earning interest. Therefore, there is a cost to spending money in the present. For example, if £1,000 were invested with a return of 10%, in 1 year's time it would be worth £1,100. If the healthcare expenditure does not occur for 1 year, then that money could be invested to obtain that 10% return in 1 year's time. If that £1,000 were to be spent in 1 year's time instead of now, it would have earned an extra £100. Therefore, spending money now is associated with a loss of investment.

Also, consider that if you have to spend £1,000 in 1 year's time, you can take £909.10 now, invest it for one year at 10% and in one year's time you will have £1,000. Therefore, the present value of £1,000 in 1 year's time is £909.10. If you were to spend that money in 2 or 5 years' time, the amount required now would be even less. This means that costs incurred now are of greater importance than costs to be incurred in the future. This is known as a 'positive time preference' (Robinson, 1993).

Therefore, future costs have to be discounted in any economic evaluation. Studies will generally discount costs if the intervention lasts more than 1 year. Not discounting costs in economic evaluations can lead to results that do not reflect real costs (Torgerson and Raftery, 1999). This is because the costs in future years will be overestimated and the intervention will appear more costly.

The method used to discount costs is the opposite of applying the compound interest formula. The UK Treasury's current recommended discount rate for public sector projects is 3.5% (see Worked example 3.2).

---

**WORKED EXAMPLE 3.2    Discounting costs**

If the costs in an economic evaluation occur over more than 1 year then they should be discounted. This example illustrates the impact of discounting the costs of an intervention using information from a theoretical hip replacement operation compared to drug treatment for a patient with osteoarthritis.

| Intervention | Costs (£) arising during | | | | |
| --- | --- | --- | --- | --- | --- |
| | Year 0 | Year 1 | Year 2 | Year 3 | Year 4 |
| Hip replacement | 5,000 | | | | |
| Painkillers (undiscounted) | 1,000 | 1,000 | 1,000 | 1,000 | 1,000 |

1.  **What are the total costs for a hip replacement?**
    The total cost for the hip replacement operation is £5,000.

2.  **What are the total costs for drug treatment?**
    The total cost for the drug treatment is £5,000.

3.  **What is the impact of discounting the costs?**
    The costs for the hip replacement all occur in the first year (now). This means that they should not be discounted.

The costs for drug treatment occur over a 5-year period. This means that they must be adjusted for discounting. In the analysis, future costs must be given less weight because they have a lower impact than an equivalent cost occurring now. The further in the future the cost, in terms of years, the less weight they are given. To do this we must use a formula to correct for

*Continued*

the discount rate, as follows:

$$D_n = \frac{1}{(1 + r)^n}$$

where $D_n$ is the discount factor for year $n$, $r$ is the discount rate and $n$ is the number of years.

The UK discount rate for costs is currently set at 3.5%. Before 2003 the discount rate was set at 5%. Different countries set different discount rates. In economic evaluations, it is common practice to vary the selected discount rate in a one-way sensitivity analysis (see Chapter 8).

Using the formula and the 3.5% discount rate we can calculate the discount factors for each year as follows:

$D_0 = 1/(1 + 0.035)^0 = 1$

$D_1 = 1/(1 + 0.035)^1 = 0.966$

$D_2 = 1/(1 + 0.035)^2 = 0.934$

$D_3 = 1/(1 + 0.035)^3 = 0.902$

$D_4 = 1/(1 + 0.035)^4 = 0.871$

The discount factor can also be obtained from a published set of discount factors, which can be obtained from HM Treasury website.

The discounted costs are calculated by multiplying the discount factor by the costs for each year.

| Intervention | Costs (£) arising during | | | | | |
|---|---|---|---|---|---|---|
| | Year 0 | Year 1 | Year 2 | Year 3 | Year 4 | Total |
| Hip replacement | 5,000 | | | | | 5,000 |
| Painkillers (discounted) | 1,000 | 1,000 × 0.966 = 966 | 1,000 × 0.934 = 934 | 1,000 × 0.902 = 902 | 1,000 × 0.871 = 871 | 4,673 |

This example shows that when discounting is taken into account, drug treatment over a 5-year period is cheaper than a hip replacement.

## Inflation

Inflation should not be confused with discounting. A healthcare intervention stretching over a number of years, such as a breast cancer screening service, will be affected by inflation. Prices increase in the future, but generally they do so for all resources. This means that the relative prices do not change, so future inputs can be valued at current prices and discounted by a real rate of interest (Robinson, 1993). It is important to be careful when looking at older costing information, as this will have to be adjusted for inflation to present-day prices.

## Cost of illness

The cost of illness is the personal cost of acute or chronic disease. The cost to the patient may be economic, social or psychological, or personal loss to self, family or immediate community. This may be reflected in absenteeism, productivity, response to treatment, peace of mind, quality of life, etc. It differs from healthcare costs, meaning the societal cost of providing services related to the delivery of healthcare, rather than personal impact on individuals (Byford *et al.*, 2000).

The direct medical costs of illness include diagnosis, medical treatment, surgery and follow-up care. For example, this means that the illness cost of ischaemic heart disease will include the cost of primary care physician visits, medications, cardiologist visits, electrocardiograms and other diagnostic tests, angioplasty and cardiac surgery, emergency care hospital stays, and rehabilitation for myocardial infarction.

Indirect costs of illness are lost time or wages incurred by patients and their unpaid caregivers.

Intangible costs of illness are the pain and suffering associated with illness.

The point of treating a patient with a disease is to reduce these costs of illness. There is considerable uncertainty about estimating the cost of illness, and it is easy to underestimate the true cost (Byford *et al.*, 2000). However, it can be useful when planning budgets. To estimate the cost of illness as accurately as possible, it is necessary to make sure that good information is available for disease prognosis and treatment methods. Some examples of cost of illness studies are given on p. 63 in the Further reading list.

••••••••••••••••••••••••••••••••••••••••••••••••••••••••••••••••••

**SELF-DIRECTED STUDY EXERCISES**

**EXERCISE 1:** Thinking about costs

Several treatments exist to treat fungal toenail infections. Four oral medicines used are drugs A, B, C and D. The table below shows the costs (£) associated with treating 100 patients with each of these four treatments:

|  | Drug A | Drug B | Drug C | Drug D |
|---|---|---|---|---|
| Drug acquisition | 400 | 1200 | 600 | 900 |
| Laboratory tests required | 900 | 300 | 900 | 300 |
| Treatment of side effects | 1 | 3 | 70 | 0 |
| Total costs (£) | 1301 | 1503 | 1570 | 1200 |

- What categories of costs have and have not been included here?
  **Answer:** Included: some direct medical costs, but not staff costs or fixed costs. Excluded: direct non-medical costs, indirect costs, intangible costs.
- If you were told that all these treatments were equally effective, which would you choose? Explain your reasons.
  **Answer:** Drug D, because if all the treatments have the same efficacy, then we should use the cheapest option (this is cost-minimisation analysis; see Chapter 5).

**EXERCISE 2:** Calculating costs

You have the following information from a trial:

|  | Anaesthetic A | Anaesthetic B |
|---|---|---|
| Number of patients | 220 | 220 |
| Drug costs per patient (£) (includes costs of anaesthetics **and** drugs used to treat nausea and vomiting) | 12.0 | 25.0 |
| Disposable equipment costs (needles, syringes, etc.) per patient (£) | 3.0 | 2.0 |
| Mean length of operation (min) | 24 | 30 |
| Staff costs (£/h) | 70 | 70 |
| Operating theatre overheads (lighting, heating, etc.) (£/h) | 80 | 80 |

**Calculate the following for Anaesthetic A and for Anaesthetic B:**

A.   Variable cost per patient
B.   Semifixed cost per patient

C. Fixed cost per patient
D. Total cost per group
E. The marginal cost of treating one more patient.

**Answers**

| Question | Anaesthetic A | Anaesthetic B |
|----------|---------------|---------------|
| A | £15 | £27 |
| B | £28 | £35 |
| C | £32 | £40 |
| D | £16,500 | £22,440 |
| E | £15 | £27 |

**EXERCISE 3:** Understanding the costs in a published economic evaluation

In this section we examine the use of costs in a published economic evaluation (Jones *et al.* Economic evaluation of hospital at home versus hospital care: cost minimisation analysis of data from randomised controlled trial. *Br Med J* 1999; 319: 1547–1550). The authors of this study have reported detailed costing methods and results. Not every published costing study or economic evaluation will provide the reader with an equivalent quantity or quality of cost information.

You may wish to read this paper and then try to complete the assessment below. You may want to try this exercise alone, or in a group.

This UK study compared the costs of early discharge from hospital to a 'hospital at home' scheme with those of standard continued acute hospital admission in a group of elderly patients in an acute hospital requiring only nursing and/or rehabilitative care.

When examining the costs presented in this study, it is necessary to identify the following:

• Perspective
• Costs included
• Methods used to collect cost information
• Time horizon
• Use of discounting.

**How did Jones *et al.* (1999) report these aspects of cost information?**

1. The perspectives used in this study were those of the NHS, the social services and the patient. The most detailed handling of costs was from the NHS perspective, and this covered both primary and secondary care. Social services costs consisted of the cost of social work and domiciliary care provision.

Patients reported that their lighting, heating and laundry costs were increased by the hospital at home scheme, although this was not quantified in the paper.

2.  Direct medical costs included in the study for the hospital at home patients were:
    a.  Fixed costs: capital costs associated with the scheme's health centre base, overheads (local scheme management and administration, car leasing and travel costs, local community trust costs);
    b.  Staff costs (nursing, physiotherapy, occupational therapy, general practitioner), hospital hotel costs, residential care, patient transport provided by the NHS;
    c.  Variable costs (consumables and equipment hired to community trust).
    Patients who were allocated to the standard hospital admission group had their length of stay recorded.

3.  Direct non-medical costs were social work and domiciliary care provision costs.

4.  The methods used to collect resource use data were:
    a.  Fixed costs not reported;
    b.  Nurses' and therapists' hours from patients' notes and a work study;
    c.  Variable costs not reported.
    Patients who were allocated to the standard hospital admission group had their costs allocated using a standard cost per patient day from the hospital's accounting department.

    Therefore, it can be seen that one arm of the study used bottom-up costs and the other arm used top-down costs.

5.  The time horizon used was 3 months.

6.  Discounting was not carried out because the time horizon for the study was less than 1 year.

••••••••••••••••••••••••••••••••••••••••••••••••••••••••••••••••••••••••••••••

## References

Byford S, Raftery J (1998). Economics notes: Perspectives in economic evaluation. *Br Med J* 316: 1529–1530.

Byford S, Torgerson D, Raftery J (2000). Cost of illness studies. *Br Med J* 320: 1335.

Drummond MF, O'Brien B, Stoddart GL, Torrance GW (1997). *Methods for the Economic Evaluation of Healthcare Programmes*, 2nd edn. Oxford: Oxford University Press, Chapter 4.

Feldstein M (1981). *Hospital Costs and Health Insurance*. Cambridge, MA: Harvard University Press.

HM Treasury. The Green Book. Annex 6. *http://greenbook.treasury.gov.uk/*.

Hodgeson TA (1994). Costs of illness in cost effectiveness analysis: a review of the methodology. *PharmacoEconomics* 6: 536–552.

Jones J, Wilson A, Parker H, *et al.* (1999). Economic evaluation of hospital at home versus hospital care: cost minimisation analysis of data from randomised controlled trial. *Br Med J* 319: 1547–1550.

Palmer S, Raftery J (1999). Economics notes: Opportunity cost. *Br Med J* 318: 1551–1552.

Raftery J (2000). Economics notes: Costing in economic evaluation. *Br Med J* 320: 1597.

Robinson R (1993). Costs and cost minimisation analysis. *Br Med J* 307: 726–728.

Smith DH, Gravelle H (2001). The practice of discounting in economic evaluations of healthcare interventions. *Int J Technol Assessment Healthcare* 17: 236–243.

Torgerson DJ, Spencer A (1996). Marginal costs and benefits. *Br Med J* 312: 36–36.

Torgerson DJ, Raftery J (1999). Discounting. *Br Med J* 319: 914–915.

## Further reading

MeReC Briefing, An introduction to health economics, Part 1. September 2000, Issue 13, National Prescribing Centre. http://www.npc.org.uk.

Cocquyt V, Moeremans K, Annemans L, Clarys P, Van Belle S (2003). Long-term medical costs of postmenopausal breast cancer therapy. *Ann Oncol* 14: 1057–1063.

Gurkan I, Faust AF, Mears SC, Wenz JF (2004). Epidemiology and financial burden of hip fractures. *Curr Opin Orthop* 15: 8–11.

Krauth C, Jalilvand N, Wlete T, Busse R (2003). Cystic fibrosis: cost of illness and considerations for the economic evaluation of potential therapies. *PharmacoEconomics* 21: 1001–1024.

# 4

# Measuring patient outcomes for use in economic evaluations

## Introduction

The process of healthcare is undertaken so that people can benefit from the intervention. Current patients benefit directly from interventions such as hip replacement surgery or taking medication for hypertension. Healthcare also has a wider impact on the health of the population. For example, both current patients and other people benefit from interventions such as vaccinations, tuberculosis treatment and smoking cessation programmes. An economic evaluation looks at all the implications of deciding to choose one way of providing care over another, not just the costs. This means that any effect the service, good or bad, has on the patient or customer, needs to be investigated.

> *Benefits, outcomes and consequences refer to the effect on the patient, not the effect on people providing the service. Cost is not an outcome measure.*

In order to assess the benefit of healthcare, correct identification and measurement of patient outcomes is essential in health economics. An understanding of these outcomes is a prerequisite for economic evaluation. This chapter defines and describes the main categories of outcome measure used: effectiveness, quality of life, utility, and expressing benefits as monetary values (contingent valuation, or 'willingness to pay'), and appraises the importance of using the appropriate outcome measure. The issue of patient outcome measurement is a complex one and some of the challenges are examined here. Published studies will be used to illustrate key issues.

## Effectiveness

Effectiveness is the outcome of an intervention or service measured in natural units. These can be general outcome measures, such as:

- Cases successfully diagnosed
- Cases successfully treated
- Life years saved
- Life years gained.

It is also possible to use clinical indicators, such as:

- Number of asthma attacks avoided
- Pain-free days
- Change in infection rate
- Percentage reduction in blood pressure
- Effect on nausea and vomiting frequency.

These measures are relatively simple to use and are often reported in clinical trials of interventions. They are therefore the most common type of outcome measure and the most frequently used in economic evaluation. They are sometimes called *intermediate* outcome measures because there is the *implication* that changes in them will extrapolate to an effect on the patient's ultimate health status. For example, a study of diet-based lipid-lowering therapy in the prevention of coronary heart disease could use the drop in plasma cholesterol level to assess the effectiveness of this intervention. It is assumed that by reducing a person's cholesterol level, the risk of developing coronary heart disease is reduced. We know that this assumption is true because there is epidemiological evidence to support the link between cholesterol levels and coronary heart disease. Years of life saved could also be used if the study is designed to follow patients over a longer period.

### Example of effectiveness

Table 4.1 reports the results from a trial that compared daily recombinant human deoxyribonuclease (rhDNase), alternate-day rhDNase and hypertonic saline for treating children with cystic fibrosis (Grieve *et al.*, 2003). The primary outcome measure was forced expiratory volume in one second ($FEV_1$), a measure of lung function.

The results show that rhDNase was more effective at improving lung function than hypertonic saline, but there was no difference between the two different dosage schedules for rhDNase.

**Table 4.1** Clinical effectiveness of treatments for children with cystic fibrosis (adapted from Grieve *et al.*, 2003)

| Treatment | Daily rhDNase | Alternate-day rhDNase | Hypertonic saline |
|---|---|---|---|
| Percentage improvement in FEV$_1$ (SD) | 14 (27)* | 12 (19)* | 0 (27) |

*$p < 0.05$ compared with hypertonic saline.

## Quality of effectiveness information

Effectiveness information is generally available from the medical and health services research literature. The quality of that information is critical: poor information means that any economic analysis using that information will also be of poor quality. This book cannot provide a detailed discussion of the assessment of quality of evidence: the interested reader is directed to NHS Centre for Research and Dissemination (CRD) Report 4: *Undertaking Systematic Reviews* (2001). However, studies can be categorised using accepted *hierarchies of evidence*. A commonly used grading is:

I   Properly randomised controlled trial

II-1a   Controlled trial with pseudo-randomisation (alternate allocation, allocation by birth date or case note number)

II-1b   Controlled trial without randomisation

II-2a   Cohort prospective study with concurrent controls

II-2b   Cohort prospective study with historical controls

II-2c   Cohort retrospective study with concurrent controls

II-3   Case–control retrospective study

III   Large differences from comparisons between time and/or places with and without intervention (in some circumstances these may be equivalent to level I or II)

IV   Opinions of respected authorities, based on clinical experience, descriptive studies, or reports of expert committees (CRD, 2001).

### Bias and randomised controlled trials

It can be seen that *randomised controlled trials* (RCTs) are considered to be the highest grade, or quality, of evidence. Proper randomisation of patients to control and treatment groups in clinical trials is essential to minimise *bias*. Randomisation is what enables the trial to detect the efficacy of the intervention while controlling for variations in patient factors, such as age, sex or health status. Assessment of the quality of study design is often referred to as *internal validity*. If a study has internal validity, this means it has been designed well and is able to answer the question it was designed to answer. For example, in the cystic fibrosis study reported above, internal validity would have been reduced if the severity of illness of the patients in each treatment arm was different.

*Relevance of randomised controlled trials*

RCTs and other studies are often used to inform practice. In this situation, it is necessary to assess the relevance of the study to your practice situation. This is also called *external validity* or *generalisability*. RCTs are controlled studies and so may not reflect your practice if the patients or treatment processes are different. This will limit how useful the RCT effectiveness information is to you. For example, in the cystic fibrosis study reported above, relevance to you would have been reduced if you were treating adults with cystic fibrosis because the trial only examined effectiveness in children.

**Effectiveness versus efficacy**

*Efficacy* is the consequence (benefit) of a treatment under ideal and controlled clinical outcomes and is the outcome that is measured in RCTs. This assesses the benefit and harm of the intervention when all other factors are controlled. However, real life does not behave like an RCT. In practice, different types of patients from those in the trial may receive the intervention. Treatment processes may be different: the patient may receive different doses of a drug, or be monitored less intensively than those in the trial. These factors mean that the intervention is likely to be less effective in practice than in RCTs. *Effectiveness* is the therapeutic consequence of a treatment in real-world conditions. The effectiveness of a treatment or service is often lower than its efficacy, and so using RCT information may overestimate the impact of the intervention. Many researchers are attempting to overcome this problem by designing RCTs that reflect practice more closely. These are sometimes called *pragmatic* RCTs.

**Limitations of effectiveness measures**

A problem with effectiveness measures is that there may be more than one outcome reported for a particular treatment or service. For example, an analgesic may be more effective than another at relieving pain, but cause more nausea. Does one choose the analgesic with more power, or the one with a lower incidence of nausea? So, effectiveness measures are limited because they only measure one part of an outcome and may not reflect the overall impact of the intervention on the patient's health-related quality of life (HRQoL). For example, in the cystic fibrosis study reported above, we know that $FEV_1$ was improved by the interventions. However, we do not know whether that improvement was large enough to improve the patient's HRQoL, so it is an intermediate measure of outcome, where we are assuming that improvements in lung function improve overall health status. Also, we do not know whether the treatments were associated with unwanted side effects. There may be side effects that are sufficiently bad to affect the patient's health status, or so bad that they refuse to have the treatment at all. Finally, we do not know whether the improvement in lung function now will continue into the future and extend the life expectancy of the patient (see Worked example 4.1).

Many effectiveness measures are disease specific, such as lung function, and so cannot be used to compare outcomes for different disease states. For example, it would not be possible to use lung function to assess the outcome of an operation for a ruptured Achilles tendon. The only *generic* effectiveness measure is mortality and associated life-years lost or gained.

### Mortality used as an effectiveness measure

Mortality has been used to measure the effectiveness of treatments in patients. Examples of this are the studies looking at the use of aspirin after myocardial infarction, lipid-lowering agents in coronary heart disease, and the treatment of hypertension in patients with diabetes.

Mortality is a useful outcome measure because it is objective and easy to measure. However, there are problems associated with it. First, people may die from causes other than that of interest to the study, which can mask mortality linked to the intervention of interest and thus confound the results. Second, most illnesses affect quality of life rather than mortality, and so quality of life improvements due to interventions will not be detected or included in the economic evaluation. Third, mortality is a relatively insensitive measure that requires a study with many patients followed up over a long period of time. Finally, people of different ages and sex have different risks of mortality, so it is important that patient groups have similar age and sex profiles if they are to be compared.

*Example of mortality used as an effectiveness measure*

Table 4.2 reports the results from a trial that examined the mortality of men aged 45–54 with pre-existing coronary heart disease, and assessed the impact of lipid-lowering drugs on that mortality (Pharoah and Hollingworth, 1996). This table shows that using these drugs reduces mortality in this patient group. If 1000 men were treated for 10 years, three deaths would be prevented.

The limitations of the use of mortality can be seen in this example. First, it takes up to 10 years' follow-up in a very large group of patients to detect a change in mortality. Also, people may die from another cause, which can confound the results.

It is likely that treating patients with these drugs reduced the progression of many of them to coronary heart disease. Therefore, the health status of many patients was probably improved by the intervention, such that they could carry on working or their normal daily activities. This important effect of the treatment is not picked up by measuring mortality only.

Everybody dies eventually, so it is actually premature mortality we are trying to reduce, such that individuals are able to live out an acceptable lifespan. Therefore, if a premature death is prevented – for example by lipid-lowering drugs – we have saved years of life for an individual. Therefore, mortality can be converted into *life-years saved* or *life-years gained*. Using standard life tables, it is possible to work out the expected lifespan for an individual of a particular age and sex. For example, Gray *et al.* (2001) report that a group of hypertensive diabetic patients with a mean age of 56 taking atenolol had a mean (95% CI) life expectancy of 20.0 (17.4, 23.3) years.

**Table 4.2** Mortality of men aged 45–54 with pre-existing coronary heart disease, and the impact of lipid-lowering drugs on that mortality (adapted from Pharoah and Hollingworth, 1996)

| *Type of mortality* | *Treatment* | | | |
|---|---|---|---|---|
| | *No treatment* | | *With treatment* | |
| | *Coronary heart disease* (%) | *All cause* (%) | *Coronary heart disease* (%) | *All cause* (%) |
| Mortality at 1 year | 2.41 | 5.07 | 1.40 | 4.06 |
| Mortality at 10 years | 7.22 | 13.57 | 4.19 | 10.54 |

**WORKED EXAMPLE 4.1**    A theoretical worked example of using effectiveness measures

Patients with chronic renal failure who are on haemodialysis suffer from profound anaemia, which is often extremely debilitating. This is due to a reduction in their production of erythropoietin and loss of blood during haemodialysis. Historically, these patients have been managed by the use of blood transfusions. Now, synthetic erythropoietin is available. It is considered to be highly effective, but is very expensive. So, the alternatives are either to give erythropoietin or to give blood transfusions when the patient's haemoglobin level is below 8 g/dl.

Effectiveness data for the two alternatives available from the literature suggest that erythropoietin can maintain haemoglobin levels above 8 g/dl for 91% of the year, whereas blood transfusions maintain levels for 76% of the year.

1.    **What is the implicit assumption being made by the use of this outcome measure?**
      The assumption is that this is a desirable outcome because the reversal of anaemia will increase the patient's energy levels and hence their quality of life. What is the difference in effectiveness of the two alternatives, for 1000 patients?

      Erythropoietin keeps the Hb level >8 g/dl for 15%
          more of the year than do blood transfusions
          = 54.75 days per patient per year
          = 54 750 days per 1000 patients per year.

## Quality of life

The limitations associated with effectiveness measures have led researchers to develop ways of measuring the whole impact of a disease or treatment on a patient. The following sections describe some of these approaches.

Most modern medicine improves quality rather than quantity of life. Using clinical indicators carries the implication that changes in these will extrapolate to an effect on the patient's quality of life (QoL). However, there is an increasing awareness that it is necessary to measure the impact of healthcare on an individual's QoL, or HRQoL, at least.

Measuring QoL is methodologically complex. There are many functional, social, psychological, cognitive and subjective factors that affect QoL, a full discussion of which is beyond the scope of this chapter. The interested reader is directed to Fitzpatrick *et al.* (1992). QoL measures can be divided into generic and disease specific. *Disease-specific measures* have been developed for patients with chronic diseases, such as the Arthritis Impact Measurement Scale (AIMS) for rheumatoid arthritis, which includes looking at grip strength and morning stiffness. Such measures can only be used to assess patients or treatments within those disease states.

*Generic measures* are not so sensitive within an individual disease state. They are more useful when looking at groups of patients who may have different illnesses, and can be used to compare outcomes in different patient groups. One of the most widely used is the Short Form (SF)-36 health survey (Garratt *et al.*, 1993). This looks at:

- Physical functioning
- Physical role
- Bodily pain
- General health
- Vitality
- Social functioning
- Emotional role
- Mental health.

Typical questions asked include:

Does your health limit you in these activities?

|  | *Yes Limited a lot* | *Yes Limited a little* | *No Not limited at all* |
|---|---|---|---|
| Walking more than a mile | ○ | ○ | ○ |
| Bathing or dressing yourself | ○ | ○ | ○ |
| Lifting or carrying groceries | ○ | ○ | ○ |

Using these types of tool is more time-consuming than using effectiveness measures, but can give a much better indication of the impact of the treatment or service on the patient's QoL.

In the example of the study of lipid-lowering drugs in men aged 45–54 with pre-existing heart disease, a tool such as the SF-36 health survey could assess the effect of reducing the incidence of coronary heart disease on the QoL of the patients who have the treatment. The Nottingham Health Profile (NHP) has been widely used. This is discussed in more detail by Robinson (1993).

The limitation with some generic quality of life measures, such as the NHP, is that they provide a profile of patients' QoL. Although they are informative, these measures are not presented on interval or ratio scales and cannot be analysed quantitatively, and so are not useful in economic evaluations.

## Utility

Utility is the value attached by an individual to a specific level of health or a specific health outcome. Different individuals may attach different values to the same health state. For example, some people may be prepared to tolerate a lot of nausea to allow them to be pain free. Others may prefer to tolerate more pain and reduce the level of nausea. The important concept here is that utility measurement allows patients to value their health status based on their own preferences.

Like generic QoL measures, utility can be used when looking at groups of patients who may have different illnesses, and can be used to compare outcomes in different patient groups. Utility measures go beyond generic quality of life measures because they are based on interval scales and thus enable quantitative comparison. Simply, utility is used to attach a numerical value to the value a person has for a particular health state.

Imagine that treatment A improves a group of patients' health by an average of 6 points on a utility scale, and that treatment B improves a group of patients' health by an average of 3 points. Treatment A can be said to be twice as effective as treatment B. However, treatment A might be surgery for a ruptured Achilles tendon and treatment B might be rhDNase for cystic fibrosis. This example shows that utility can be used to compare outcomes for very different treatments in very different patient groups.

The specific methods used to derive utility are complex and are still under development. They are preference-based, which means that they allow individuals to indicate the direction and strength of their preference for a particular health state. People are asked to attach values to multiattribute health states. This means that the health state contains physical, emotional, social and mental health domains.

Attaching values to health states can be carried out using *standard gamble* or *time trade-off* methods, or a *rating scale*. The last is rarely used.

**Figure 4.1** Visual analogue scale (VAS).

To understand these methods it is necessary to be familiar with visual analogue scales (VAS). Figure 4.1 illustrates a typical VAS (you can also see a vertical VAS resembling a thermometer at http://www.euroqol.org).

Mark on the scale where you think indicates how you feel now (1). This seemingly straightforward exercise combines your physical and all other aspects of health, and it is your assessment of how much that health state means to you.

To help you understand this, try the following: mark on the VAS where you would value your health state if you had pneumonia (2). The difference between (1) and (2) is the difference in your health state, as valued by you. So, if you had pneumonia, and you were given some antibiotics to cure it, that difference in health state would be the health gain obtained by the drugs.

### Standard gamble

The *standard gamble* (Petrou, 2001) is considered by some health economists to be the gold standard for utility valuation because it is based on decision-making under conditions of uncertainty, and therefore mirrors real life more closely, as well as healthcare decision-making. In this approach, an individual is asked to choose between the following:

- The certainty of surviving for a fixed period in a defined health state, usually a state of ill health
- A gamble between a probability ($p$) of surviving for the same period without disability or a probability ($1 - p$) of immediate death.

The probability ($p$) is varied until the person shows no preference (is indifferent) between the certain option and the gamble. The probability at which the person is indifferent defines the utility of that person for the health state being considered, on a scale between 0 and 1, where the endpoints are death and perfect health. Gudex (1994) offers a complete guide to using the standard gamble (see Worked example 4.2).

**WORKED EXAMPLE 4.2** Using standard gamble

Standard gamble starts with a description of the health state under evaluation. In this example, the health state is dialysis for end-stage renal disease. The respondent, for example a patient, is asked to read the scenario and then asked to consider a choice, which involves comparing two alternatives. Alternative 1 is living in a certain health state – for example end-stage renal disease – for 10 years. Alternative 2 involves a risky treatment that has a chance (gamble) of immediate death, such as renal dialysis. The probability of immediate death is varied until the respondent is unable to choose between the two alternatives.

Consider Figure 4.2, which shows the standard gamble.

1.  **What state, A or B, would you choose?**
    We will assume you chose state B, which has a 100% chance of perfect health for 10 years and success from dialysis.

The probability values are usually presented using probability wheels (Figure 4.3).

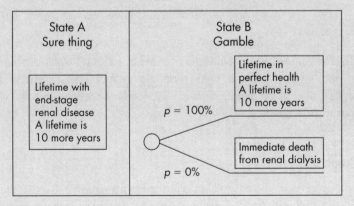

**Figure 4.2** A standard gamble.

*Continued*

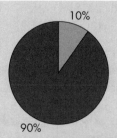
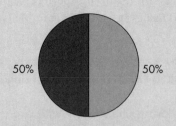

10% chance of immediate death
90% chance of lifetime in perfect health

50% chance of immediate death
50% chance of lifetime in perfect health

**Figure 4.3** Probability wheels.

2. **The probability of death from dialysis has now been increased to 90%. What state would you choose?**
   We will assume you chose state A in this instance.

3. **The probability of death from dialysis has now been decreased to 10%. What state would you choose?**
   We will assume you chose state B in this instance.

   This exercise is repeated, changing the probability of immediate death from dialysis. The exercise is complete when you cannot choose between the two states. Imagine this occurred when the probability of death from dialysis was 55%.

4. **What is the utility value generated from this exercise?**
   The utility value is then = probability healthy. That is, the utility value of being treated with dialysis is 0.55. For a published example of the use of the standard gamble, see p. 89, Further reading.

   The limitations of the standard gamble are that it is time-consuming, that people have difficulty understanding probabilities, and that how people value health states can be influenced by how the questions are phrased or presented.

### Time trade-off

This method was developed as a simpler alternative to the standard gamble, specifically for use in healthcare. In this method, people are asked to consider the relative amounts of time they would be willing to trade to survive in a range of health states. They are asked to choose between spending a certain amount of time in a defined state of ill health, or moving to a shorter but healthier life. The duration survival in the healthier state is varied until the person is indifferent between the two options. At this point, that person's utility for the health state can be calculated (see Worked example 4.3).

*Person trade-off* is a related technique that involves naming a group of individuals (reference group) who are returned to full health from a health state such as renal failure. The value of dialysis for renal disease can then be valued by asking how many people (*y*) have to be returned to full health from this health state to be regarded as equivalent to the health gain in the *x* members of the reference group. The value of dialysis for renal disease is then calculated as *x/y* (Ubel *et al.*, 2000)

---

**WORKED EXAMPLE 4.3**   Using time trade-off (TTO)

TTO starts with a description of the health state under evaluation. In this example, the health state is dialysis for end-stage renal disease. The respondent, for example a patient, is asked to read the scenario and then asked to consider a choice. The time in perfect health is varied until the respondent cannot choose between the two alternatives.

| State A | | State B |
|---|---|---|
| You have chronic renal failure<br>To stay alive you need to have dialysis<br>This dialysis is provided at a local hospital<br>You will live for 10 years in this health state | OR | 10 years in perfect health |

1.   **What state, A or B, would you choose?**
   We will assume you chose state B, perfect health for 10 years.

2.   **The time in perfect health has now been reduced to 1 year. What state would you choose?**
   We will assume you chose state A in this instance.

*Continued*

This exercise is repeated, changing the amount of time in perfect health but making sure it is always less than the time in health state A. The exercise is complete when you cannot choose between the two states. Imagine this occurred when the time in perfect health was 5 years.

3.  **What is the utility value generated from this exercise?**
    The utility value relative to perfect health is calculated by dividing the time in health state B by the time in health state A. That is, 5 years/10 years = a utility value of 0.5 for being treated with dialysis at hospital.

For a published example of the use of time-trade-off, see p. 89, Further reading.

Groome *et al.* (1999) compare standard gamble with time trade-off for assessing utility values for treatments for end-stage renal disease.

### Preference-based multiattribute health status measurement

The first main method used to attach values to health states was developed by Rosser *et al.* (1982). It is described in more detail by Robinson (1993), but has been largely superseded by other methods. Three main methods are used: Euroqol (EQ-5D), Quality of Well-Being (QWB) and Health Utilities Index (HUI). These methods, and the multiattribute utility theory underpinning them, are described in detail by Drummond *et al.* (1997). EQ-5D is described below.

### EQ-5D

The EQ-5D (Dolan, 1997; Euroqol Group, 1991) is a standardised instrument for use as a measure of health outcome (see http://www. euroqol.org). Applicable to a wide range of health conditions and treatments, it provides a simple descriptive profile and a single index value for health status that can be used in the clinical and economic evaluation of healthcare as well as population health surveys. EQ-5D has been specially designed to complement other quality of life measures, such as the SF-36, the Nottingham Health Profile (NHP), the Sickness Impact Profile (SIP), or disease-specific measures.

EQ-5D has five dimensions: mobility, self-care, usual activities, pain/discomfort and anxiety/depression. There are three levels per dimension

**Table 4.3** EQ-5D dimensions (from http://www.euroqol.org)

---

**EQ-5D**

By placing a tick in one box in each group below, please indicate which statements best describe your own health state today.

**Mobility**

| | |
|---|---|
| I have no problems in walking about | ☐ |
| I have some problems in walking about | ☐ |
| I am confined to bed | ☐ |

**Self-care**

| | |
|---|---|
| I have no problems with self-care | ☐ |
| I have some problems washing or dressing myself | ☐ |
| I am unable to wash or dress myself | ☐ |

**Usual activities** (e.g. work, study, housework, family or leisure activities)

| | |
|---|---|
| I have no problems with performing my usual activities | ☐ |
| I have some problems with performing my usual activities | ☐ |
| I am unable to perform my usual activities | ☐ |

**Pain/discomfort**

| | |
|---|---|
| I have no pain or discomfort | ☐ |
| I have moderate pain or discomfort | ☐ |
| I have extreme pain or discomfort | ☐ |

**Anxiety/depression**

| | |
|---|---|
| I am not anxious or depressed | ☐ |
| I am moderately anxious or depressed | ☐ |
| I am extremely anxious or depressed | ☐ |

---

and respondents/patients describe themselves within this system. The EQ-5D dimensions are shown in Table 4.3 (from http://www.euroqol.org).

This means there are 243 possible health states plus unconscious. This is what some of these health states look like:

- *Health State 11111*
    - No problems walking about
    - No problems with self-care
    - No problems performing usual activities
    - No pain or discomfort
    - Not anxious or depressed.
- *Health State 21111*
    - Some problems walking about
    - No problems with self-care
    - No problems performing usual activities
    - No pain or discomfort
    - Not anxious or depressed.

The EQ-5D health state may be converted to a score using published values. The time trade-off approach was used to assign the scores, which can be obtained from a University of York Discussion Paper (Kind, 1999). This document gives detailed information about how the scores were obtained from a survey of the UK population.

*Health State 11111*
This is assigned a score of 1.00 and represents perfect health.
*Health State 21111*
This is assigned a score of 0.85 and represents a condition considered to be less than perfect health.

These scores can be used as a 'weighted health index' (Kind *et al.*, 1998). They give a numerical value that provides a score for the *quality* of life in a given health state. The score can be used in the calculation of a *quality-adjusted life year* (QALY).

### Quality-adjusted life years

All the approaches above give utility measures that range from 0 to 1, where the higher the score, the better the health-related quality of life is considered to be. These utility measures are used to generate quality-adjusted life-years. A QALY combines survival periods (quantity of life) with health status valuations (quality of life) to provide a standard unit for measuring health gain.

One QALY is 1 year in perfect health. Because it is measured on an interval scale, one QALY could also be 2 years at 'half' perfect health. If you value health states using QALYs, you can compare different treatments. This method would let you compare the health gain from hip replacements with those due to antidepressant treatment, even though the clinical indicators for these conditions are very different.

### Healthy year equivalents

An alternative to the QALY is the healthy year equivalent (HYE), which uses a two-stage lottery method and which may better represent individual preferences (Jefferson *et al.*, 1996). It is also suggested that HYEs are equivalent to QALYs that have been derived from the time trade-off method.

### A theoretical worked example using QALYs

Utility data for the two alternatives available from the literature suggest that patients maintained on erythropoietin value their health states at a higher level than those maintained on blood transfusions. In a study

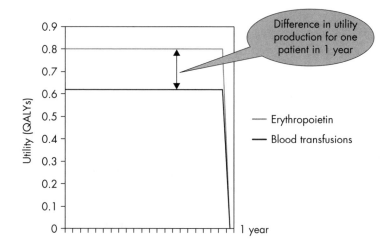

**Figure 4.4** Illustration of QALYs produced by erythropoietin and blood transfusions.

100 patients stated their utility for a treatment period of 10 years. The utility value for each year (when valued from 0 to 1) on erythropoietin was 0.80, whereas on blood transfusions it was 0.62. Figure 4.4 shows how those QALYs can be represented graphically.

What is the difference in utility production of the two alternatives, i.e. how many extra QALYs are produced by erythropoietin per year of treatment, for 1000 patients?

Incremental difference in utility
= 0.80 − 0.62
= 0.18 QALYs per patient per annum
= 180 QALYs per 1000 patients per annum.

## Whose utility values should be used?

Utility values can be obtained from healthcare professionals, patients and the general public. There are advantages and disadvantages associated with each group.

- Healthcare professionals are more informed about the health states and interventions but may provide a biased value owing to their continued exposure to that illness or intervention. Healthcare professionals have been shown to assign lower ratings than patients or the general public (Carter *et al.*, 1976; Saigal *et al.*, 1999).
- Patients are informed about the health states and interventions they have experienced. They will not be informed about interventions

they have not experienced. Patients tend to attach higher values to health states than do healthcare professionals (Carter *et al.*, 1976; Saigal *et al.*, 1999) and the general public (Shackman *et al.*, 2002). This may be because people in a health state gradually develop ways of dealing or coping with that health state, whereas the general public are less informed or are valuing their fear of experiencing that health state. Sometimes the health state has to be valued by proxy, such as the health state of a newborn baby or a person with advanced Alzheimer's disease. Therefore, it is important to remember that proxy values may be lower than the patient's values would have been.

- The general public provides societal values, which may be preferable to inform public policy decision-making. These values will be a mix of informed and uninformed views, and may provide lower values than patients would have done.

### Problems with QALYs and HYEs

There are many advantages to using utility to assess health. Utility measures allow comparison of health states between different illnesses and interventions. They assess many different dimensions of health, including physical, social and cognitive function, psychological wellbeing and pain. The valuations are generally based on societal preferences, which minimises bias. However, there is much criticism concerning the design and application of QALYs and HYEs. Some of the questions asked are:

- Are they valid? (Do they measure what they say they measure?)
- Are they reliable? (Are they reproducible and consistent?)
- Are they responsive (to subtle changes in health status)?
- Are they independent of the time spent in the health status?
- Are QALYs stable over time and between cultures?
- Are they ageist?
- Whose (patients, general population, healthcare professionals, etc.) values matter?
- Do they place sufficient value on life and life-saving?
- Is really possible to compare QALYs across disease states or studies when the methods are so sensitive to change?

The debate about using utility and QALYs to value health states and inform healthcare policy decision-making is wide ranging, and involves healthcare professionals, health economists, other health services researchers, ethicists, politicians and policy-makers, patients and the general public. It is beyond the scope of this book to present this debate, so some further reading is suggested. Drummond *et al.* (1997) present a concise summary of the key points in the debate.

## Expressing benefits as monetary values

Another method of measuring outcome is to convert these benefits to a monetary value. The contingent valuation (CV), or 'willingness to pay' (WTP) method, elicits monetary values for items not typically traded in private markets, such as health. Valuation is based on the contingency of the existence of the hypothetical market for health. CV accounts for both health and non-health effects and is thus considered to be a more comprehensive measure of the effects of a healthcare technology. For example, non-health benefits may include patients' preferences for consideration of their dignity, or aspects associated with the process of an intervention, such as location.

In simple terms, this method seeks to elicit how much an individual would be willing to pay to avoid an illness or obtain the benefits of a treatment. CV is increasingly being applied to elicit preferences regarding the use of medicines, for example in hypertension, lipid-lowering and depression. WTP has been used to elicit preferences for the avoidance of side effects with antidepressants, identifying those 'most troublesome' to patients (O'Brien *et al.*, 1995). Blurred vision and tremor were the side effects considered most troublesome and were associated with the highest WTP values to avoid them.

## Example of willingness to pay

Imagine you have a headache. You can have medicine A or medicine B. You are given the following information:

- Medicine A and medicine B are equally effective for alleviating headache.
- Medicine A makes 1 in 10 people feel sick.
- Medicine B makes 3 in 10 people feel sick.
- Which medicine do you prefer?
- How much would you be 'willing to pay' to have medicine A?

This exercise is not asking you to guess how much medicine A or medicine B costs: it is asking you to put yourself into the situation (health state) resulting from taking one of the two medicines. Both will cure your headache, but medicine B has a higher risk of nausea associated with it. What value, in pounds, do you attach to the reduced risk of feeling sick?

How would your selection and willingness to pay change if you were told that medicine A cures 50% of headaches and medicine B cures 90% of headaches? Now you will have to decide whether you are willing to risk an increased chance of nausea for an increased chance of cure (make a trade-off) (see Worked example 4.4).

---

**WORKED EXAMPLE 4.4**   Using WTP

Let us go back to the erythropoietin example we looked at earlier.

A willingness-to-pay study for the two alternatives available from the literature suggests that patients maintained on erythropoietin are 'willing to pay' for the extra perceived health benefits over blood transfusions. Fifty patients in a study stated that they would be willing to pay a mean of £2,000 a year for the extra health benefits associated with erythropoietin.

**What is the difference in benefit between the two alternatives, expressed in monetary terms, i.e. how much are patients willing to pay for the health benefits of erythropoietin per year of treatment, for the 1000 patients?**

Change in benefit = £2,000 more benefit per annum
                    per patient when given erythropoietin

Change in benefit = £2,000,000 more benefit per annum per
                    1000 patients when given erythropoietin.

---

## Methodological issues concerning WTP

Current empirical evidence and reviews suggest that the ideal design for a CV study remains unresolved (Klose, 1999). Some main issues are discussed below and some further reading is suggested.

### Value elicitation methods

Values for WTP can be obtained in different ways, and there is research suggesting that the method used affects the WTP value given. The dichotomous choice (DC) – or 'take it or leave it' (TIOLI) – method has been recommended by the US National Oceanic and Atmospheric Administration. Respondents are asked whether they are willing to pay a single amount, which is varied through the necessarily large sample. Although this is supposed to be closest to real market decisions, it may be open to 'yea-saying' bias. The use of 'bidding' can lead to starting point bias, and the use of 'payment cards' can lead to range bias, despite higher response and completion rates. The impact of range bias has been investigated and studies have reported that if the range is doubled the WTP values increase.

### Payment vehicles

Similarly, there is no consensus regarding payment vehicles, which is a particular concern in publicly funded health systems, where it may lead to strategic bias. This is a risk in the UK, where respondents may give very high or very low values to have an effect on service implementation. It is also suggested that respondents have an incentive to state high values for their preferred alternative, as they do not expect any individual charges. However, the evidence to support this proposed bias is lacking. Although healthcare is generally publicly funded in the UK, there is an increasing contribution from the individual. Therefore, it does not necessarily follow that the payment vehicle used in UK WTP studies must be taxation.

### Income and WTP

Reviews of empirical WTP studies have all concluded that income is closely related to WTP values, as the marginal utility of income reduces as income increases.

### Hypothetical nature of WTP

The primary concern for both advocates and critics of WTP is the hypothetical nature of the scenarios, the contingent market, and hence the valuations elicited. Great efforts are made in studies to develop realistic scenarios with understandable language and minimum bias. However, there is concern that respondents have difficulty responding because of the hypothetical nature of the questions. Uncertainty about the validity of this hypothetical market arises from its contingent nature causing artificiality. There are concerns that the values are constructed in response to the questions, and that they do not exist before they are measured. Furthermore, it is not clear whether expressed values bear any relation to actual values or predict future behaviour. At present there is no healthcare study that has compared hypothetical WTP responses with actual market rates, and so the debate must remain unresolved.

## Quality adjusted life years and willingness to pay

QALYs and WTP are both preference-based measures used to value health outcomes. They can both be used to inform decisions about healthcare resource allocation. However, the one that is used may affect those decisions differently, because there is evidence to suggest that they are not equivalent measures of outcome (Bala *et al.*, 1998). The reasons for this are partly the large differences in how the values are constructed, and partly because the way in which the questions are asked has to be so different.

## Discounting outcomes

It is accepted without question that costs should be discounted when the intervention under evaluation extends over a period of more than 1 year (see Chapter 3). However, there is no accepted practice regarding whether benefits should be discounted and the appropriate discount rate to use. Gold *et al.* (1996) provide an extensive discussion of the arguments for and against discounting health effects. The common 'official' view is that costs and benefits should be discounted at the same rate (Smith and Gravelle, 2001). One argument for taking this approach is that a consistent method of estimating the present value of costs and effects is used. Benefits should be discounted no matter what the unit of measurement. To illustrate, a study using QALYs should discount the benefits. Similarly, a study using the proportion of appropriate referrals to a GP should also employ a discount rate. The calculation used is the same as that used to discount costs (see Chapter 3). A sensitivity analysis should always be used to explore the impact of the discount rate on the robustness of the findings from the economic evaluation.

••••••••••••••••••••••••••••••••••••••••••••••••••••••••••••••••

**SELF-DIRECTED STUDY EXERCISE**

Go to http://www.euroqol.org to find out more about EQ-5D and how it can be used. You will find an example of the tool on:
http://www.euroqol.org/scoring/score_firstpage_example.htm.

••••••••••••••••••••••••••••••••••••••••••••••••••••••••••••••••

# References

Bala M, Wood L, Zarkin G, *et al.* (1998). Valuing outcomes in healthcare: a comparison of willingness to pay and quality adjusted life years. *J Clin Epidemiol* 51: 667–676.

Carter WB, Bobbitt RA, Bergner M, *et al.* (1976). Validation of an interval scaling: the Sickness Impact Profile. *Health Serv Res* 11: 516–528.

Dolan P (1997). Modeling valuations for EuroQol health states. *Med Care* 35: 1095–1108.

Drummond MF, O'Brien B, Stoddart GL, Torrance GW (1997). *Methods for the Economic Evaluation of Healthcare Programmes*. Oxford: Oxford University Press.

Euroqol Group (1991). Euroqol: a new facility for the measurement of health related quality of life. *Health Policy* 16: 199–208.

Fitzpatrick R, Fletcher A, Gore S, *et al.* (1992). Quality of life measures in healthcare. I: Applications and issues in assessment. *Br Med J* 305: 1074–1077.

Garratt A, Ruta D, Abdalla M, *et al.* (1993). The SF-36 health survey questionnaire: an outcome measure suitable for routine use within the NHS? *Br Med J* 306: 1440–1444.

Gold ME, Siegel JE, Russell LB, Weinstein MC (1996). Cost-effectiveness in health and medicine. Oxford: Oxford University Press.

Gray A, Clarke P, Raikou M, *et al.* (2001). An economic evaluation of atenolol versus captopril in patients with type 2 diabetes (UKPDS 54). *Diabetic Med* 18: 438–444.

Grieve R, Thompson S, Normand C, *et al.* (2003). A cost effectiveness analysis of rhDNase in children with cystic fibrosis. *Int J Technol Assessment Healthcare* 19: 71–79.

Groome PA, Hutchinson TA, Tousignant P, Hanley JA (1999). The repeatability of three methods for measuring prospective patients' values in the context of treatment choice for end-stage renal disease. *J Clin Epidemiol* 52: 849–860.

Gudex C (1994). *Standard Gamble User Manual: Props and Self-completion Methods*. York: University of York Centre for Health Economics.

Jefferson T, Demicheli V, Mugford M (1996). *Elementary Economic Evaluation in Healthcare*. London: BMJ Books.

Kind P, Dolan P, Gudex C, Williams A (1998). Variations in population health status: results from a United Kingdom national questionnaire survey. *Br Med J* 316: 736–741.

Kind P, Hardman G, Macran S (1999). UK Population norms for EQ-5D. York: Centre for Health Economics Discussion Paper, 172.

Klose T (1999). The contingent valuation method in healthcare. *Health Policy* 47: 97–123.

NHS Centre for Reviews and Dissemination (2001). *Undertaking Systematic Reviews of Research on Effectiveness: CRD's Guidance for Carrying Out or Commissioning Reviews*. CRD Report 4, 2nd edn. York: University of York.

O'Brien BJ, Novosel S, Torrance G, Streiner D (1995). Assessing the economic value of a new antidepressant. A willingness-to-pay approach. *PharmacoEconomics* 8: 34–35.

Petrou S. What are health utilities? *www.evidence-based-medicine.co.uk*, 2001; Volume 1, number 4.

Pharoah P, Hollingworth W (1996). Cost effectiveness of lowering cholesterol concentration with statins in patients with and without pre-existing coronary heart disease. *Br Med J* 312: 1443–1448.

Robinson R (1993). Cost–utility analysis. *Br Med J* 307: 859–862.

Rosser R, Kind P, Williams A (1982). Valuation of quality of life: some psychometric evidence. In: Jones-Lee MW (ed). *The Value of Life and Society*. Amsterdam: Elsevier.

Saigal S, Stoskopf B, Feeny D, *et al.* (1999). Differences in preferences for neonatal outcomes among healthcare professionals, parents and adolescents. *JAMA* 281: 1991–1997.

Schackman B, Goldie S, Freedberg K, *et al.* (2002). Comparison of health state utilities using community and patient preference weights derived from a survey of patients with HIV/AIDS. *Med Decision Making* 22: 27–38.

Smith DH, Gravelle H (2001). The practice of discounting in economic evaluations of healthcare interventions. *Int J Technol Assessment Healthcare* 17: 236–243.

Ubel P, Richardson J, Menzel P (2000). Societal value, the person trade-off, and the dilemma of whose values to measure for cost-effectiveness analysis. *Health Econ* 9: 127–136.

## Further reading

Bell CM, Chapman RH, Stone PW, *et al.* (2001). An off-the-shelf help list: a comprehensive catalogue of preference scores from published cost–utility analyses. *Med Decision Making* 21: 288–294.

Brooks R (1996). EuroQol: the current state of play. *Health Policy* 37: 53–72.

Dolan P, Gudex C, Williams A (1996). The time trade-off method: results from a general population study. *Health Econ* 5: 141–154.

Dolan P, Gudex C, Kind P, Williams A (1996). Valuing health states: a comparison of methods. *J Health Econ* 15: 209–231.

Fitzpatrick R, Fletcher A, Gore S, *et al.* (1992). Quality of life measures in healthcare. I: Applications and issues in assessment. *Br Med J* 305: 1074–1077.

Fitzpatrick R, Davey C, Buxton MJ, Jones DR (1998). Evaluating patient-based outcome measures for use in clinical trials. *Health Technol Assessment* 2: 1–86.

Gafni A (1994). The standard gamble method: what is being measured and how it is interpreted. *Health Serv Res* 29: 207–224.

Green C, Brazier J, Deverill M (2000). Valuing health-related quality of life. A review of health state valuation techniques. *PharmacoEconomics* 17: 151–165.

Green C (2001). On the societal value of healthcare: what do we know about the person trade-off technique? *Health Econ* 10: 233–243.

Harris J (1987). QALYfying the value of life. *J Med Ethics* 13: 117–123.

Klose T (1999). The contingent valuation method in healthcare. *Health Policy* 47: 97–123.

MeReC Briefing, An introduction to health economics, Part 1. September 2000, Issue 13, National Prescribing Centre. http://www.npc.org.uk.

Nord E, Pinto J-L, Richardson J, *et al.* (1999). Incorporating societal concerns for fairness in numerical valuations of health programmes. *Health Econ* 8: 25–39.

Roset M, Badia X, Mayo NE (1999). Sample size calculations in studies using the EuroQol 5D. *Qual Life Res* 8: 539–549.

Ryan M, Scott DA, Reeves C, *et al.* (2001). Eliciting public preferences for health-care: a systematic review of techniques. *Health Technol Assessment* 5(5): 1–186.

Saigal S, Stoskopf B, Feeny D, *et al.* (1999). Differences in preferences for neonatal outcomes among healthcare professionals, parents and adolescents. *JAMA* 281: 1991–1997 [standard gamble used].

Schulz M, Chen J, Woo H, *et al.* (2002). A comparison of techniques for eliciting patient preferences in patients with benign prostatic hyperplasia. *J Urol* 168: 155–159 [time trade-off used].

Torgerson D, Raftery J (1999). Economics notes: measuring outcomes in economic evaluations. *Br Med J* 318: 1413; plus subsequent correspondence (*Br Med J* 1999; 319: 705–706).

Torrance GW (1986). Measurement of health state utilities for economic appraisal: a review. *J Health Econ* 5: 1–30.

Viscusi W (1995). Discounting health effects for medical decisions. In: Sloan F, ed. *Valuing Healthcare: Costs, Benefits, and Effectiveness of Pharmaceuticals and Other Medical Technologies*. New York: Cambridge University Press, 125–147.

# 5

# Cost-effectiveness analysis

## Introduction

There is often more than one way of doing something in healthcare. For example, there may be two different drugs that can be used to treat depression, or two surgical techniques for the management of dysmenorrhoea. Note that interventions may be compared against each other (for example antibiotic A against antibiotic B) or against a 'do nothing' scenario.

There are different ways in which we can choose one of these options. We may decide to pick the more effective surgical technique, or we may decide to select the less costly antidepressant. Economic evaluation is a generic term for techniques that are used to identify, measure and value both the costs and the outcomes of healthcare interventions. An economic evaluation is concerned with identifying the *differences* in costs *and* outcomes between options. It can be defined as a study that *compares the costs and benefits of two or more alternative interventions*; so, the main components are *costs* and *benefits*. In economics language, this provides information on the production–function relationship; that is, how the inputs are related to the outputs (outcomes) (Robinson, 1993a). Economic evaluation can be used to inform decision-making, and can provide information to assist in answering the following questions:

- What services to provide, when and at what level?
- How to provide such services?
- Where to provide such services?

There are three methods of economic evaluation:

- Cost-effectiveness analysis (CEA)
- Cost–utility analysis (CUA)
- Cost–benefit analysis (CBA).

These methods differ in the type of outcome measure used, and are described, with examples, in the next three chapters. Cost-minimisation analysis (CMA) is used when the outcomes of different options are equivalent, and so the less costly option should be selected. CMA can take place in any of the three main types of economic evaluation.

An alternative method of economic evaluation sometimes used is cost–consequence analysis. This method individually reports the results of different outcomes in terms of their different natural units.

This chapter examines the use of *cost-effectiveness* analysis in medicines and healthcare services, which is the most common form of economic evaluation. If the outcomes of different options are measured in the same natural units, but have different effectiveness, cost-effectiveness analysis is the appropriate economic evaluation technique. The structure and purpose of cost-effectiveness analysis and the circumstances under which this method is appropriate are explained. Before beginning this chapter, you will need to understand the concepts covered in Chapters 3 and 4.

### The components of economic evaluation

It is clear that economic evaluations can be understood in terms of the inputs (costs) and outputs (benefits or outcomes) of a healthcare intervention (Figure 5.1). Therefore, an economic evaluation requires the systematic identification of costs and consequences of the healthcare interventions to be compared (Figure 5.2). Sources of information on costs and consequences are described in more detail in Chapter 8.

Any healthcare intervention can be seen as a process in this way. Figure 5.3 illustrates how an operation can be shown as a process with inputs (resources consumed) and outputs (effect on the patient).

Think of a healthcare intervention with which you are familiar, either through your clinical practice or through research or reading. Identify the

**Figure 5.1** Components of economic evaluation.

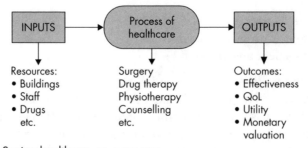

**Figure 5.2** Seeing healthcare as a process.

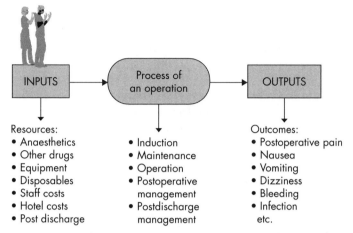

**Figure 5.3** An example of a healthcare process: the process of an operation.

inputs and outputs of this intervention. Can you think of an alternative way of reaching the same output in the same group of patients?

### Outcome measures in cost-effectiveness analysis

In CEA, outcomes are reported in a single unit of measurement, and are given in natural units, for example mmHg for blood pressure reduction, or life years gained by transplantation (Robinson, 1993b). The outcome measure is common to both alternatives, but may be achieved to different degrees (i.e. there is a difference in effectiveness).

An economic evaluation could examine the use of coronary artery bypass graft (CABG) surgery for ischaemic heart disease compared with medical (drug therapy only) management. The effectiveness of both treatment methods can be measured using mortality at 10 years. Evidence suggests that it is likely that mortality will be lower if CABG is used. Therefore, cost-effectiveness analysis is the appropriate method to use because the outcome is common to the two alternatives, but there is a difference in effectiveness.

### Incremental economic analysis

In cost-effectiveness analysis (and cost–utility analysis) you will come across the regular use of incremental economic analysis. This is a systematic method for identifying the difference (increment) in costs and outcomes between two healthcare interventions. The following questions are always asked:

- What is the difference in cost between the interventions?
- What is the difference in outcome between the interventions?

The answers to these questions allow the derivation of the incremental cost-effectiveness ratio (ICER). Incremental cost/outcome ratios may be calculated using the following equation:

$$\frac{Cost_1 - Cost_2}{Outcome_1 - Outcome_2}$$

$Outcome_1$ is the number of patients successfully treated with intervention 1.

$Outcome_2$ is the number of patients successfully treated with intervention 2.

$Cost_1$ is the cost of treating patients with intervention 1.

$Cost_2$ is the cost of treating patients with intervention 2.

The ICER expresses the cost required to achieve each extra unit of outcome. When one alternative is more effective but requires more resources, the ICER must be calculated. In the situation when one alternative is more effective and less costly, this alternative is the dominant therapy. When there is dominance, ICERs do not need to be generated (see Worked example 5.1).

**WORKED EXAMPLE 5.1** Incremental economic analysis

An economic evaluation could examine the first-line management of community-acquired pneumonia using antibiotics A or C. The effectiveness for both treatment methods can be measured using 'infections successfully treated first line'.

The incremental economic analysis is carried out in the following way:

**What are the costs associated with treatment with**
a)   Antibiotic A     [$Cost_A$]
b)   Antibiotic C     [$Cost_C$]?

*Continued*

**What are the outcomes associated with**
a)   Antibiotic A   [Outcome$_A$]
b)   Antibiotic C   [Outcome$_C$]?

**What is the difference in cost between using antibiotic A and antibiotic C?**
[Cost$_A$ − Cost$_C$]

**What is the difference in outcome between using antibiotic A and antibiotic C?**
[Outcome$_A$ − Outcome$_C$]

**ICER for treating community-acquired pneumonia with antibiotic A instead of antibiotic C:**

$$\frac{[\text{Cost}_A - \text{Cost}_C]}{[\text{Outcome}_A - \text{Outcome}_C]}$$

Theoretical costs of treatment

|  | Cost of treating 100 patients (£) | Effectiveness (percentage treatment of infections) |
| --- | --- | --- |
| Antibiotic A | 7,000 | 75 |
| Antibiotic C | 8,000 | 80 |

So, it costs £1,000 more to treat 100 patients with antibiotic C. Five more pneumonias are successfully treated with antibiotic C. Therefore, the ICER is £200 per extra pneumonia successfully treated with antibiotic C.

## Ways of using outcome data in incremental economic analysis

ICERs present the cost per unit of outcome. This could be cost per life year gained, cost per death averted, cost per case successfully diagnosed, or cost per patient successfully treated. It can also be cost per mmHg reduction or cost per percentage point improvement in lung function.

For example, in the cost-effectiveness analysis of rhDNase in children with cystic fibrosis discussed in Chapter 4, the outcome measure was percentage improvement in FEV$_1$. In their study, the authors report the ICER to be £200 per 1% gain in $FEV_1$ (Grieve *et al.*, 2003). This approach is often used in CEA. The advantage of this outcome measure is that it is objective and generally accepted as 'true'. However, sometimes it is not easy to interpret the clinical significance of this type of ICER. An improvement of 1% in $FEV_1$ is not likely to be clinically significant. Therefore, we might be more interested in knowing the ICER for an improvement of 10% or 20% in $FEV_1$, which is more likely to be clinically significant. The ICER will also be correspondingly larger.

Another approach would be to convert the results into numbers of patients successfully treated. We can easily explain this if we consider the cost-effectiveness analysis of rhDNase in children with cystic fibrosis again. Clinicians working in the management of people with cystic fibrosis consider that a clinically significant improvement in $FEV_1$ is 10% or greater (Suri *et al.*, 2001). Therefore, an alternative approach would be to examine the change in $FEV_1$ of each patient in the study and allocate them to 'successfully treated' or 'unsuccessfully treated'. Then the ICER could be calculated on the basis of patients rather than percentage change in $FEV_1$. The disadvantage of this method is that it may introduce subjective judgements about whether a patient has been treated successfully or not.

## Using an incremental cost-effectiveness ratio to make a decision

After reading Worked example 5.1, you may now ask yourself: which antibiotic do you think should be chosen by the healthcare decision-maker? This example illustrates that carrying out incremental cost-effectiveness analysis does not necessarily provide an obvious option: this will only happen when dominance occurs, where it is clear that the more effective, less costly option should be selected. However, the decision-maker usually has to select between the more costly, more effective option and the less costly, less effective option.

The generation of the ICER allows us to see how much extra cost is incurred for the extra benefit. It is then left to the decision-maker to make a value judgement as to whether they think that the extra benefit is worth the extra cost. In the example above, the decision-maker must decide whether they think that the extra case of pneumonia successfully treated with antibiotic C is worth £200. This is a disadvantage of cost-effectiveness analysis.

Economists use ICERs extensively in CEA, and this and later chapters illustrate how they are used and interpreted. Non-economist healthcare decision-makers may find ICERs less easy to understand, or to apply to their decision-making process. In this situation, it is always useful to present the differences in costs and outcomes as well as the ICER. This is called presenting *disaggregated* results. In the worked example above, disaggregated results are presented as: 'it costs £1,000 more to treat 100 patients with antibiotic C. Five more pneumonias are successfully treated with antibiotic C.'

The advantage of presenting the ICER is that it is a ratio, and does not change for one comparison whether you are treating 10 patients or 1000.

## Should the incremental cost-effectiveness ratio be large or small?

The larger the ICER, the more money is required to buy each unit of outcome. Therefore, as an ICER becomes larger, the intervention is said to be less cost-effective. For example, a CEA of reducing cholesterol concentration with statins generated cost per life year gained for different types of patients in which the drugs may be indicated (Pharoah and Hollingworth, 1996). Table 5.1 shows the different ICERs generated for these different groups of patients.

It can be seen that different groups of patients had very different ICERs. To generate one additional life year in women aged 45–54 with a history of angina and cholesterol 5.5–6.0 mmol/l it would cost £361,000. This is 60 times what it would cost to generate one additional life year in men aged 55–64 with a history of myocardial infarction and cholesterol above 7.2 mmol/l.

**Table 5.1** ICERs for lowering cholesterol concentration with statins in different groups of patients (adapted from Pharoah and Hollingworth, 1996)

| Patient group | ICER (£ per life year gained) |
|---|---|
| Women aged 45–54, history of angina, cholesterol 5.5–6.0 mmol/l | £361,000 |
| Men aged 45–64, no history of heart disease, cholesterol >6.5 mmol/l | £136,000 |
| All patients, history of heart disease, cholesterol >5.4 mmol/l | £32,000 |
| Men aged 55–64, history of myocardial infarction, cholesterol >7.2 mmol/l | £6,000 |

Therefore, although statins are effective and safe in all these groups of patients, they have very different levels of cost-effectiveness. It is generally accepted that healthcare providers cannot afford to treat all patients in whom statin treatment is likely to be effective. The implications of these different magnitudes of ICERs, in a resource-constrained healthcare system, is that they may be used to prioritise which patients receive statins.

## Cost-minimisation analysis

In CMA, the outcome of the treatments being compared is the same. Having ensured that the outcomes between the comparators are equivalent, then the approach used is to consider the costs of each option. The preferred option is the cheapest (Robinson, 1993c). For example, suppose two antibiotics, G and C, are equally effective in the treatment of *Pseudomonas* pneumonia, according to the current evidence. Therefore, we should use the least costly alternative. The following assumptions have been made:

- The two interventions are equally effective.
- We have included all the costs.
- There is no uncertainty associated with the clinical or economic parameters.

A recent economic evaluation of atenolol versus captopril in hypertensive patients with type 2 diabetes reported that there was no statistically significant difference in life expectancy between groups (Gray *et al.*, 2001). However, the mean cost per patient over the trial period was £6,485 in the captopril group and £5,550 in the atenolol group. The reduction was statistically significant and was due partly to differences in drug acquisition prices, and partly due to fewer and shorter hospitalisations in the atenolol group. The results from this CMA would suggest that atenolol should be used in preference to captopril in this group of patients (see Worked examples 5.2 and 5.3).

**WORKED EXAMPLE 5.2** Cost-effectiveness analysis 1: theoretical economic evaluation of management of anaemia in haemodialysis patients

Patients with chronic renal failure who are on haemodialysis suffer from profound anaemia, which is often extremely debilitating. This is due to

*Continued*

a reduction in their production of erythropoietin and loss of blood during haemodialysis. Historically, these patients have been managed by the use of blood transfusions. Now, synthetic erythropoietin is available, which is considered to be highly effective but is very expensive. So, the alternatives are either to give erythropoietin or to give blood transfusions when the haemoglobin level of the patient is below 8 g/dl.

Effectiveness data for the two alternatives available from the literature suggest that erythropoietin can maintain haemoglobin levels above 8 g/dl for 91% of the year, whereas blood transfusions maintain levels for 76% of the year. The effectiveness measure used here is the percentage time spent with a haemoglobin level above 8 g/dl.

In this exercise, you will carry out an economic evaluation of the management of anaemia in chronic renal failure patients.

- Assume that the economic evaluation is taking the perspective of the healthcare provider.
- You have 1000 dialysis patients who would be eligible for erythropoietin.
- You have the following cost information for the two alternatives:
  - *Costs of administration of erythropoietin*
    The average dose is 200 units/kg subcutaneously per week in three divided doses. Using prefilled syringes, this costs £106.65 per week per patient.
    Occasionally, patients have influenza-type reactions, an increase in blood pressure or a hypertensive crisis. The incidence and cost of managing these events are given below.

|  | Influenza-type reaction | Increased BP | Hypertensive crisis |
|---|---|---|---|
| Incidence (patients per year) | 1 per 10 | 1 per 10 | 1 per 500 |
| Cost of management (£) | 1.00 | 0 | 600 |

*Continued*

– *Costs of blood transfusions*

Patients whose anaemia is managed by blood transfusions have, on average, two transfusions per month. Each transfusion is typically two units of blood.

Cost per transfusion = cost of blood + cost of administration
= £130.

Occasionally patients have allergic reactions, an increase in blood pressure, or iron overload. The incidence and cost of managing these events are given below:

|  | Allergic reaction | Increased BP | Iron overload |
|---|---|---|---|
| Incidence (patients per year) | 1 per 100 | 1 per 10 | 1 per 100 |
| Cost of management (£) | 400 | 0 | 400 |

For each alternative, answer the following questions:

1. **What are the direct costs to the healthcare provider?**
   - Costs of treating with erythropoietin: acquisition costs, administration costs, management of side effects.
   - Costs of treating with transfusions: acquisition costs, administration costs, management of side effects.

2. **What are indirect costs and to whom do they accrue?**
   Cost to society of 'knock on' consequences in terms of lost productivity (i.e. patient cannot work while ill or being treated): time off work while having blood transfusions.

3. **What are intangible costs and to whom do they accrue?**
   These are costs that are hard to measure in monetary terms, e.g. the anxiety associated with having a blood transfusion, fear of needles, social stigma.

4. **How much would it cost to manage the 1000 patients for 1 year using blood transfusions?**
   Transfusion costs per patient per annum:

   $$(£130 \times 2) \times 12 = £3,120$$

*Continued*

Transfusion costs per 1000 patients per annum: £3,120,000
Side-effect costs per 1000 patients per annum:

$$(10 \times £400) + (100 \times 0) + (10 \times £400) = £8,000$$

Therefore, total costs per annum: £3,128,000

5. **How much would it cost to manage the 1000 patients for 1 year using erythropoietin?**
Erythropoietin costs per patient per annum:

$$£106.65 \times 52 = £5,545.80$$

Erythropoietin costs per 1000 patients per annum: £5,545,800.
Side-effect costs per 1000 patients per annum:

$$(100 \times £1) + (100 \times 0) + (2 \times £600) = £1,300$$

Therefore, total costs per annum: £5,547,100.

6. **What is the difference in cost of the two alternatives for the 1000 patients?**

$$£5,547,100 - £3,128,000 = £2,419,000$$

7. **What is the difference in effectiveness of the two alternatives for the 1000 patients?**
Erythropoietin keeps the Hb level over 8 g/dl for 15% more of the year than do blood transfusions:

> 54.75 days per patient per year
> = 54 750 days per 1000 patients per year.

8. **What is the implicit assumption being made by the use of this outcome measure?**
This is an intermediate measure of outcome. The assumption is that this is a desirable outcome because the reversal of anaemia will increase the patient's energy levels and hence their quality of life.

*Continued*

9.   **Calculate an incremental cost-effectiveness ratio for erythropoietin.**

$$ICER = \frac{\text{Change in cost}}{\text{Change in outcome}}$$

$$= \frac{£2,419,100}{54\ 750}$$

$$= £44.2 \text{ per extra day of Hb over 8g/dl.}$$

**WORKED EXAMPLE 5.3**   Theoretical economic evaluation of pharmacist-led clinical service to nursing homes

A group of community pharmacists wants to set up a clinical service to four local health authority (LHA)-funded nursing homes looking after 200 patients. This service involves a pharmacist visiting each nursing home once a month to assess the safety and effectiveness of individual pre-scriptions, and to set up and maintain laxative, sedative and analgesic prescribing policies. The LHA has told the pharmacists to show that this would be cost-effective.

Table 5.2 shows the results of a research study that the pharmacists have completed to measures the costs and outcomes before and after the provision of a pharmacist-led clinical service to four nursing homes.

From the results in Table 5.2, it can be seen that the health authority is saving £6,000 in prescribing costs per year. The cost of running the service is £7,680. The difference is an increase of £1,680, which will be incurred by the health authority.

$$ICER = \frac{\text{Cost}_{\text{new service}} - \text{Cost}_{\text{status quo}}}{\text{Effect}_{\text{new service}} - \text{Effect}_{\text{status quo}}}$$

$$= \frac{£1,680}{6 \text{ hospital admissions}} \text{ or } \frac{£1,680}{9 \text{ GP call-outs}}.$$

This can be expressed using the following ICERs:

- The new service reduces hospital admissions at a cost of £280 per admission averted.
- The new service reduces GP call-outs at a cost of £187 per call-out averted.

The health authority still has to decide what to do …

*Continued*

**Table 5.2** Costs and outcomes associated with the provision of a pharmacist-led clinical service to four nursing homes

| Parameter of interest | Status quo (12 months prior to introduction of service) | Pharmacist-led service |
|---|---|---|
| *Fixed costs* | | |
| Capital and overheads | None | None |
| *Semifixed costs* | | |
| Pharmacist | 0 | 4 h per home per month to 4 homes = 192 h per annum = £7,680 (at £40/h) |
| *Variable costs* | | |
| Laxatives | £2,000 | £600 |
| Hypnotics | £2,200 | £1,800 |
| Analgesics | £1,800 | £1,600 |
| Other prescribing costs | £22,000 | £18,000 |
| Total prescribing costs | £28,000 | £22,000 |
| *Outcome measures* | | |
| Number of hospital admissions | 36 | 30 |
| Number of out-of-hours GP callouts | 96 | 87 |

## Cost-effectiveness planes

The ICERs that we have generated so far can be plotted on to a graph known as a *cost-effectiveness plane* (Figure 5.4).

The difference in cost is plotted against the difference in effect. Depending upon the results of the incremental economic analysis, the ICERs can be placed in any one of the four quadrants:

- *Northeast quadrant*: intervention is more effective and more costly (such as the ICER generated for antibiotic A compared to C)
- *Southeast quadrant*: intervention is more effective and less costly
- *Southwest quadrant*: intervention is less effective and less costly
- *Northwest quadrant*: intervention is less effective and more costly.

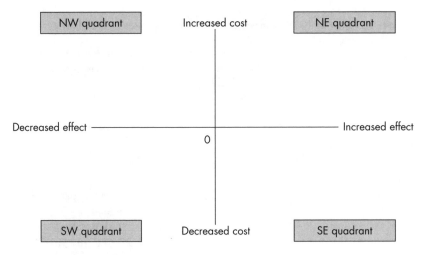

**Figure 5.4** The cost-effectiveness plane.

Interventions in the southeast quadrant should definitely be selected. Interventions in the northwest quadrant should definitely not be selected. Interventions in the southwest and northeast quadrants require value judgements to be made (see Worked example 5.4).

---

**WORKED EXAMPLE 5.4** Using the cost-effectiveness plane

In Worked example 5.1 we derived an ICER for the cost per extra pneumonia successfully treated with antibiotic C compared to antibiotic A. This ICER can be plotted on the cost-effectiveness plane, as shown in Figure 5.5. You can see that this ICER is in the northeast quadrant because antibiotic C is more effective and more costly.

---

### Sensitivity analysis

After the ICER has been generated in the primary incremental economic analysis (*base case analysis*), it is necessary to assess the robustness of these ICERs. In this situation, robustness refers to the sensitivity of ICERs to uncertainties in the data or alternative methods of analysis. If the conclusions do not change when these parameters are varied, the conclusions can be considered to be robust. The robustness of conclusions is examined using sensitivity analysis. This subject is introduced here with some simple worked examples. Further development of the subject and worked

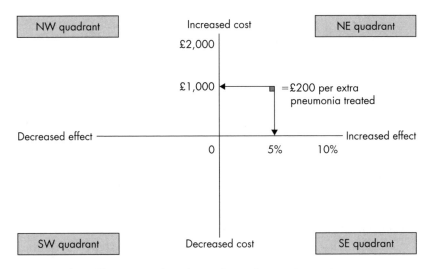

**Figure 5.5** Cost-effectiveness plane for antibiotic A vs antibiotic C.

examples are presented in Chapter 8. Probabilistic sensitivity analysis is a more advanced method and is described in more detail in Chapter 10.

Sensitivity analysis has many functions when used in an economic analysis. Every economic evaluation will contain some degree of uncertainty, imprecision or methodological controversy (Drummond *et al.*, 1997). For example, it may have been necessary to make informed guesses about missing data, or estimates may be available but be known to be imprecise. Uncertainty in the underlying assumptions, including analytical methods, weakens an analysis. The use of sensitivity analysis goes some way towards *quantifying the degree of uncertainty* existing in an economic evaluation. It also identifies areas where more research is needed to increase robustness.

There is more than one way of conducting a sensitivity analysis (Briggs *et al.*, 1994). 'Simple' sensitivity analysis varies one or more parameters across a plausible range. In *one-way sensitivity analysis*, each uncertain component is varied individually, to establish the separate effect of each on the results of the analysis. This may be sufficient if each of the uncertain components is independent of the others.

'Multi-way' sensitivity analysis varies two or more components at the same time. However, the greater number of components that are varied, the progressively more difficult it becomes to present the results of multi-way sensitivity analysis. A form of this is *scenario analysis*, which explores the implications of alternative states of the world, each of which affects a number of parameters in an evaluation.

*Threshold analysis* is concerned with identifying the critical value of parameters above or below which the conclusions of the study will change. Threshold analysis is useful in CEA for defining points at which the therapy under investigation becomes dominant.

Another method is *analysis of extremes*. This involves comparing a base case with the most pessimistic and most optimistic scenarios.

*Probabilistic sensitivity analysis* involves assuming that the values of selected parameters have a probability distribution (Grieve, 1998). The probability distribution is defined at the start of the analysis. A computer simulation is run where values of selected input parameters are chosen at random from the predefined distribution and an output distribution is produced. The output distribution shows the probability that each output, such as incremental cost or outcome, will occur.

A sensitivity analysis generally involves three steps (Drummond *et al.*, 1997):

1.  Identification of the uncertain parameters. At this stage you should look at the costs and outcomes in your analysis, and the methods used to derive them. If you have made any assumptions, or there is any uncertainty about those data, you will need to conduct a sensitivity analysis on that parameter.
2.  Specification of the plausible range over which the uncertain factors are thought to vary (from literature, expert opinion, or specified confidence interval around the mean). The range must be well defined, not arbitrary. For example, varying people's height from 3 feet to 10 feet is not a sensible range because no-one is ever going to be 10 feet tall.
3.  Calculation of study results based on the combination of most conservative and least conservative estimates. The ICER should be recalculated using the new values for the parameter (see Worked examples 5.5 and 5.6).

---

**WORKED EXAMPLE 5.5**  *One-way sensitivity analysis*

In Worked example 5.1 we derived an ICER for the cost per extra pneumonia successfully treated with antibiotic C compared to antibiotic A. Consider the following:

**Example 1**

A new trial carried out in clinical practice suggests that antibiotic C is not as effective as first thought, but that it is actually 77% effective

*Continued*

**Table 5.3** Sensitivity analysis of antibiotic A versus antibiotic C

| Analysis | Cost to treat 100 patients (£) | | Effectiveness (%) | | ICER (£)* |
|---|---|---|---|---|---|
| | Antibiotic C | Antibiotic A | Antibiotic C | Antibiotic A | |
| Base case | 8,000 | 7,000 | 80 | 75 | 200 |
| Antibiotic C 77% effective | 8,000 | 7,000 | 77 | 75 | 500 |

*Cost per extra pneumonia successfully treated with antibiotic C.

(Table 5.3). The ICER must be recalculated with this new effectiveness information.

This new ICER is larger, although antibiotic C is still more effective and more costly. This sensitivity analysis suggests that antibiotic C is less cost-effective than the base-case analysis had suggested. This new ICER can be plotted on the cost-effectiveness plane (Figure 5.6).

Figure 5.6 shows that the new ICER is above the frontier of the base-case analysis, and so this intervention is less cost-effective than previously thought. Now the decision-maker has to decide whether they think that the extra case of pneumonia successfully treated with antibiotic C is worth £500.

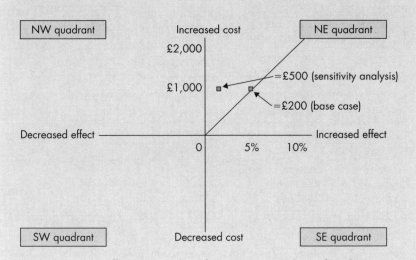

**Figure 5.6** Cost-effectiveness plane for sensitivity analysis of antibiotic A vs antibiotic C.

*Continued*

## Example 2

A new contract means that the healthcare provider is able to purchase antibiotic C at a much lower price. The new total costs are detailed in Table 5.4. The ICER must be recalculated with this new cost information.

**Table 5.4** Sensitivity analysis of antibiotic A vs antibiotic C

| Analysis | Cost to treat 100 patients (£) | | Effectiveness (%) | | ICER (£)* |
|---|---|---|---|---|---|
| | Antibiotic C | Antibiotic A | Antibiotic C | Antibiotic A | |
| Base case | 8,000 | 7,000 | 80 | 75 | 200 |
| Antibiotic C (new price) | 6,800 | 7,000 | 80 | 75 | (−40) |

*Cost per extra pneumonia successfully treated with antibiotic C.

This sensitivity analysis suggests that antibiotic C is more effective and less costly; therefore it is dominant. We would not normally calculate an ICER in this situation. However, the results of the sensitivity analysis can be plotted on the cost-effectiveness plane (Figure 5.7).

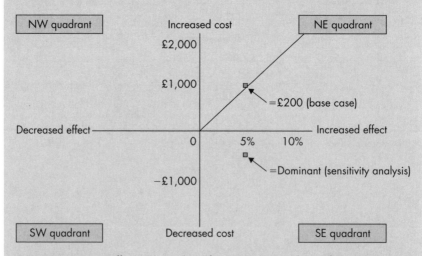

**Figure 5.7** Cost-effectiveness plane for sensitivity analysis of antibiotic A vs antibiotic C.

*Continued*

Figure 5.7 shows that the new ICER is in the southeast quadrant, where interventions are less costly and more effective. In this situation, the decision-maker is presented with the option they should choose.

**WORKED EXAMPLE 5.6**    Two-way sensitivity analysis

It may be true that the new effectiveness information and the cost information should be used together. It is possible to assess the impact of both of these pieces of information on the ICER in a two-way sensitivity analysis.

The new total costs and effectiveness are detailed in Table 5.5. The ICER must be recalculated with this new information.

This sensitivity analysis suggests that antibiotic C is more effective and less costly; therefore it is dominant. The results of the sensitivity analysis can be plotted on the cost-effectiveness plane (Figure 5.8).

Figure 5.8 shows that the new ICER is in the southeast quadrant, where interventions are less costly and more effective. This two-way sensitivity analysis suggests that choosing antibiotic C will produce two more successfully treated pneumonias at a reduction of £200 in costs. In this situation, the decision-maker is presented with the option they should choose.

**Table 5.5** Two way sensitivity analysis of antibiotic A versus antibiotic C

| Analysis | Cost to treat 100 patients (£) | | Effectiveness (%) | | ICER (£)* |
|---|---|---|---|---|---|
| | Antibiotic C | Antibiotic A | Antibiotic C | Antibiotic A | |
| Base case | 8,000 | 7,000 | 80 | 75 | 200 |
| Antibiotic C (new price) | 6,800 | 7,000 | 77 | 75 | (−100) |

*Cost per extra pneumonia successfully treated with antibiotic C.

Continued

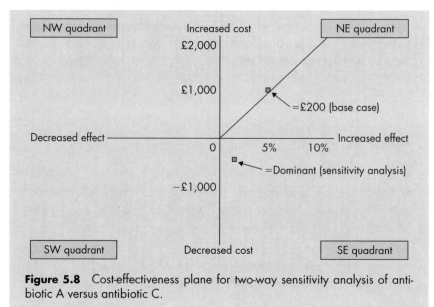

**Figure 5.8** Cost-effectiveness plane for two-way sensitivity analysis of antibiotic A versus antibiotic C.

Examples of probabilistic sensitivity analysis are presented in Chapter 10.

## A final note

This chapter has introduced the concept of cost-effectiveness analysis. This term is often used incorrectly to refer to all forms of economic evaluation, but it is a particular technique. CEA is the most common form of economic evaluation because it can use existing published studies for effectiveness data. The techniques used in this analytical method are developed in Chapters 8 and 10. CEA is useful for selecting between two interventions that treat the same illness. However, it is less useful when the treatments being considered have different types of outcome. Also, it is of limited use when an intervention has an impact on both quality and quantity of life. The next two chapters explore how this complex problem is being addressed.

• • • • • • • • • • • • • • • • • • • • • • • • • • • • • • • • • • • • • • • • • • • • • • • • • • • • • • • • • • •

### SELF-DIRECTED STUDY EXERCISES

### EXERCISE 1: Calculating an ICER

Several treatments exist to treat fungal toenail infections. Four oral medicines used are drugs A, B, C and D. The table below shows the costs (£) associated with treating one patient with each of these four treatments:

|  | Drug A | Drug B | Drug C | Drug D |
|---|---|---|---|---|
| Total costs (£) | 1,301 | 1,503 | 1,570 | 1,200 |

If you were then given the following effectiveness information about drugs C and D for a population of 100 patients, which of these two treatments would you choose?

| Agent | Efficacy in treating fungal toenail infections |
|---|---|
| Drug C | 90%* |
| Drug D | 80%* |

*Significant difference in efficacy.

$$\text{ICER for drug C} = \frac{\text{Cost (drug C)} - \text{Cost (drug D)}}{\text{Outcome (drug C)} - \text{Outcome (drug D)}}$$

$$= \frac{1,570 - 1,200}{10} = \frac{370}{10} = \frac{100(1,570 - 1,200)}{90 - 80} = \frac{37,000}{10}$$

$$= £3,700 \text{ per extra successfully treated case.}$$

Either could be recommended, depending on the driving force for the choice. Is cost containment most important? Then choose drug D. Is improved patient outcome most important? Then choose drug C.

## EXERCISE 2: Calculating an ICER

You have the following information from a trial:

|  | Anaesthetic A | Anaesthetic B |
|---|---|---|
| Number of patients | 220 | 220 |
| Drug costs per patient (£) (includes costs of anaesthetics **and** drugs used to treat nausea and vomiting) | 12.0 | 25.0 |
| Disposable equipment costs (needles, syringes, etc.) per patient (£) | 3.0 | 2.0 |
| Mean duration of operation (min) | 24 | 30 |
| Staff costs (£/h) | 70 | 70 |
| Operating theatre overheads (lighting, heating, etc.) (£/h) | 80 | 80 |
| Number of patients who **do not** experience nausea or vomiting | 180 | 200 |

Calculate the following for anaesthetic A and for anaesthetic B:

1.   Total cost per group
2.   Incremental cost-effectiveness ratio between anaesthetics A and B.

**Answers**

| Question | Anaesthetic A | Anaesthetic B |
|---|---|---|
| 1. | £16,500 | £22,440 |
| 2. | £297 per nausea/vomiting episode avoided | |

3.   Draw a cost-effectiveness plane and place the ICER you have calculated on that graph. You should have a point plotted in the northeast quadrant (Figure 5.9).

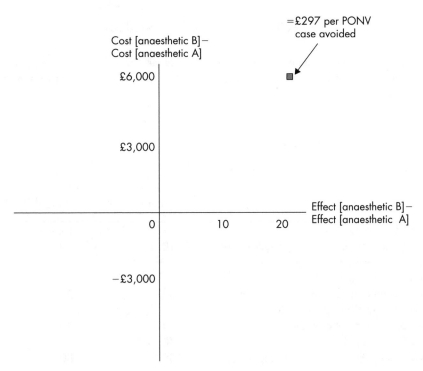

**Figure 5.9** Cost-effectiveness plane for anaesthetic A vs anaesthetic B. PONV, postoperative nausea and vomiting.

## References

Briggs A, Sculpher M, Buxton M (1994). Uncertainty in the economic evaluation of healthcare technologies: the role of sensitivity analysis. *Health Econ* 3: 95–104.

Drummond MF, O'Brien B, Stoddart GL, Torrance GW (1997). *Methods for the Economic Evaluation of Healthcare Programmes*, 2nd edn. Oxford: Oxford University Press.

Gray A, Clarke P, Raikou M, *et al.* (2001). An economic evaluation of atenolol versus captopril in patients with type 2 diabetes (UKPDS 54). *Diabetic Med* 18: 438–444.

Grieve A (1998). Issues for statisticians in pharmaco-economic evaluations. *Stat Med* 17: 1715–1723.

Grieve R, Thompson S, Normand C, *et al.* (2003). A cost effectiveness analysis of rhDNase in children with cystic fibrosis. *Int J Technol Assessment Healthcare* 19: 71–79.

Pharoah P, Hollingworth W (1996). Cost effectiveness of lowering cholesterol concentration with statins in patients with and without pre-existing coronary heart disease. *Br Med J* 312: 1443–1448.

Robinson R (1993a). Economic evaluation and healthcare: what does it mean? *Br Med J* 307: 670–673.

Robinson R (1993b). Cost-effectiveness analysis. *Br Med J* 307: 793–795.

Robinson R (1993c). Costs and cost minimisation analysis. *Br Med J* 307: 726–728.

Suri R, Metcalfe C, Lees B, *et al.* (2001). Comparison of hypertonic saline and alternate-day or daily recombinant human deoxyribonuclease in children with cystic fibrosis: a randomised trial. *Lancet* 358: 1316–1321.

## Further reading

Black WC (1990). The CE plane: a graphic representation of cost-effectiveness. *Med Decision Making* 10: 212–214.

MeReC Briefing, An introduction to health economics, Part 1. September 2000, Issue 13, National Prescribing Centre. http://www.npc.org.uk.

Robinson R (1993). The policy context. *Br Med J* 307: 994–996.

## Further published examples of cost-effectiveness analysis

Ben-Menachem T, McCarthy BD, Fogal R, *et al.* (1996). Prophylaxis for stress-related gastrointestinal hemorrhage: a cost effectiveness analysis. *Crit Care Med* 24: 338–345.

Burman WJ, Dalton CB, Cohn DL, *et al.* (1997). A cost-effectiveness analysis of directly observed therapy vs self-administered therapy for treatment of tuberculosis. *Chest* 112: 63–70.

Cantor JC, Morisky DE, Green LW, *et al.* (1985). Cost-effectiveness of educational interventions to improve patient outcomes in blood pressure control. *Prev Med* 14: 782–800.

Elliott RA, Payne K, Moore JK, *et al.* (2003). Clinical and economic choices in anaesthesia for day surgery: a prospective randomised controlled trial. *Anaesthesia* 58: 412–421.

Gaynes BI, Deutsch TA (1998). Cost-effectiveness of topical 0.03% flurbiprofen in outpatient cataract surgery as measured by surgical time and vitreous loss. *Am J Health Syst Pharmacol* 55: S23–S24.

Goodman CA, Coleman PG, Mills AJ (1999). Cost-effectiveness of malaria control in sub-Saharan Africa. *Lancet* 354: 378–385.

Katz DA, Cronenwett JL (1994). The cost-effectiveness of early surgery versus watchful waiting in the management of small abdominal aortic aneurysms. *J Vasc Surg* 19: 980–991.

Kempen JH, Frick KD, Jabs DA (2001). Incremental cost effectiveness of prophylaxis for cytomegalovirus disease in patients with AIDS. *PharmacoEconomics* 19: 1199–1208.

Lennox AS, Osman LM, Reiter E, *et al.* (2001). Cost effectiveness of computer tailored and non-tailored smoking cessation letters in general practice: randomised controlled trial. *Br Med J* 322: 1396–1400.

Logan AG, Milne BJ, Achber C, *et al.* (1981). Cost-effectiveness of a worksite hypertension treatment program. *Hypertension* 3: 211–218.

# 6

## Cost–utility analysis

### Introduction

In a cost–utility analysis (CUA) the outcomes of the two alternatives are measured using utility values, that is, the value attached to the health states produced by the two interventions. The value may be attached by patients, health professionals or the general population, but the last is preferred. CUA is actually a form of cost-effectiveness analysis but utility is used instead of natural units to measure outcomes (Robinson, 1993).

This chapter examines the use of CUA in medicines and healthcare services. If the outcomes of different options are measured using utility, CUA is the appropriate economic evaluation technique. The structure and purpose of CUA and the circumstances under which this method is appropriate are explained. Before beginning this chapter, you will need to understand the concepts covered in Chapters 3 and 4. Incremental economic analysis, cost-effectiveness planes and sensitivity analysis were covered in Chapter 5 and apply in exactly the same way in CUA.

### Outcome measures in cost–utility analysis

In CEA the results of the incremental economic analysis are measured in terms of cost per additional unit of outcome, such as life years gained, or improvements in lung function. In CUA the results are measured in the same way, but the ICER is presented as the cost per additional QALY. QALYs are the most commonly used measures in CUA (see Worked example 6.1).

**WORKED EXAMPLE 6.1** Economic evaluation of management of anaemia in haemodialysis patients

Patients with chronic renal failure who are on haemodialysis suffer from profound anaemia, which is often extremely debilitating. This is due

*Continued*

to a reduction in the production of erythropoietin in these patients, and loss of blood during haemodialysis. Historically, these patients have been managed by the use of blood transfusions. Now, synthetic erythropoietin is available. It is considered to be highly effective, but is very expensive. So, the alternatives are to either give erythropoietin or to give blood transfusions when the patient's haemoglobin level is below 8 g/dl.

**Cost information** (see Chapter 5 for detailed calculation)

Total costs to manage the 1000 patients for 1 year using blood transfusions: £3,128,000.

Total costs to manage the 1000 patients for 1 year using erythropoietin: £5,547,100.

**Outcome information**

Utility data for the two alternatives available from the literature suggest that patients maintained on erythropoietin value their health states at a higher level than those maintained on blood transfusions. In a study, 100 patients stated that for a treatment period of 10 years, their utility value for each year (when valued from 0 to 1) on erythropoietin was 0.80, whereas on blood transfusions it was 0.75.

1. **What is the difference in cost between the two alternatives for the 1000 patients?**
   £2,419,100.

2. **What is the difference in utility production of the two alternatives, i.e. how many extra QALYs are produced by erythropoietin per year of treatment, for the 1000 patients?**

   Change in utility = 0.80 − 0.75
                        = 0.05 QALYs per patient per annum
                        = 50 QALYs per 1000 patients per annum.

   Figure 6.1 illustrates the difference in utility production for the two alternatives.

*Continued*

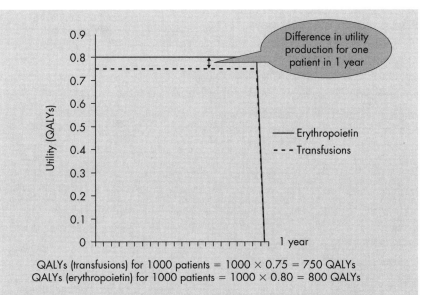

QALYs (transfusions) for 1000 patients = 1000 × 0.75 = 750 QALYs
QALYs (erythropoietin) for 1000 patients = 1000 × 0.80 = 800 QALYs

**Figure 6.1** Utility produced over 1 year for erythropoeitin vs blood transfusions.

3. **Calculate an incremental cost–utility ratio for erythropoietin.**

$$\text{ICER} = \frac{\text{Change in cost}}{\text{Change in outcome (utility)}}$$
$$= \frac{£2,419,100}{50}$$
$$= £48,382 \text{ per extra QALY gained by erythropoietin.}$$

This cost per QALY can be plotted on a cost-effectiveness plane (Figure 6.2). You can see that this ICER is in the northeast quadrant because erythropoietin is more effective and more costly.

## Using cost–utility analysis to allocate resources to different services

Worked example 6.1 shows how QALYs can be used in a CUA to generate costs per QALY. However, in that example we were trying to decide between two ways of treating the same illness. We could also have used a common outcome such as the presence of anaemia, and the resulting economic evaluation would have been a CEA (see Chapter 5, worked examples). It is more difficult to compare two healthcare interventions that do not have comparable outcome measures. CEA cannot

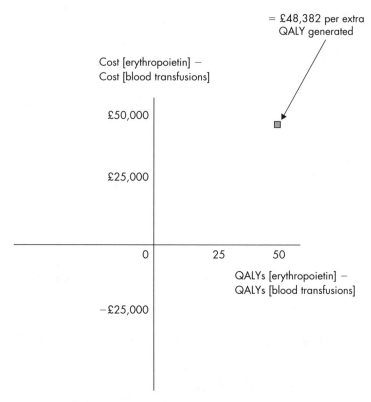

**Figure 6.2** Cost-effectiveness plane for erythropoietin vs blood transfusions.

be used in this situation, and we have to use an outcome measure that can be used across different diseases, such as QALYs. CUA can be used to generate costs per QALY in different disease areas, and so diseases with different clinical outcomes can be compared. This means that CUA can be used to allocate resources to different services. Worked example 6.2 illustrates how this can be carried out.

**WORKED EXAMPLE 6.2** Cost–utility analysis of two different types of service

A group of community nurses (Group A) wants to set up an asthma patient monitoring service for a GP practice which has 200 asthma patients.

*Continued*

Results from a study suggest that the practice will have cost reductions and the patients will have improved outcomes (Table 6.1).

**Table 6.1** Impact of a nurse-led asthma monitoring service

| Costs and outcome measures for 1 year | Before asthma service | With asthma service | Difference |
|---|---|---|---|
| Prescribing costs (£) | 20,000 | 16,000 | −4,000 |
| Hospital costs (£) | 2,000 | 1,000 | −1,000 |
| Nurse service costs (£) | 0 | 4,000 | 4,000 |
| Total costs (£) | 22,000 | 21,000 | −1,000 |
| Emergency hospital admissions due to asthma | 20 | 10 | −10 |

Another group of community nurses (Group B) wants to set up an ischaemic heart disease (IHD) patient monitoring service for the same GP practice, which has 250 IHD patients. Results from a study suggest that the service will be cost neutral and the patients will have improved outcome (Table 6.2).

**Table 6.2** Impact of a nurse-led ischaemic heart disease monitoring service

| Costs and outcome measures for 1 year | Before IHD service | With IHD service | Difference |
|---|---|---|---|
| Prescribing costs (£) | 25,000 | 20,000 | −5,000 |
| Hospital costs (£) | 10,000 | 5,000 | −5,000 |
| Nurse service costs (£) | 0 | 10,000 | 10,000 |
| Total costs (£) | 35,000 | 35,000 | 0 |
| Emergency hospital admissions due to chest pain | 50 | 25 | −25 |

The practice has to decide whether to reduce emergency admissions due to asthma by 10 a year and save £1,000, or reduce emergency admissions due to chest pain by 25 a year at no change in costs to the practice.

*Continued*

**How can the GP objectively compare and choose between improving the health of asthma and IHD patients?**

Groups A and B elicit utility values from the 200 asthma and 250 IHD patients. Time trade-off was used to elicit the utility values and these were used to calculate QALYs.

The groups obtain the following results:

|  | Asthma patients | IHD patients |
|---|---|---|
| Mean QALYs before intervention | 0.75 | 0.60 |
| Mean QALYs after intervention | 0.85 | 0.75 |
| Incremental QALY change caused by intervention | 0.10 | 0.15 |

The results refer to a 1-year period. The asthma patients improved their quality of life per year by 0.10 QALYs each. The IHD patients improved their quality of life per year by 0.15 QALYs each.

Incremental cost-effectiveness ratio (ICER):

$$\frac{\Delta Cost}{\Delta QALY} = \frac{Cost_{IHD\ service} - Cost_{asthma\ service}}{QALY_{IHD\ service} - QALY_{asthma\ service}}$$

$$= \frac{0 - (-1000)}{(250 \times 0.15) - (200 \times 0.10)} = \frac{1000}{17.5}$$

$$= £57\ per\ QALY\ gained\ from\ the\ IHD$$
service over the asthma service.

If the GP practice funds the IHD service it will cost them £1,000 per year more than the asthma service, but they will obtain 17.5 more QALYs for their patients.

## Using cost–utility analysis to choose between life-saving and life-improving interventions

In the worked examples above, extra QALYs were generated by improving the quality of life of a group of patients. However, QALYs also can be used to choose between treatments where there are different levels of life-saving or life-improving effect.

To help understand this idea, we can consider the example of medical versus surgical treatment for hip joint disease. This painful condition progressively reduces an individual's mobility until they are unable to walk, and causes considerable pain. It can be managed medically with analgesics, which ease the pain but do not halt the progression of the disease. Alternatively, a total hip replacement can be carried out which improves mobility and reduces pain considerably. There is, however, a small risk of death associated with the operation (1%). In Figure 6.3, the theoretical QALYs associated with this example are presented. You can see that people who have surgical intervention (and survive the perioperative period) have a longer life expectancy, probably due to improved mobility leading to improved general health.

It is possible to work out how many QALYs are produced by each treatment option by measuring the area under the curve for each of the three possible events (Table 6.3).

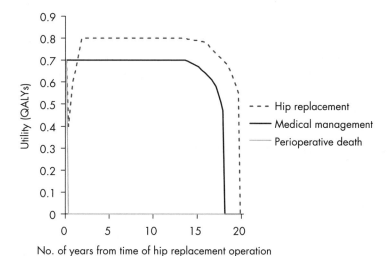

No. of years from time of hip replacement operation

**Figure 6.3** Theoretical QALY profile for medical and surgical management of hip joint disease.

**Table 6.3** Number of QALYs generated by treatments for hip joint disease

| Event | Number of QALYs* |
| --- | --- |
| Surgical management, perioperative death | 0.1 |
| Surgical management, lives for 20 years | 15.1 |
| Medical management, lives for 18 years | 12.0 |

*Theoretical estimates.

**Table 6.4** Theoretical costs and QALYs generated by treatments for hip joint disease

| Option | Number of QALYs | Costs (£)* |
|---|---|---|
| Surgical management | $(99 \times 15.1 + 1 \times 0.1) = 1495$ | 1,500,000 |
| Medical management | $(100 \times 12.0) = 1200$ | 1,000,000 |
| Difference | 295 | 500,000 |

*Theoretical estimates.

It is possible to carry out an incremental economic analysis. If we have a group of 100 people with hip joint disease, they can either have medical treatment and live for 18 years, or they can have surgical management. In this case, one person will die perioperatively, and 99 will live for 20 years. Table 6.4 shows the costs and QALYs for the two treatment options.

Surgical management generates 295 more QALYs at an increased cost of £500,000, so the cost per QALY is £1,695.

One very well known example of this type of economic evaluation was a study carried out by Williams (1985), who assessed treatment options for patients with different severities of angina. This was the first widely disseminated use of QALYs in evaluating healthcare; it caused widespread debate, and is recommended to the interested reader.

## The effect of discounting quality adjusted life years in cost–utility analysis

In Chapter 4, discounting outcomes was discussed. This is an area of health economics where there is not complete agreement on the 'correct' method. Therefore, CUAs often present their results in both undiscounted and discounted form. This means that the discount rate applied to costs that occur over a number of years is also applied to the outcomes. The incremental economic analysis is then carried out on these discounted values.

Discounting QALYs can have a significant impact on the ICERs generated. An economic evaluation looked at the economic impact of four disease-modifying treatments (interferon-β and glatiramer acetate) for relapsing–remitting and secondary progressive multiple sclerosis (MS) (Chilcott et al., 2003). In this analysis, the authors examined the clinical course of the disease over 20 years (length of life and quality of life during that 20 years) and calculated how many QALYs this was equivalent to. They also costed the treatment of patients with MS over 20 years. From your knowledge of discounting you can already see that discounting costs

**Table 6.5** Undiscounted and discounted cost per QALY gained compared with conventional treatment for MS (adapted from Chilcott *et al.*, 2003)

| Treatment | Undiscounted cost per QALY (£) | Cost per QALY (costs and QALYs discounted at 6%) (£) |
|---|---|---|
| Interferon-$\beta_{1a}$ 6 MIU/week (Avonex) | 42,041 | 73,137 |
| Interferon-$\beta_{1a}$ 22 μg/week (Rebif) | 60,963 | 105,718 |
| Interferon-$\beta_{1a}$ 44 μg/week (Rebif) | 71,732 | 124,034 |
| Interferon-$\beta_{1b}$ 8 MIU/week (Betaferon) | 49,664 | 86,127 |
| Glatiramer acetate 20 mg/week (Copaxone) | 97,636 | 168,539 |

and benefits over such a long period is going to have a great effect on the final ICERs. Table 6.5 shows the results from the analysis.

It is clear that discounting costs and benefits has increased the ICERs, sometimes by as much as 75%. This means that the intervention is not as cost-effective as it first appeared.

Different researchers may use different discount rates, which means that the results from two studies may not be comparable. For example, a study looked at the cost-effectiveness of combination antiretroviral therapy for HIV disease (Freedberg *et al.*, 2001). The authors examined the economic impact of using a combination of three or more drugs compared with no therapy in patients with a mean CD4 count of 87/mm$^3$. The incremental cost per QALY gained was $23,000 (£14,490), using a discount rate of 3%. If they had used a discount rate of 6%, as in the study by Chilcott *et al.* (2003), they would have produced a higher cost per QALY gained.

## Making decisions using cost–utility analysis

In this chapter we have generated some theoretical costs per QALY and reported some from the literature. The interventions have ranged from the management of anaemia in dialysis patients, treatment of hip joint disease, asthma, ischaemic heart disease and multiple sclerosis. However, although the diseases and their effects on patients' health are very different, the analyses have all generated a common ICER: a cost per QALY. This means that we can compare these costs per QALY and can rank them in terms of their respective costs per QALY gained.

Interventions that generate the most QALYs will have lower costs per QALY. Therefore, treatments for young people will tend to have lower costs per QALY than treatments for old people or for people with a

**Table 6.6** Cost per QALY for combination antiretroviral therapy for HIV disease (adapted from Freedberg *et al.* (2001).

| Initial CD4 count | Improvements in QALYs (3% discount rate) | Cost per QALY (£) |
|---|---|---|
| 50/mm$^3$ | 1.23 | 16,380 |
| 200/mm$^3$ | 1.90 | 10,710 |
| 500/mm$^3$ | 1.96 | 8,820 |

shortened life expectancy. An example of this is the study by Freedberg *et al.* (2001). They calculated costs per QALY for combination antiretroviral therapy in HIV disease *vs* no therapy in patients with different CD4 counts. In HIV disease, the lower the CD4 count the more advanced the disease, and life expectancy drops with CD4 count. Table 6.6 shows the cost per QALY for three different categories of CD4 count.

These results show that the cost per QALY increases as the CD4 count drops. This means that treatment is considered to be less cost-effective as the disease becomes more advanced. Therefore, the recommendation could be only to treat patients until their CD4 count drops below a certain level.

## QALY league tables

Cost–utility (effectiveness) analysis assumes that the decision-maker wants to maximise the possible numbers of QALYs gained from an intervention. This is the principle behind the use of QALY league tables. In 1985, Williams first suggested the idea of using a league table approach to decide which programmes should be funded. He explained that further refinements in methods of economic evaluation and additional data would be required to use this approach to inform decision-making. The league table involves ranking a list of interventions in order of cost per QALY. Comparisons may then be made between different interventions, such as renal transplant and insulin for diabetes.

Using this approach requires a definition of the decision-maker's maximum willingness to pay for an improvement in one QALY. This has been also been called the 'ceiling ratio'. Artificial ceiling ratios have been recommended in the literature. Problems associated with QALY league tables have led to extensive debate. The interested reader should read Drummond *et al.* (1993) and Briggs and Gray (2000), who provide a useful discussion on the role, if any, of league tables.

Published league tables of CUAs need to be interpreted and used with great caution. It is difficult to compare different costs per QALY as there is no 'gold standard' in many aspects of CUA methods. Often the same perspectives are not used, costing methods are not comparable, the same method of generating QALYs has not been used, and the discounting methods used are not the same.

Johannesson (1995) gives a good explanation of decision rules used in cost–utility (effectiveness) analysis. The use of CUA by decision-making bodies such as the National Institute for Clinical Excellence (NICE) is discussed in Chapter 9.

••••••••••••••••••••••••••••••••••••••••••••••••••••••••••••••••••••••••

**SELF-DIRECTED STUDY EXERCISES**

**EXERCISE 1**: Calculating a cost per QALY

Several treatments exist to treat fungal toenail infections. Four oral medicines used are drugs A, B, C and D. The table below shows the costs (£) associated with treating one patient with each of these four treatments:

|                  | Drug A | Drug B | Drug C | Drug D |
|------------------|--------|--------|--------|--------|
| Total costs (£)  | 1,301  | 1,503  | 1,570  | 1,200  |

You then find some evidence to suggest that two of these agents have differing effects on patients' quality of life owing to difference in their side-effect profiles. This evidence is summarised below:

| Agent  | Increase in QALYs per patient per year |
|--------|----------------------------------------|
| Drug C | 0.10                                   |
| Drug D | 0.05                                   |

**What is the difference in utility production of the two alternatives, per year of treatment, for the 100 patients?**

0.05 QALYs per patient per year = 5 QALYs per 100 patients per year.

**Calculate an incremental cost–utility ratio for drug C compared with drug D.**

$$\text{ICER} = \frac{\text{Cost (drug C)} - \text{Cost (drug D)}}{\text{Outcome (drug C)} - \text{Outcome (drug D)}}$$

$$= \frac{100(1,570 - 1,200)}{10 - 5} = \frac{37,000}{5}$$

$$= £7,400 \text{ per extra QALY.}$$

Draw a cost-effectiveness plane and place the ICER you have calculated on that graph. You should have a point plotted in the northeast quadrant (Figure 6.4).

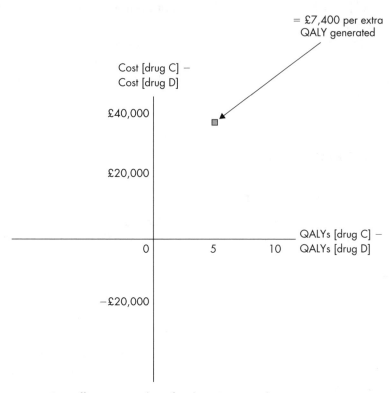

**Figure 6.4** Cost-effectiveness plane for drug C versus drug D.

**Which treatment will you recommend to your Trust, and why?**

Either could be recommended, depending on the driving force for the choice. Is cost containment most important? Then choose drug D. Is improved patient outcome most important? Then choose drug C.

. . . . . . . . . . . . . . . . . . . . . . . . . . . . . . . . . . . . . . . . . . . . . . . . . . . . . . . . . . . . . . . . . . . . .

## References

Briggs A, Gray A (2000). Using cost effectiveness information. *Br Med J* 320: 246.

Chilcott J, McCabe C, Tappenden P, *et al.* (2003). Modelling the cost effectiveness of interferon beta and glatiramer acetate in the management of multiple sclerosis. *Br Med J* 326: 522–525.

Drummond M, Torrance G, Mason J (1993). Cost-effectiveness league tables: more harm than good? *Soc Sci Med* 37: 33–40.

Freedberg K, Losina E, Weinstein M, *et al.* (2001) The cost-effectiveness of combination antiretroviral therapy for HIV disease. *N Engl J Med* 344: 824–831.

Johannesson M (1995). The relationship between cost-effectiveness analysis and cost–benefit analysis. *Soc Sci Med* 41: 483–489.

Robinson R (1993). Cost–utility analysis. *Br Med J* 307: 859–862.

Williams A (1985). The economics of coronary artery bypass grafting. *Br Med J* 291: 326–329.

## Further reading

Arnesen T, Trommald M (2004). Roughly right or precisely wrong? Systematic review of quality of life weights elicited with the time trade-off-method. *J Health Serv Res Policy* 9: 43–50.

Gerard K (1992). Cost–utility in practice. A policy-maker's guide to the state of the art. *Health Policy* 21: 240–249.

Greenberg D, Pliskin JS (2002). Preference-based outcome measures in cost–utility analyses: A 20-year overview. *Int J Technol Assessment Health Care* 18: 461–466.

Oliver A, Healey A, Donaldson C (2002). Choosing the method to match the perspective: economic assessment and its implications for health-services efficiency. *Lancet* 359: 1771–1774.

Petrou S, Malek M, Davey P (1993). The reliability of cost–utility estimates in cost per QALY league tables. *PharmacoEconomics* 13: 287–292.

## Further published examples of cost–utility analysis

Brisson M, Edmunds WJ (2003). Varicella vaccination in England and Wales: cost utility analysis. *Arch Dis Child* 88: 862–869.

Harris RA, Washington AE, Nease RF, Kuppermann M (2004). Cost utility of prenatal diagnosis and the risk-based threshold. *Lancet* 363: 276–282.

Patel A, Knapp M, Perez I, *et al.* (2004). Alternative strategies for stroke care: cost effectiveness and cost utility analyses from a prospective randomised controlled trial. *Stroke* 35: 196–203.

Sharma S, Bakal J (2004). Cost–utility analysis: calculation of the value of cyclosporin A for the treatment of severe dry eye. *Evidence-based Eye Care* 5: 58–59.

Stein K, Dalziel K, Walker A, *et al.* (2003). Screening for hepatitis C in genitourinary medicine clinics: a cost utility analysis. *J Hepatol* 39: 814–825.

Walker A, Sirel JM, Marsden AK, *et al.* (2003). Cost effectiveness and cost utility model of public place defibrillators in improving survival after prehospital cardiopulmonary arrest. *Br Med J* 327: 1316–1319.

# 7

# Cost–benefit analysis

## Introduction

In a cost–benefit analysis (CBA) the outcomes of the two alternatives are measured using monetary values, that is, the monetary value attached to the health states produced by the two interventions. The value may be attached by patients, health professionals or by the general population, but the last is preferred. This is not difficult for some outcomes, e.g. loss of earnings; it is more difficult to attach a monetary value to death, disability, distress or uncertainty. If the study has not used a human capital approach or willingness-to-pay (WTP) study, then it is not a CBA. Authors who have reported benefits in terms of costs savings, such as the savings associated with a reduction in the number of inpatient days because of use of an antibiotic, have not done a formal cost–benefit analysis.

CBA is different from cost-effectiveness analysis or cost–utility analysis because the inputs and outputs of the process are measured in the same units. This means that ICERs do not have to be generated. CBA is used for a similar purpose to CUA. It can be used to compare two healthcare interventions that do not have comparable outcome measures, and thus help decide how to allocate resources to those interventions. In fact, CBA is considered to be the most comprehensive method of economic evaluation because it allows the returns on investment in health to be compared with the returns obtained from investments in other areas of the economy (Robinson, 1993).

CBA uses economic welfare theory to inform the evaluation of interventions. This means that a societal viewpoint is taken. An intervention is shown to be worthwhile from a societal viewpoint when the benefits of the intervention exceed the costs. This may be interpreted to mean that those who may be expected to gain from the intervention are (hypothetically) able to compensate those who will lose because of it. The losers in this instance would be those who had to pay for the intervention. However, the gainers may not be able to compensate the losers if the intervention is a relatively minor one in terms of its effect on society. The interested reader should refer to Sugden and Williams (1979) for a comprehensive description of the theory behind CBA.

This chapter examines the use of CBA in medicines and healthcare services. If the outcomes of different options are measured using monetary values, CBA is the appropriate economic evaluation technique. The structure and purpose of CBA and the circumstances under which this method is appropriate are explained. Before beginning this chapter, you will need to understand the concepts covered in Chapters 3 and 4.

## Outcome measures in cost–benefit analysis

In CBA, results of the economic analysis are measured in terms of a monetary valuation of outcome. This can be done using the human capital approach, but is most commonly done using individuals' observed or stated preferences. This means how much they are willing to pay for a service, or how much they are willing to accept for a poorer outcome (or risk of a poorer outcome) (see Worked example 7.1).

**WORKED EXAMPLE 7.1** Economic evaluation of management of anaemia in haemodialysis patients

Patients with chronic renal failure who are on haemodialysis suffer from profound anaemia, which is often extremely debilitating. This is due to a reduction in the production of erythropoietin in these patients, and loss of blood during haemodialysis. Historically, these patients have been managed by the use of blood transfusions. Now, synthetic erythropoietin is available. It is considered to be highly effective, but is very expensive. So, the alternatives are either to give erythropoietin or to give blood transfusions when the patient's haemoglobin level is below 8 g/dl.

**Cost information** (see Chapter 5 for detailed calculation)

Total costs to manage the 1000 patients for 1 year using blood transfusions: £3,128,000.

Total costs to manage the 1000 patients for 1 year using erythropoietin: £5,547,100.

**Outcome information**

A willingness-to-pay study for the two alternatives available from the literature suggests that patients maintained on erythropoietin are

*Continued*

'willing to pay' for the extra perceived health benefits over blood transfusions. In a study, 50 patients stated that they would be willing to pay a mean of £2,000 a year for the extra health benefits associated with erythropoietin.

1. **What is the difference in cost between the two alternatives for the 1000 patients?**
   £2,419,100.

2. **What is the difference in benefit between the two alternatives, expressed in monetary terms, i.e. how much are patients willing to pay for the health benefits for erythropoietin per year of treatment, for the 1000 patients?**

   Change in benefit = £2,000 more benefit per annum per patient when given erythropoietin.

   Change in benefit = £2,000,000 more benefit per annum per 1000 patients when given erythropoietin.

3. **What is the overall net benefit of erythropoietin compared with blood transfusions?**

   Overall net benefit = Change in benefit − Change in cost
   = 2,000,000 − 2,419,000
   = −£419,000.

   Therefore, the overall net benefit from giving erythropoietin is −£419,000.

   If the net benefit is negative, the net cost (to society) is positive, so the preferred option must be the blood transfusions.

## Using cost–benefit analysis to allocate resources to different services

Worked example 7.1 shows how WTP can be used in a CBA to generate net benefit. However, in that example we were trying to decide between two ways of treating the same illness. We could also have used a common outcome such as the presence of anaemia, and the resulting economic evaluation would have been a CEA (see Chapter 5, worked examples). It is more difficult to compare two healthcare interventions that do not have comparable outcome measures. CEA cannot be used in this situation, and we have to use an outcome measure that can be used across different diseases, such as WTP. CBA can be used to generate net benefit in different disease areas, and so diseases with different clinical outcomes can be compared. This means that CBA can be used to allocate resources to different services. Worked example 7.2 illustrates how this can be carried out.

**WORKED EXAMPLE 7.2**  Cost–benefit analysis of two different types of service

A group of community nurses (Group A) wants to set up an asthma patient monitoring service for a GP practice which has 200 asthma patients. Results from a study suggest that the practice will have cost reductions and the patients will have improved outcomes (Table 7.1).

**Table 7.1** Impact of a nurse-led asthma monitoring service

| Costs and outcome measures for 1 year | Before asthma service | With asthma service | Difference |
|---|---|---|---|
| Prescribing costs (£) | 20,000 | 16,000 | −4,000 |
| Hospital costs (£) | 2,000 | 1,000 | −1,000 |
| Nurse service costs (£) | 0 | 4,000 | 4,000 |
| Total costs (£) | 22,000 | 21,000 | −1,000 |
| Emergency hospital admissions due to asthma | 20 | 10 | −10 |

Another group of community nurses (Group B) wants to set up on ischaemic heart disease (IHD) patient monitoring service for the same GP practice, which has 250 IHD patients. Results from a study suggest that the service will be cost neutral and the patients will have improved outcome (Table 7.2).

**Table 7.2** Impact of a nurse-led ischaemic heart disease monitoring service

| Costs and outcome measures for 1 year | Before IHD service | With IHD service | Difference |
|---|---|---|---|
| Prescribing costs (£) | 25,000 | 20,000 | −5,000 |
| Hospital costs (£) | 10,000 | 5,000 | −5,000 |
| Nurse service costs (£) | 0 | 10,000 | 10,000 |
| Total costs (£) | 35,000 | 35,000 | 0 |
| Emergency hospital admissions due to chest pain | 50 | 25 | −25 |

*Continued*

The practice has to decide whether to reduce emergency admissions due to asthma by 10 a year and save £1,000, or reduce emergency admissions due to chest pain by 25 a year at no change in costs to the practice.

**How can the GP objectively compare and choose between improving the health of asthma and that of IHD patients?**

Groups A and B elicit WTP values from the 200 asthma and 250 IHD patients (Table 7.3).

**Table 7.3** WTP values for asthma and IHD patients

| Service | Mean WTP per patient (£) | Range of WTP values (£) | Total WTP for group (£) |
|---|---|---|---|
| Asthma monitoring (200 patients) | 250 | 50–1,500 | 50,000 |
| IHD monitoring (250 patients) | 350 | 40–2,500 | 87,500 |

**What do these results mean?**

The asthma patient group has a combined WTP of £50,000. The IHD patient group has a combined WTP of £87,500. Therefore, £37,500 more benefit will be obtained by funding the IHD monitoring service.

Net cost to society = Cost of service − Benefit of service.

The asthma service costs −£1000 and provides £50,000 of benefit. The IHD service costs £0 and provides £87,500 of benefit. This equates to − £51,000 for the asthma service and − £87,500 for the IHD service. Therefore the IHD service provides £36,500 more benefit. It has an incremental net cost of − £36,500 to society.

So, this CBA would suggest that, because both services have a net negative cost (positive net benefit) to society, both are 'worth it'. It would then go on to recommend the IHD service over the asthma service.

## Making decisions using cost–benefit analysis

Theoretically, CBA is the best and most comprehensive form of economic evaluation. It is able to attach value to both health and non-health effects of an intervention. Non-health benefits can include how patients feel about the process of care. This is also called *process utility*.

Another non-health benefit is the anxiety associated with interventions or diagnostic tests. The importance to patients of non-health effects is clearly illustrated in a study examining patients' willingness to pay for autologous blood donation (where the patient provides their own blood for future use) compared with allogeneic blood donation (where the patient receives blood from another person) (Lee *et al.*, 1998). The willingness to pay of respondents informed about the actual differences in risk of adverse effects far outweighed the cost of the service. The authors estimated that it costs up to $48 (£30) more to provide a unit of autologous blood rather than allogeneic blood. However, depending on the estimation method used, people were prepared to pay a median of $750–1,100 (£473–693) to receive autologous blood. Autologous blood donation offers virtually no health benefits, but evidently has substantial non-health benefits in terms of 'peace of mind'.

However, very few CBAs have been carried out in healthcare. In fact, many economic evaluations calling themselves CBAs are only costing studies, because they do not attach a monetary value to patient outcomes.

Attaching monetary values to health is controversial. There are many methodological problems associated with measuring WTP. People's answers are affected by ability to pay and their experience. The way in which values are elicited can affect the size of the values. In theory, individuals should be adept at valuing something in monetary terms, but are individuals living with publicly funded healthcare able to do this? A future area of research is looking at estimating the perceived value of an expected health improvement, such as an improvement of one QALY. To do this the WTP for a QALY must be estimated.

McIntosh *et al.* (1999) outline some recent advances in the methods of CBA and discuss the use of contingent valuation (willingness to pay) and conjoint analysis (discrete choice experiments) to value the benefit in monetary terms.

..........................................................................................

**SELF-DIRECTED STUDY EXERCISE** – examining a CBA in depression

Read the paper by O'Brien BJ, Novosel S, Torrance G and Streiner D (1995). Assessing the economic value of a new antidepressant. A willingness-to-pay approach. *PharmacoEconomics* 8: 34–45.

This study assessed the value of a new antidepressant relative to existing tricyclic antidepressants (TCAs). TCAs have equivalent efficacy to the new antidepressant but a worse side-effect profile. Seven key side effects were identified from the published literature. This study aimed to assess whether the additional benefits (reduced risk of side effects) are worth the extra cost of the drug.

1.   **Whose preferences did they elicit?**

     The study asked current patients to express their views. Patients ($n = 95$) with mild or moderate depression were recruited from outpatient clinics at Canadian psychiatric hospitals.

2.   **Whose preferences were excluded from this study?**

     The study did not explore the views of future patients or other perspectives such as those of clinicians, pharmacists or other healthcare professionals.

3.   **What approach did they use to obtain monetary values?**

     The study used an open-ended willingness-to-pay approach. Respondents were asked to estimate the maximum they would be willing to pay each month for a new drug that would reduce the chance of experiencing a side effect. Each of the seven side effects was valued separately. This was combined with a 'bid-up' approach. This was an attempt to elicit the absolute maximum that each respondent was willing to pay to receive the benefits of the new antidepressant.

4.   **How did they estimate economic value of the new antidepressant?**

     This study used a cost–benefit framework. This means that the difference in costs between the new drug and existing antidepressants is compared to the benefit of the new drug that was measured using willingness to pay.

     The overall willingness to pay for reducing all seven side effects was not measured directly. There is no agreed approach on how to combine individual willingness-to-pay values. The ideal approach would have been to ask respondents to state one value, but the authors felt that this would have been too cognitively demanding. The authors estimated the overall benefit using the seven willingness-to-pay values for reducing the risk of the seven side effects. Two approaches were used to indirectly estimate the overall willingness-to-pay value.

Upper WTP value = Mean of all seven WTP values for each side effect.

Lower WTP value = Mean of the largest WTP value from each respondent.

5.  **Which antidepressant would you recommend for inclusion in your drug formulary?**
    Use the information in Table 7.4 to calculate your answer.

**Table 7.4** Willingness to pay for drugs in depression (O'Brien et al., 1995)

| Drug | Drug cost per month ($Can) | Mean WTP per month for new drug ($Can) | |
|---|---|---|---|
| | | $WTP_{upper}$ | $WTP_{lower}$ |
| New drug | 61.5 | 117.6 | 36.2 |
| $TCA_a$ | 9.9 | 117.6 | 36.2 |
| $TCA_d$ | 75.6 | 117.6 | 36.2 |
| $TCA_c$ | 76.8 | 117.6 | 36.2 |

A number of approaches could be used to answer this question. One approach is to use the 'net-benefit' decision rule. The drug with a net benefit greater than zero should be selected.

   Net benefit = WTP − Net cost.

Using the $WTP_{upper}$ values:

   Net benefit for new drug compared to $TCA_a$ = 117.6 − (61.5 − 9.9)
   = 66

   Net benefit for new drug compared to $TCA_d$ = 117.6 − (61.5 − 75.6)
   = 131.7

   Net benefit for new drug compared to $TCA_c$ = 117.6 − (61.5 − 76.8)
   = 132.9

The new drug shows a net benefit value greater than zero. Using this information the new drug should be added to the formulary because patients value reduced numbers of side effects and the drug is of equivalent efficacy to existing TCAs.

Using the $WTP_{lower}$ values:

   Net benefit for new drug compared to $TCA_a$ = 36.2 − (61.5 − 9.9)
   = −15.4

$$\text{Net benefit for new drug compared to TCA}_d = 36.2 - (61.5 - 75.6)$$
$$= 50.3$$

$$\text{Net benefit for new drug compared to TCA}_c = 36.2 - (61.5 - 76.8)$$
$$= 51.5$$

The new drug shows a net benefit value greater than zero for two of the three comparisons. Using this information it is not clear whether the new drug should be added to the formulary.

## References

Lee S, Liljas B, Neumann P, *et al.* (1998). The impact of risk information on patients' willingness to pay for autologous blood donation. *Med Care* 36: 1162–1173.

McIntosh E, Donaldson C, Ryan M (1999). Recent advances in the methods of cost–benefit analysis in healthcare. Matching the art to the science. *PharmacoEconomics* 15: 357–367.

O'Brien BJ, Novosel S, Torrance G, Streiner D (1995). Assessing the economic value of a new antidepressant. A willingness-to-pay approach. *PharmacoEconomics* 8: 34–45.

Robinson R (1993). Cost–benefit analysis. *Br Med J* 307: 924–926.

Sugden R, Williams AH (1979). *The Principles of Practical Cost–Benefit Analysis.* Oxford: Oxford University Press.

## Further reading

Diener A, O'Brien B, Gafni A (1998). Healthcare contingent valuation studies: a review and classification of the literature. *Health Econ* 7: 313–326.

Donaldson C (1990). Willingness to pay for publicly provided goods: a possible measure of benefit? *J Health Econ* 9: 103–118.

Hutton J (1993). Cost–benefit analysis in healthcare decision-making. *Health Econ* 1: 213–216.

Johannesson M (1996). A note on the relationship between ex ante and expected willingness to pay for healthcare. *Soc Sci Med* 42: 305–311.

Johannesson M, Johansson P-O, Jonsson B (1992). Economic evaluation of drug therapy. *PharmacoEconomics* 1: 337.

Johannesson M, Jonsson B (1991). Economic evaluation in healthcare: Is there a role for cost–benefit analysis? *Health Policy* 17: 1–23.

Klose T (1999). The contingent valuation methods in healthcare. *Health Policy* 47: 97–123.

Morrison GC, Gyldmark M (1992). Appraising the use of contingent valuation. *Health Econ* 1: 233–243.

Olsen JA, Smith RD (2001). Theory versus practice: a review of 'willingness-to-pay' in health and healthcare. *Health Econ* 10: 39–52.

Reardon G, Pathak DS (1989). Contingent valuation of pharmaceuticals and pharmacy services – methodological considerations. *J Soc Admin Pharmacy* 6: 83–91.

Reutzel TJ, Furmaga E (1993). Willingness to pay for pharmacist services in a Veterans Administration Hospital. *J Res Pharm Econ* 5: 89–114.

Smith RD (2000). The discrete-choice willingness-to-pay question format in health economics: should we adopt environmental guidelines? *Med Decision Making* 20: 194–206.

Williams A (1974). The cost–benefit approach. *Br Med Bull* 20: 252–256.

## Further published examples of cost–benefit analysis

Hsu H-C, Lin RS, Tung TH, Chen THH (2003). Cost–benefit analysis of routine childhood vaccination against chickenpox in Taiwan: decision from different perspectives. *Vaccine* 21: 3982–3987.

Sculpher M, Manca A, Abbott J, *et al.* (2004). Cost effectiveness analysis of laparoscopic hysterectomy compared with standard hysterectomy: results from a randomised trial. *Br Med J* 328: 134–137.

Van Voorhis BJ, Syrop CH (2000). Cost-effective treatment for the couple with infertility. *Clin Obstet Gynecol* 43: 958–973.

Wu G, Lanctot KL, Herrmann N, *et al.* (2003). The cost–benefit of cholinesterase inhibitors in mild to moderate dementia: a willingness-to-pay approach. *CNS Drugs* 17: 1045–1057.

# 8

# Introduction to the use of decision analysis in economic evaluations

## Introduction

Decisions are made all the time in healthcare where the results of those decisions are not certain. For example, if you treat a person with pneumonia using an antibiotic, there may be an 80% chance it will work. However, you cannot be 100% sure that it will work, so there is uncertainty about the effectiveness of that antibiotic. Therefore, the decision to treat that patient is made under conditions of *uncertainty*.

This chapter identifies areas where there is uncertainty in healthcare decision-making and describes the process of designing an economic evaluation using decision analysis. Using worked examples, the reader will be shown how to design a simple decision-analytical model and apply data to such a model to derive incremental cost-effectiveness ratios.

*Decision analysis is a systematic approach to decision-making under conditions of uncertainty*

## What are the sources of uncertainty?

When a decision is made in healthcare, there is uncertainty around the outcome of that decision. There are lots of ways in which uncertainty can exist:

- Diagnosis: for example, diagnostic tests do not always give the correct result.
- Natural history of the disease: not everyone with the same disease will feel the same way or will suffer the same ill effects of that illness; for example, not everyone with hypertension will eventually have a myocardial infarction.
- Treatment efficacy and effectiveness: no treatment is 100% effective, so there is always a chance it will not work in everyone; for example, as antidepressant drugs.

- The development of adverse events: some people show side effects or allergic responses to drugs, such as penicillins.
- Resources consumed by treatment options: if a treatment does not work in a particular patient, you may have to try something else and use more drugs and other healthcare resources, as in treating pneumonia or depression, for example.
- Unit cost of resources: the price of services changes over time and between places; for example, drugs, staff time.

The common theme in these examples is that you can never predict exactly what is going to happen when you make a decision, but a decision must be made. This is what is meant by decision-making under conditions of uncertainty. In fact, most decisions we make are made under conditions of uncertainty, whether they are about healthcare or other aspects of our lives. Deciding to cross the road or deciding to get married are also conditions associated with uncertainty.

## Probability: the language of uncertainty

It is not possible to remove uncertainty from the decision-making process, but it is possible to quantify it. Knowing the level of uncertainty can influence our decision. For example, if you were about to cross a road and you were told that you had a 20% risk of death, would you still cross? In decision analysis we represent uncertainty by using probabilities. Probability can have many related meanings:

- Number between 1 and 0 expresses likelihood of event: for example, what is the probability of successfully treating a urinary tract infection (UTI) with trimethoprim?
- Probability as proportion in a population: for example, what is the probability of having appendicitis if you are between 11 and 16 years old?
- Probability as a measure of strength of belief: we all use the words 'possibly' and 'probably' as subjective measures of probability.

### Principles of probability

The sum of probabilities of all possible outcomes of a chance event is always 1. If the probability of an antibiotic successfully treating a case of pneumonia is 0.8, then the probability that it will not work must be 0.2.

There may be three or more possible outcomes of a decision. For example, the possible outcomes of a total hip replacement operation may be survival with improved mobility, survival with no improvement in mobility, or perioperative death. If the probability of perioperative death is 1% (0.01) and the probability of survival with improved mobility is 85% (0.85), then the probability of survival with no improvement in mobility must be 14% $(1 - (0.01 + 0.85) = 0.14)$.

It is also possible to link more than one uncertain event so that we can calculate how likely both are to occur. These can either be *joint* or *conditional* probabilities.

## Joint probabilities

*Joint probabilities* occur when one event is not linked to another. For example, say we have two events, A and B, that can occur in the same person. The incidence of one is not affected by the incidence of the other, so they are said to be *independent* events. The probability of both occurring is:

$p(\text{A and B}) = p(\text{A} \times \text{B})$.

See Worked example 8.1.

---

**WORKED EXAMPLE 8.1** Joint probabilities

**What is the probability of picking a man from the population in Manchester who is both hypertensive ($p = 0.09$) and has arthritis ($p = 0.02$)?**

The probability of this happening is $0.09 \times 0.02 = 0.0018$ (0.18%).

However, the probability of having arthritis is not affected by whether the person has hypertension or not. Therefore, the probability of picking a man from the population in Manchester who is not hypertensive ($p = 1 - 0.09$) and has arthritis ($p = 0.02$) is $(1 - 0.09) \times 0.02 = 0.0182$ (1.82%).

---

## Conditional probabilities

*Conditional probabilities* occur when the probability of one event has an effect on the probability of the other. The probability of event E occurring, given that F has already occurred, is:

$p(\text{E and F}) = p(\text{E/F}) \times p(\text{F})$.

See Worked example 8.2.

---

**WORKED EXAMPLE 8.2**    Conditional probabilities

**What is the probability of picking a man from the population in Manchester who is hypertensive ($p = 0.09$)?**

**And then what is the probability that the man is also diabetic, given that the probability of having diabetes when you are hypertensive is 0.05? If you are not hypertensive, the probability of having diabetes is 0.04.**

This situation is different because there is a higher probability of a person having diabetes if they have hypertension than if they are normotensive, because the pathologies of these two diseases are linked.

Therefore, the probability of picking a man who is hypertensive and has diabetes = $0.09 \times 0.05 = 0.0045$ (0.45%).

The probability of picking a man who is not hypertensive and has diabetes = $(1 - 0.09) \times 0.04 = 0.0364$ (3.64%).

---

For further reading on probability theory, the interested reader is directed to Weinstein and Feinberg (1980).

## Sources of probability estimates in decision analysis

When a decision is made regarding healthcare resource allocation, information from different sources is used about effectiveness, costs, etc. This combining of information to inform a decision is called 'synthesis'. Information can come from a range of qualities of source. The better quality the data, the more confidently we can rely on them to inform our decision-making. Information can come from:

- Clinical trials
- Epidemiological studies
- Clinical series
- Best-guess estimates.

Chapter 4 describes hierarchies of evidence. For further explanations on assessing the quality of evidence, the interested reader is directed to NHS

Centre for Reviews and Dissemination (2001) and Fitzpatrick *et al.* (1998). In decision analysis, when we talk about 'good-quality' data, we are actually saying that the data have quantified levels of uncertainty. Randomised controlled trials (RCTs) are the best-designed studies for looking at the effectiveness of treatments and quantifying levels of uncertainty. Usually, the results obtained from such studies can be believed more confidently than those from other types of study. The principal source of uncertainty is variability within the population of interest with respect to safety, effectiveness and cost. The associated uncertainty can be handled by sampling from the appropriate population and applying standard statistical methods to obtain an estimate representative of that population (randomised sampling to give *stochastic data*). The study design is an RCT or randomised epidemiological observational study. The uncertainty associated with stochastic data is expressed as confidence intervals, whether it is safety, effectiveness or cost data. RCTs give a mean estimate of effectiveness and also quantify the amount of uncertainty around that mean estimate in the form of a 95% confidence interval (1.96 standard deviations) (see Worked example 8.3).

**WORKED EXAMPLE 8.3**

Patients with type 2 diabetes who have their hypertension treated with captopril are shown to have a mean life expectancy (undiscounted) of 19.4 years, with a 95% confidence interval of 16.9–22.6 years (Gray *et al.*, 2001). This means that there is a 5% chance that the real life expectancy of these patients lies outside the range 16.9–22.6 years. We are 95% certain that the life expectancy lies within that range.

**Has this removed the uncertainty associated with effectiveness?**

No, it has quantified it. Therefore, we have a quantitative measure of uncertainty. Any decisions based on these effectiveness data must take into account the fact that the true expectancy may lie anywhere between 16.9 and 22.6 years, and there is a very small probability (<5%) that the life expectancy might actually be outside this range.

This way of expressing uncertainty can be used for safety and cost data as well.

### Using non-RCT data in economic evaluations

RCT data are preferred because they are stochastic and control for bias. Precision, or lack of it, can be quantified, and it is possible to draw statistical inferences from the sample to the population from which the data are drawn.

Once data sources are not randomly assigned then the data are not stochastic, and so confidence intervals cannot be used because statistical inferences cannot be made in this way. These forms of data are called *deterministic data*. However, they are still associated with uncertainty, which still needs to be quantified. So, it is necessary to find another way to address and quantify uncertainty. In other words, this means that another way must be found to define the range within which the parameter in question might occur (see Worked example 8.4).

---

**WORKED EXAMPLE 8.4**   Cost of a GP consultation

If a study requires the cost of a GP consultation, there are two ways of obtaining those data. The first is to measure the amount of time and resources used for a random sample of consultations to produce a stochastic data set. However, this is time-consuming and costly. Another way might be to estimate from interview with a GP how long a consultation usually takes and what is used during that consultation. A cost could then be estimated for a 'typical' consultation. The problem associated with this type of data is that you do not know what the range of true values is because you only have one point estimate, and so it is impossible to calculate a range or 95% confidence intervals.

**How do you quantify uncertainty in this situation?**

• You could ask the GP to estimate the longest and shortest consultations.
• You could consult the literature for other estimates.

So, you have to define your own ranges of uncertainty. Therefore, you cannot be as confident about these data as the stochastic data because you do not have such a reliable measure of uncertainty.

---

Cost data in economic evaluations are much more likely to be deterministic data. The use of this type of data usually reduces the precision of point estimates. Sensitivity ranges have to be employed instead of statistical ranges. These are less satisfactory because of their subjectivity. This is discussed in more detail on p. 158, Probabilistic sensitivity analysis.

## Use of decision analysis to design economic evaluations

The aim of economic analysis of an intervention is to determine whether, under specified conditions, it is cost-effective. Economic evaluation can be considered to consist of four stages. The first is the derivation of the research question. The principles of decision analysis are used to define the research question and express the intervention as a decision-analytical pathway. In decision analysis we use expected value decision-making, where we characterise each uncertain event by a single number, and illustrate the decisions and uncertain events diagrammatically with a *decision tree* (decision-analytical model).

The second stage is to obtain economic and clinical evidence to apply to the decision-analytic model. In *primary economic evaluation* the data come from primary sources. This is either a prospective study attached to an RCT or an observational study. In *secondary economic evaluation*, the sources of data are published evidence. Systematic review of economic and clinical data is used to find and assess information to combine with the decision-analytical model.

The third stage is the combination of clinical and economic parameters within the decision model framework to derive cost/outcome ratios. This involves the analysis of the incremental effect of an intervention on overall resource use and patient outcome, compared with alternatives.

In the fourth stage, the robustness of these ratios is examined using sensitivity analysis to determine how much variation in which parameters has most effect on the conclusions drawn.

So, in summary, the process of economic evaluation is:

1. Derive (identify and structure) the research question.
2. Identify and obtain cost and clinical evidence.
3. Incremental economic analysis.
4. Sensitivity analysis.

The specific methods used in the four stages are presented in more detail below.

To make the process clearer, we will build a decision-analytical model (or decision tree) as we work through the text (see Worked example 8.5).

**WORKED EXAMPLE 8.5**

There are two different classes of drug used to treat depression: selective serotonin-reuptake inhibitors (SSRIs) and tricyclic antidepressants (TCAs). TCAs have been around for a long time and SSRIs are relatively new, tending to have higher acquisition costs. We would like to know whether other reductions in costs make SSRIs less costly overall, or maybe they are more effective in treating depression.

Our research question is:

*Are SSRIs more cost-effective than TCAs in the treatment of depression?*

## Building an economic evaluation, stage 1

In economic evaluation, the framework of decision analysis is used to derive the research question. Decision-analytical models provide a clear and intuitive framework within which an economic question can be developed. The ideal decision-analytical model is that which most closely resembles real-life situations without being prohibitively complex. The use of decision analysis enables the research question to be identified and bound within a set of explicit conditions. This requires that the intervention and any alternatives are described in terms of inputs, process and outputs (see Chapter 5). The perspective or viewpoint of the analysis is defined at this point. Evaluations may assume the viewpoint of a single provider, the health service, the patient or society (see Chapter 3). The perspective affects what costs are included. The time horizon affects at which points within the intervention process the evaluation begins and ends.

### Inputs to the decision-analytical model

The input to the process is the patient group appropriate for the intervention. The intervention process begins with the decision of whether the patient is appropriate for treatment or not. The next stage is to describe all alternative treatments under consideration. A 'no-treatment' option should be included if appropriate. In all alternatives, all stages of the intervention process need to be stated, including drug regimens used, as well as doses and durations of treatment; any investigational or diagnostic tests routinely required; information about interventions such as operations, physiotherapy, counselling; and so on.

### Events occurring in the decision-analytical model

The stages at which treatments may be altered or discontinued need to be known, as does under which criteria these occur and what, if any, alternative treatment is implemented. Probabilistic events expressed as chance nodes define the intervention process. The side effect or complication rates of each alternative and how they are treated are required to assess full economic impact.

### The outputs of the decision-analytical model

The final component of the decision-analytical pathway is patient outcome (see Chapter 4). An ideal outcome measure provides a measure of the impact of the treatment on quantity and quality of life. In practice intermediate outcomes are often used, as multiattribute outcome measures are methodologically complex and time-consuming to collect. The outcome measure used determines the type of economic evaluation. If two alternatives are equally effective, they need only be differentiated by their economic impact, giving rise to cost-minimisation analysis. The use of a linear, unidirectional measure of outcome to compare effectiveness, such as life years gained, gives rise to cost-effectiveness analysis (see Chapter 5). When multiattribute measures of outcome are used which combine measures of impact in both quantity and quality of life to produce measures of utility, the evaluation is a cost–utility analysis (see Chapter 6). Where benefits are expressed in monetary terms, the evaluation is a cost–benefit analysis (see Chapter 7).

  Once the components of the research question have been identified, they are structured in a logical and temporal sequence.

  In summary, the stages that need to be completed here are:

* Characterisation of the intervention or service under investigation (and the alternatives)
* Definition of the study perspective
* Detailed description of the process of intervention/service, inputs (resources and unit costs) and outputs (patient outcomes).

Once these stages have been completed, we can build our decision tree.

### Building a decision tree

A decision tree has five principal components:

1.  *Starting point*: at which point in the process we begin the evaluation of the intervention.
2.  *All treatment alternatives under investigation*: the different strategies under investigation.
3.  *Decision nodes* ■: there should only be one decision node: the policy decision of whether to use one strategy or the other.
4.  *Chance nodes* ●: these are uncertain events and will have probability values attached to them.
5.  *Outcome/time horizon* ◀: the outcome being used must be defined and the point at which evaluation ends (time horizon).

The decision tree in Figure 8.1 shows two alternatives for treating urinary tract infections (UTIs).

The starting point is the patient group who have been diagnosed with a UTI that now needs to be treated. At the decision node, the policy decision is whether to treat this group of patients with the standard current treatment (drug T) or whether to use a newer, more costly agent, drug C. There is no 'do nothing' option here because current practice is to treat symptomatic UTIs, to alleviate symptoms, and also to prevent complications such as pyelonephritis. It would, however, be possible to include more antibiotics in the model and have more arms in the tree, if it were felt to be necessary.

The probabilistic event here is whether or not the antibiotic is successful in treating the infection. It would also be possible to expand the tree by including the probabilistic events of side effects and withdrawal from treatment. The endpoint of the evaluation is whether the antibiotic is successful or not, and the time horizon would probably be quite short – about 7 days in this intervention. The 'unsuccessful' arm could be expanded to include the probability of success of the second-line agent, or even the probability that the patient develops pyelonephritis and kidney failure. In this situation, the time horizon would have to be extended.

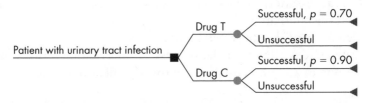

**Figure 8.1** Decision tree for treating a urinary tract infection.

It is clear that this decision tree is a simplified version of reality. You can see that we can make it much more complicated if we want to. However, the model needs to be manageable as well, and there must be data available to attach to all the chance nodes. So, to include an arm relating to the probability of pyelonephritis, we must actually have information on that probability.

See Worked example 8.6.

**WORKED EXAMPLE 8.6**    Stage 1 (Are SSRIs more cost-effective than TCAs?)

We need to identify:

- The alternatives under investigation;
- Perspective of the study;
- The process of intervention.

### Alternatives under investigation

SSRI versus TCA.

### Perspective of the study

This is the healthcare provider, as they will be paying for treatment. Depression is generally managed initially in the community, but there may be some management in secondary care when patients do not respond to treatment, so the perspective must cover both.

### Process of intervention

We need to ask and answer questions a), b) and c) below:

a)  **What is likely to happen when a patient presents to their GP with depression?**
    Some of the events that may occur:

    - They may be given an antidepressant (an SSRI or a TCA).
    - The drug may or may not be tolerated by the patient.
    - The drug may or may not be effective.
    - If the drug is ineffective or not tolerated, the patient may be started on another drug.
    - If the second-line treatment does not work the patient may be given adjunctive therapy, such as counselling in the surgery.

*Continued*

- The patient may be referred to a psychiatrist and they may have outpatient or inpatient care.
- The patient may have a relapse.

b)   **What is the outcome of the process? What are the events that may happen during treatment of depression and how will we measure if the treatment has been successful?**
The outcome that is desired is the successful treatment of the depression without relapse. Assessment of this outcome will probably require specialised outcome assessment.

Undesirable outcomes are side effects, inefficacy and relapse.

c)   **What resources are used, and where do we get the unit costs? Don't forget here that the resources used need to include those used to deal with treatment failures.**
Resources used will be medicines, GP's time, psychiatrist's time, hospital facilities. Unit costs will be needed for drugs, time of healthcare professionals, and hospital treatment and hotel costs.

Now we can build our decision tree. We need to identify the components of the decision tree for our research question.

- *Starting point:* Patient diagnosed with major depressive disorder (MDD);
- *Alternatives:* TCA and SSRI;
- *Decision node:* SSRI or TCA (policy decision);
- *Chance nodes:* Withdrawal due to intolerance; withdrawal due to lack of efficacy; relapse of MDD symptoms;
- *Outcome:* Drug effective as episodic treatment and no relapse in first year;
- *Time horizon:* 1 year.

Once we have identified these components, we can build our decision tree. It will look something like Figure 8.2.

This decision tree looks quite complex. The branches of the SSRI part of the tree are identical to the branches of the TCA part of the tree. However, the information we attach to each branch will not be identical.

Of course, this is a simplified version of reality. We can always make it much more complicated if we want to.

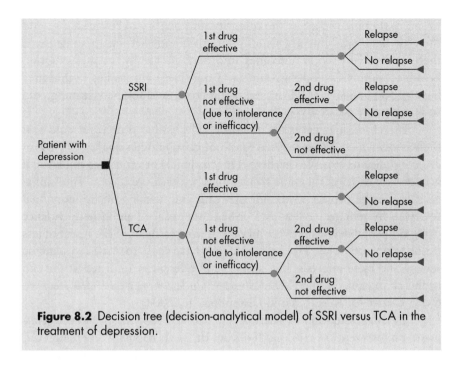

**Figure 8.2** Decision tree (decision-analytical model) of SSRI versus TCA in the treatment of depression.

## Building an economic evaluation, stage 2

The second stage in an economic evaluation is to obtain the clinical and economic evidence required to fill the decision-analytical model. It is necessary to be able to account for all effects on the patient and all changes in resource use. Therefore, the final outcome of the patient should be assessed, not just intermediate outcomes. All resource use associated with an intervention should be identified and costed.

In secondary economic analysis the source is published research. It is essential that the most robust evidence be used. Robust evidence can be considered to consist of data that have been collected using rigorously designed methods. The most robust source is held to be RCTs. Secondary data are preferably obtained from RCTs. However:

* The doctor cannot be sure that his patient is like the patient in the RCT.
* New treatments develop, policies emerge.
* RCTs simplify reality.
* RCTs cannot generate answers for all variables required to make a decision (e.g. unit costs, utility values).

In many therapeutic areas the quantity and quality of resource use and the cost data available are usually far from satisfactory. In some areas there is also very poor outcomes information. Ideally, in this situation health economists will design and carry out their own studies so that they have good quality data. However, this is costly and time-consuming, and so is often not possible.

Therefore, it is necessary to utilise all possible sources of data and then assess which are appropriate (and of good enough quality) for use in an economic analysis. When there is much clinical or economic evidence, it is necessary to select the most robust data by literature review. Traditional reviews can be subject to the idiosyncratic impressions of the individual reviewer. Systematic review and critical appraisal of published evidence using simple guidelines provide an objective assessment of the research less prone to reviewer bias. This book does not have space to discuss systematic review and meta-analysis, but some useful references are listed at the end of this chapter, including *CRD Report 4: Undertaking Systematic Reviews* (NHS Centre for Research and Dissemination, 2001).

The ideal situation is where all clinical and economic evidence relating to an intervention are collected from the same robustly designed RCT. Unfortunately, this is unlikely to occur at present in most therapeutic areas. Therefore, it is necessary to use alternative data sources, which may include less rigorously designed studies. Case–control studies, observational studies, routinely collected data, or data collected from 'expert panels' are common alternative sources.

See Worked example 8.7.

---

**WORKED EXAMPLE 8.7**   Stage 2 (Are SSRIs more cost-effective than TCAs?)

Costs required:

- Drug costs (first choice and substitution)
- GP appointment costs
- Adjunctive therapy costs (e.g. counselling)
- Secondary care costs (e.g. hospital stay, electroconvulsive therapy (ECT), outpatient appointments).

Indirect costs (days lost from work) and intangible costs (anxiety arising from relapse) are not required because this evaluation is not using a societal perspective.

Clinical evidence required:

- Withdrawal rates due to intolerance and lack of efficacy
- Relapse rates.

## Building an economic evaluation, stage 3

The third stage in economic evaluation is to combine the clinical and economic evidence with the decision-analytical model. Clinical probabilities and resource use along each pathway are combined to derive the probabilistic cost for each pathway. The first stage is to build a *base case*. This combines the clinical outcome point estimates with the economic cost associated with each stage of the model. If one of the alternatives is more effective and less costly, it is termed the *dominant therapy*. When one alternative is more effective but requires more resources, the cost required to achieve each extra unit of outcome is calculated.

If the outcome measure is single and unidirectional, this provides an incremental cost-effectiveness ratio (ICER). The lower the value, the more cost-effective the alternative.

In cost–utility analysis the cost/outcome ratio should provide a measure of the cost to obtain one more unit of multiattribute outcome, such as QALYs. When this outcome measure is not available, the outcome measures used must be justified. If outcome measures used are only intermediate outputs, such as number of cases detected or a decrease in infection rate, this must be stated.

See Worked examples 8.8 and 8.9.

---

**WORKED EXAMPLE 8.8** Theoretical example of use of a decision tree in an incremental economic analysis of the treatment of blue finger syndrome

Several drugs are indicated for a very distressing condition known as 'blue finger syndrome', where patients' fingers turn dark blue for no reason. The drugs used are associated with lots of side effects. Some people cannot tolerate the drugs (this means they have side effects that are so bad they have to stop taking them) or the drugs may not work. If these things happen, they will be referred to their local out-patient clinic to see a finger specialist. This may be an important factor in the ultimate choice of therapy. You are the adviser to your local healthcare provider. They want to know whether to use indigocillin or navytriptyline when a person presents to their GP with blue finger syndrome. About 200 people per year present with blue finger syndrome.

*Continued*

You have the following information from a trial:

| Agent | Withdrawal rates due to intolerance or inefficacy (%) | Normal treatment cost per patient per year (£) |
|---|---|---|
| Indigocillin | 40* | 250.00 |
| Navytriptyline | 60* | 10.00 |

*Significant difference in efficacy.
The additional cost of treating a patient who withdraws from either drug per year is £500.

Figure 8.3 shows the decision-analytical model for this intervention. The information above allows us to calculate how many of the 200 patients will go down each arm of the model. We also know how much each arm costs for one patient. Therefore, we can calculate how much each arm costs in total. This is shown on the model.

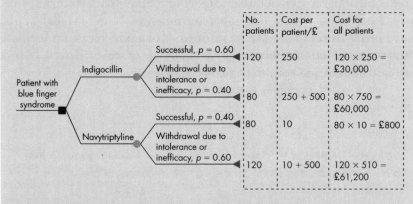

**Figure 8.3** Decision-analytical model of indigocillin versus navytriptyline for blue finger syndrome.

Now we can calculate the ICER for this evaluation:

$$ICER = \frac{Cost_{indigocilin} - Cost_{navytriptyline}}{Outcome_{indigocilin} - Outcome_{navytriptyline}}$$

$$= \frac{90,000 - 62,000}{120 - 80} = \frac{28,000}{40}$$

= £700 per extra person successfully treated.

**WORKED EXAMPLE 8.9**    Stage 3 (Are SSRIs more cost-effective than TCAs?)

$$\text{ICER} = \frac{\text{Cost}_{SSRI} - \text{Cost}_{TCA}}{\text{Outcome}_{SSRI} - \text{Outcome}_{TCA}}$$

## Building an economic evaluation, stage 4

The fourth stage of economic evaluation is the assessment of the *robustness* of the ICERs derived. In this situation, robustness refers to the sensitivity of ICERs to uncertainties in the data or methods of analysis. The importance of uncertainty will depend upon the extent to which it affects the appropriate decision. Although the base-case estimates of an economic evaluation may indicate that a particular intervention is cost-effective, inherent uncertainties in the analysis could mean that in reality the intervention is not cost-effective after all.

If the conclusions about cost-effectiveness do not change when these parameters are varied, the conclusions can be considered to be *robust*. The robustness of conclusions is examined using sensitivity analysis.

Sensitivity analysis has many functions when used within an economic analysis:

- Uncertainties in point estimates from clinical and cost data, or in underlying assumptions, including extrapolation of data or use of different analytical methods, weaken an analysis. Sensitivity analysis goes some way towards quantifying the degree of uncertainty.
- The use of sensitivity analysis identifies areas where more research is required to increase robustness.
- Sensitivity analysis can improve the generalisability of a study.

The following sections describe how sensitivity analysis is used to deal with these issues.

### Inherent uncertainty in clinical and cost data

As discussed earlier, clinical evidence is much more likely than economic evidence to be available as stochastic data. Economic evidence, if available at all, is often reported as deterministic data. Uncertainty surrounding the available resource use data is often very significant owing to inadequacy of the point estimates. It is necessary to assess the impact of variation of these estimates. The variation examined should reflect realistic ranges of the point estimate.

Stochastic data are able to use 95% confidence intervals to provide a range. Studies that provide a source or explanation for the ranges used are likely to be of more use to decision-makers than studies using an arbitrary range in their sensitivity analysis.

The ranges that are derived for deterministic data must be justified. This is because the ranges determine how much the parameter is varied in a sensitivity analysis. Therefore, the conclusions of the economic evaluation might be changed by the sensitivity analysis.

For example, on p. 144 in the section on using non-RCT data in economic evaluations we were attempting to obtain the cost of a GP consultation. Say that you have obtained an estimate from an interview with one of the GPs from the practice, thereby providing you with a deterministic point estimate for the cost of a GP consultation of £20. However, you know that in other areas of the country this ranges from £15 to £35. Therefore, it would be appropriate in a sensitivity analysis to vary the value from £15 to £35. However, there is no reason to vary the value from, say, £5 to £100, because this range is meaningless.

### Extrapolation of data or endpoints

Extrapolation in economic evaluation can occur where the economic evaluation has used an intermediate endpoint of outcome and extrapolated that endpoint to a final health outcome.

Examples of assumptions:

- Reduction in blood cholesterol reduces heart disease
- Treatment of depressive symptoms reduces suicide
- Appropriate prescribing of inhalers improves QoL in asthma patients.

There is uncertainty in the natural history of diseases, so the relationship between the clinical indicator and the final outcome will be an estimated parameter.

The second form of extrapolation is where data are extrapolated beyond the primary data source, for example extrapolating the results of a 1-year trial to patients' entire lifetimes by modelling the profile of survival curves.

### Choice of analytical method

The analytical methods used in an economic evaluation consist of a range of techniques, including methods of measuring and valuing resource consequences and health outcomes, and the choice of costs and benefits to include in an evaluation. In a number of areas there is no consensus, such as the inclusion of indirect costs and discounting methods.

A common problem is the different methods used to cost the same intervention. In many cases, values for the same parameter from different studies are costed so differently that they cannot be realistically compared. This problem is also encountered when clinical data are combined or compared.

Problems can arise in the following ways:

- Different patient populations used (age, sex, diagnosis, comorbidity)
- Different treatment practices used (e.g. diagnostic methods)
- Different effectiveness measures used (e.g. depression scales, schizophrenia scales).

The issues discussed so far relate to the intrinsic validity of the study. Sensitivity analysis needs to be carried out to test the intrinsic validity and robustness of the conclusions derived.

## Generalisability of results

Generalisabiltiy is concerned with the extent to which the results of a study, as they apply to a particular population/context, hold true for another population or in a different context.

A key form of this type of uncertainty concerns whether the results of a study conducted on one group of patients is also valid for another group. Differences in relative prices/costs, demography and epidemiology of disease, availability of healthcare resources, incentives to healthcare professionals and institutions, and variations in clinical practice may all affect the relative cost-effectiveness of the same healthcare technology, both in different countries and within the same country.

Another form of uncertainty relating to generalisability is the extent to which the cost-effectiveness observed in a trial would hold true in routine clinical practice. It is well known that experimental trial designs may impose atypical patterns of care on patients: that is, a clinical trial may lack external validity, and a technology shown to be cost-effective on the basis of data from a trial may no longer prove so when data based on routine clinical practice are considered. The design of pragmatic practice-based clinical trials increases external validity. However, even in these trials, monitoring will be more comprehensive and compliance among patients will be affected by the knowledge that they are taking part in a trial.

### Probabilistic sensitivity analysis

Probabilistic sensitivity analysis is used to generate mean expected costs and outcomes and statistical measures of expected variance around the mean. This allows an estimation to be made of the probability and extent to which uncertainty and variation in the data used affect the absolute and relative costs and outcomes. For this analysis each variable is assigned a base case or average value and a distribution of possible values. This more complex method is described in Chapter 10.

See Worked examples 8.10 and 8.11.

**WORKED EXAMPLE 8.10**   Stage 4 (Are SSRIs more cost-effective than TCAs?)

**What parameters do you think may be associated with uncertainty and should be varied in a sensitivity analysis?**
- Definitions of MDD?
- Variations in efficacy?
- Efficacy and effectiveness?
- Local variations in maintenance of MDD?
- Variations in costs of therapy?

**WORKED EXAMPLE 8.11**   An economic evaluation using decision analysis

Now that you have built your decision model, we are going to use it. The following example provides information about the treatment of depression. Use the information you have been given to derive an ICER ratio for drug F versus drug I.

Your local healthcare provider intends to mount an awareness campaign about depression in your town, targeting local newspapers, GPs, pharmacies, women's groups, social services and so on. They expect to pick up about 2000 extra depression cases by doing this.

For the purposes of this exercise, imagine that you are an adviser for your healthcare provider. They want you to recommend whether they should treat these new patients first with a TCA (drug I) or an SSRI (drug F).

*Continued*

You have the following information:

## Costs

| | |
|---|---|
| Drug costs (first choice and substitution) per year | Drug I: £7<br>Drug F: £280 |
| GP appointment costs | £20 per consultation |
| Adjunctive therapy costs (e.g. counselling) | £50 per session |
| Secondary care costs (e.g. hospital stay, ECT, outpatient appointments) | £200 per day in hospital<br>£50 per outpatient appointment<br>£75 per ECT session |

## Process of care for people with depression

Treatment pattern for the first year of successfully treated patients who do not withdraw or relapse:

• One year's course of first-choice drugs
• Six GP visits.

Treatment pattern for the first year of patients who withdraw due to inefficacy or side effects:

• If they fail initially on drug F they are changed to drug I.
• If they fail initially on drug I they are changed to drug F.
• Assume that patients withdraw an average of 1 month after beginning the new drug.
• If they fail again, assume the second drug failure is another month later. They are referred to hospital, where an average referral involves six outpatient appointments and 1 day in hospital.
• All patients who withdraw will have 12 GP visits over the first year.

Treatment pattern for the first year of patients who relapse on first or second treatment:

• Assume that patients relapse an average of 6 months from beginning of first treatment.

*Continued*

- Relapsed patients are referred to hospital, where an average referral involves four outpatient appointments and 1 day in hospital.
- They will have 12 GP visits.

### Clinical evidence

|                                          | Drug F | Drug I |
|------------------------------------------|--------|--------|
| Withdrawal rates due to intolerance      | 0.20   | 0.40   |
| Withdrawal rates due to lack of efficacy | 0.20   | 0.20   |
| Relapse rates                            | 0.20   | 0.30   |

To complete the analysis, you need to answer the following questions:

- How much would it cost the healthcare provider to treat 2000 patients with drug I?
- How many of these patients would be successfully treated at the end of 1 year?
- How much would it cost the healthcare provider to treat 2000 patients with drug F?
- How many of these patients would be successfully treated at the end of 1 year?

To help you complete this exercise, we will refer to the five possible outcomes for each treatment option as Relapse, No relapse, Second relapse, Second no relapse and Failure. You need to fill in the columns of Table 8.1.

### Completing the incremental economic analysis

*Cost per patient for each arm (drug F)*

Relapse:

$$(280 \times 0.5) + (4 \times 50) + (1 \times 200) + (12 \times 20)$$
$$= £780 \times 240 \text{ patients} = £187,200$$

No relapse:

$$(280 \times 1) + (6 \times 20) = £400 \times 960 \text{ patients} = £384,000$$

*Continued*

**Table 8.1** Template for base-case economic analysis of drug F versus drug I

|  | Drug I | | Drug F | |
| --- | --- | --- | --- | --- |
|  | Number of patients | Total cost | Number of patients | Total cost |
| Relapse |  |  |  |  |
| No relapse |  |  |  |  |
| Second relapse |  |  |  |  |
| Second no relapse |  |  |  |  |
| Failure |  |  |  |  |
| Total cost of alternative |  |  |  |  |
| Successfully treated patients |  |  |  |  |
| Difference in cost |  |  |  |  |
| Difference in outcome |  |  |  |  |
| Cost per extra successfully treated patient |  |  |  |  |

Second relapse:

$$(280 \times (1/12)) + (7 \times (5/12)) + (4 \times 50) + (1 \times 200) + (12 \times 20)$$
$$= £666 \times 96 \text{ patients} = £63,957$$

Second no relapse:

$$(280 \times (1/12)) + (7 \times (11/12)) + (12 \times 20)$$
$$= £270 \times 224 \text{ patients} = £60,424$$

Failure:

$$(280 \times (1/12)) + (7 \times (1/12)) + (6 \times 50) + (1 \times 200) + (12 \times 20)$$
$$= £764 \times 480 \text{ patients} = £366,720$$

*Cost per patient for each arm (drug I)*

Relapse:

$$(7 \times 0.5) + (4 \times 50) + (1 \times 200) + (12 \times 20)$$
$$= £643.5 \times 240 \text{ patients} = £154,440$$

*Continued*

No relapse:

$$(7 \times 1) + (6 \times 20) = £127 \times 560 \text{ patients} = £71,120$$

Second relapse:

$$(280 \times (5/12)) + (7 \times (1/12)) + (4 \times 50) + (1 \times 200) + (12 \times 20)$$
$$= £757 \times 144 \text{ patients} = £109,044$$

Second no relapse:

$$(280 \times (11/12)) + (7 \times (1/12)) + (12 \times 20)$$
$$= £497 \times 576 \text{ patients} = £286,416$$

Failure:

$$(280 \times (1/12)) + (7 \times (1/12)) + (6 \times 50) + (1 \times 200) + (12 \times 20)$$
$$= £764 \times 480 \text{ patients} = £366,720$$

See Table 8.2.

**Table 8.2** Completed base-case economic analysis of drug F versus drug I

|  | Drug I | | Drug F | |
|---|---|---|---|---|
|  | Number of patients | Total cost | Number of patients | Total cost |
| Relapse | 240 | £154,440 | 240 | £187,200 |
| No relapse | 560 | £71,120 | 960 | £384,000 |
| 2nd relapse | 144 | £109,044 | 96 | £63,957 |
| 2nd no relapse | 576 | £286,416 | 224 | £60,424 |
| Failure | 480 | £366,720 | 480 | £366,720 |
| Total cost of alternative |  | £987,740 |  | £1,062,301 |
| Successfully treated patients | 1136 |  | 1184 |  |
| Difference in cost |  | £74,561 | | |
| Difference in outcome |  | 48 | | |
| Cost per extra successfully treated patient |  | **£1,553.35** | | |

*Continued*

**Which antidepressant are you going to recommend they use first in these patients?**

How would your results be affected if the following treatments were changed:

- A hospital stay included 2 days and two sessions of ECT.
- All failed patients had monthly counselling sessions.
- You used drug D (£70 per year, assume same efficacy) instead of drug I?

## Markov modelling

A simple decision tree may not be capable of modelling chronic disease states. A model trying to represent a chronic disease, such as relapsing–remitting multiple sclerosis, must be capable of reflecting changes in and out of health states. These may be referred to as random processes that evolve over time. They are random because we do not know when they will occur in the disease progression. Markov models are particularly useful for representing the use of interventions to manage chronic health states. The interested reader is directed towards a useful introduction to Markov modelling by Briggs and Sculpher (1998).

A decision-analytical model may become unnecessarily complex, as patients will move in and out of health states many times. An alternative method for presenting these events is shown in Figure 8.4. This shows a simplified version of what can happen to a person with relapsing–remitting multiple sclerosis. When they are symptom free there is a probability they will have a relapse, stay symptom free or die. When they are experiencing symptoms, there is a probability they will become symptom free, the relapse may continue, or they may die. When a patient dies, they cannot return to the other health states. Therefore, death is referred to as the 'absorbing' state.

Markov models therefore simulate the natural history of a chronic illness such as multiple sclerosis in a population of patients over a period of time, and its associated risk of relapse, remission and death.

The population of patients moves through the model over time. The model will estimate how many patients are in remission, have relapsed or have died at any given time. Probabilities of moving from one state to another will be obtained from sources such as RCTs and systematic reviews. One cycle will be assumed to last a length of time relevant to

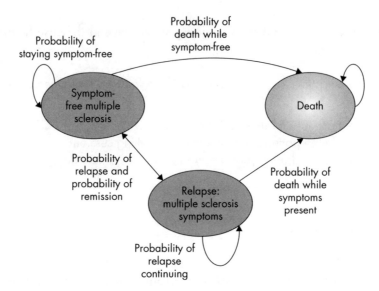

**Figure 8.4** Markov model for economic analysis of the prevention and management of relapsing–remitting multiple sclerosis.

that particular disease, such as 6 months, and transitions are usually assumed to occur halfway through the cycle.

Basic Markov models are 'memoryless' and a model more closely reflects real life if the patient's history is taken into account when assessing the probability of moving between health states (transition probabilities). For example, in relapsing–remitting multiple sclerosis the probability of relapse and death increases with time and age, and this can be incorporated into the model such that probability becomes a function of time spent within a state. This can also allow death from other causes to be included.

The time horizon of the model will often be a long period of time – sometimes the lifetime of the patient – for both costs and outcomes, and there will be a requirement for discounting.

Markov models can be used in the economic evaluation of alternative treatments when the impact of those treatments on transition probabilities is known. Figure 8.5 shows a Markov model for the progression of osteoporosis in postmenopausal women.

This model has two different types of health state, apart from the absorbing state 'death': stable states and transient states. A stable state is one in which a patient can remain for more than one cycle of the model. A transient state is one in which a patient cannot remain for more than one cycle. In Figure 8.5, the stable states are 'healthy',

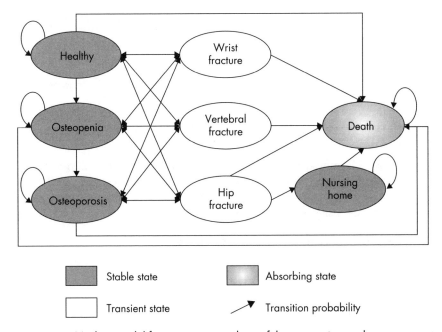

| | Stable state | | Absorbing state |
| --- | --- | --- | --- |
| | Transient state | | Transition probability |

**Figure 8.5** Markov model for economic analysis of the prevention and management of osteoporosis.

'osteopenia', 'osteoporosis' and 'nursing home', and the transient states are 'wrist fracture', 'vertebral fracture' and 'hip fracture'.

..........................................................................

**SELF-DIRECTED STUDY EXERCISES**

**EXERCISE 1:** Using a decision tree to carry out an economic evaluation

The decision tree in Figure 8.6 shows two common alternatives for treating urinary tract infections (UTIs).

1. **If you were to treat 250 patients with one of these antibiotics, which of the following columns of numbers of patients going down each pathway would you expect?**

| | A | B | C | D |
| --- | --- | --- | --- | --- |
| Treated successfully with drug T | 70 | 175 | 87.5 | 175 |
| Treated unsuccessfully with drug T | 30 | 75 | 37.5 | 30 |
| Treated successfully with drug C | 90 | 225 | 112.5 | 225 |
| Treated unsuccessfully with drug C | 10 | 25 | 12.5 | 10 |

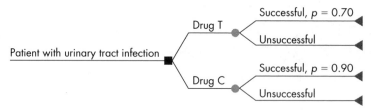

**Figure 8.6** Decision tree for treating a urinary tract infection.

It costs £2 in drug costs to treat a patient with drug C and 20p to treat a patient with drug T. A GP visit costs £10, and every patient has one GP visit. The added cost of unsuccessful treatment is £30 per patient (the cost of another GP visit and more expensive antibiotics).

2.  **The cost of treating the 250 patients with drug T is:**

    - A £50
    - B £2,550
    - C £3,450
    - D £4,800.

3.  **The cost of treating the 250 patients with drug C is:**

    - A £500
    - B £3,000
    - C £3,300
    - D £3,750.

4.  **In this example, drug C is shown to be:**

    - A More cost-effective
    - B Less cost-effective
    - C Dominant
    - D Really brilliant.

5.  **The decision tree above has:**

    - A Two chance nodes and four pathways only
    - B One chance node, two decision nodes and two pathways only
    - C One decision node and two chance nodes only
    - D One decision node, two chance nodes and four pathways only.

6.  **Which of these statements is true about the costs in the example:**

    - A The GP cost and the drug costs are variable costs
    - B The GP cost is a fixed cost and the drug costs are variable costs
    - C The drug costs are fixed costs and the GP cost is an indirect cost
    - D The drug costs are variable costs and the GP cost is an indirect cost.

7.    **This study of urinary tract infections is a:**

- A Cost-minimisation analysis
- B Cost-effectiveness analysis
- C Cost–utility analysis
- D Cost–benefit analysis.

8.    **The outcomes data for this study were collected from a randomised controlled trial and the cost data were obtained by interviewing a GP. Which of the following statements is not true:**

- A The outcomes data are probably better quality than the cost data.
- B This is a secondary economic evaluation.
- C The effectiveness of the drugs in practice is probably higher than in the clinical trial.
- D Bringing data together from different sources like this is called synthesis.

**Answers**

1. B
2. D
3. D
4. C
5. D
6. A
7. B
8. C

**EXERCISE 2:** Using decision analysis to test uncertainties in data

Read Briggs AH, Sculpher MJ, Logan RPH, *et al.* (1996). Cost effectiveness of screening for and eradication of *Helicobacter pylori* in management of dyspeptic patients under 45 years of age. *Br Med J* 312: 1321–1325.

You will see that a sensitivity analysis has been carried out on a wide range of clinical and economic parameters where it was felt there was uncertainty. The impact of this uncertainty was investigated. What impact did varying these parameters have? How important are the ranges in a sensitivity analysis?

**EXERCISE 3:** Using decision analysis in the decision-making process

Read Lilford RJ, Pauker SG, Braunholtz DA, Chard J (1998). Decision analysis and the implementation of research findings. *Br Med J* 317: 405–409.

In this paper, the authors discuss the use of a decision model for choice of treatment in case of suspected myocardial infarction (MI).

1.   What would have been the decision process in the absence of this model?
2.   Discuss the added value of this model to the decision-making process.
3.   What are the limitations associated with this approach?

••••••••••••••••••••••••••••••••••••••••••••••••••••••••••••••••••••••••

## References

Briggs A, Sculpher M (1998). An introduction to Markov modelling for economic evaluation. *PharmacoEconomics* 13: 397–409.

Fitzpatrick R, Davey C, Buxton MJ, Jones DR (1998). Evaluating patient-based outcome measures for use in clinical trials. *Health Technol Assessment* 2(14): 1–69.

Gray A, Clarke P, Raikou M, *et al.* (2001). An economic evaluation of atenolol versus captopril in patients with type 2 diabetes (UKPDS 54). *Diabetic Med* 18: 438–444.

Jefferson T, Demicheli V, Mugford M (1996). Cost effectiveness analysis and cost utility analysis. In: Jefferson T, Demicheli V, Mugford M, eds. *Elementary Economic Evaluation in Healthcare*. London: BMJ Books.

Lilford RJ, Pauker SG, Braunholtz DA, Chard J (1998). Decision analysis and the implementation of research findings. *Br Med J* 317: 405–409.

NHS Centre for Reviews and Dissemination (2001). *Undertaking Systematic Reviews of Research on Effectiveness*. CRD Report 4, 2nd edn. York: University of York.

Weinstein RC, Feinberg HV (1980). *Clinical Decision Analysis*. Philadelphia: W B Saunders.

## Further reading

Briggs AH, Sculpher MJ, Logan RPH, *et al.* (1996). Cost effectiveness of screening for and eradication of *Helicobacter pylori* in management of dyspeptic patients under 45 years of age. *Br Med J* 312: 1321–1325.

Mulrow CD (1994). Systematic reviews: rationale for systematic reviews. *Br Med J* 309: 597–599.

Grimshaw J, McAuley LM, Bero LA, *et al.* (2003). Systematic reviews of the effectiveness of quality improvement strategies and programmes. *Qual Saf Healthcare* 12: 298–303.

### Examples using Markov modelling techniques

Highland KB, Strange C, Mazur J, Simpson KN (2003). Treatment of pulmonary arterial hypertension: a preliminary decision analysis. *Chest* 124: 2087–2092.

Remak E, Hutton J, Price M, *et al.* (2003). A Markov model of treatment of newly diagnosed epilepsy in the UK: an initial assessment of cost-effectiveness of topiramate. *Eur J Health Econ* 4: 271–278.

Salomon JA, Weinstein MC, Hammitt JK, Goldie SJ (2003). Cost-effectiveness of treatment for chronic hepatitis C infection in an evolving patient population. *J Am Med Assoc* 290: 228–237.

You JHS, Chan FWH, Wong RSM, Cheng G (2003). Cost-effectiveness of two models of management for patients on chronic warfarin therapy – a Markov model analysis. *Thromb Haemost* 90: 1106–1111.

# 9

## Using economic evaluations to inform decision-making in healthcare

### Introduction

Previous chapters have explained the methods used to generate information on the economic impact of interventions. The main focus of economic evaluations is to aid decision-making. To do this, the information generated must be reliable and valid. It must also be relevant to inform decisions at both a national level, such as guidance produced by the National Institute for Clinical Excellence in the UK, and a local level, such as informing the resource allocation decisions made by local decision-makers, such as Primary Care Trusts in the UK. This is a very difficult thing to do, and very few published economic evaluations meet this objective. This chapter will discuss how economic evaluations may be used to inform practice and present the current evidence on their use for this purpose. It will also discuss the use of guidelines to inform the design of good-quality economic evaluations. Finally, the use of quality assessment criteria for evaluating published economic evaluations will be discussed.

### How may economic evaluations be used?

Economic studies have a number of potential uses in healthcare. It is generally accepted that economic evaluations should not be used to guide treatment decisions for individual patients. They are more appropriate for guiding the development of drug formularies, disease-specific guidelines, or the development of patient services. Economic evaluations may also be used to inform drug reimbursement decisions.

Healthcare interventions can potentially be assessed at two levels: nationally, guided by a structured and coordinated programme, and locally by decision-makers such as health authority or NHS Trust staff. Central decision-making will often be supported by experts capable of interpreting the design and relevance of economic studies. In the absence

**Table 9.1** Some potential uses of economic evaluation

- To justify the existence of a service
- To justify the development of a new service
- To justify the extension of an existing service
- To inform the development of clinical guidelines
- To inform which medicines to have on a formulary
- As a mandatory requirement to inform the reimbursement of medicines
- As a voluntary requirement to inform national guidance on health technologies

of national guidance – and possibly even when national guidance exists – local decision-makers may carry out their own assessment of healthcare interventions. This may be done individually or within a committee structure. Local decision-makers may often not have people in the area with the relevant expertise to critique economic evaluations, and these skills are essential if economic evaluations are going to be used in decision-making. Table 9.1 shows how the results of economic evaluations may be used to inform healthcare practice.

Applying economic evaluations in practice has been described as an iterative process, where studies are capable of generating progressively firmer estimates of cost-effectiveness. Four stages of economic analysis are suggested:

- Stage 1, when the basic clinical science is complete (early developmental)
- Stage 2, maturing innovation
- Stage 3, close to widespread diffusion
- Stage 4, to generalise the results of earlier studies to routine clinical practice (moving into practice) (Sculpher *et al.*, 1997).

The *incremental cost-effectiveness ratio* (ICER) is the main output from an economic evaluation. This is a summary measure that may be used by decision-makers allocating scarce healthcare resources (see Chapter 5). *League tables* have been used to compare the ranking of alternative healthcare interventions (see Chapter 6) (Mason *et al.*, 1996). Mauskopf *et al.* (2003) questioned the use of these league tables because of a potential lack of comparability between economic evaluations, which may have used different methods and assumptions about the choice of comparator, discount rate, time horizon, patient population, and method used to elicit utilities. These methodological differences may limit the usefulness of decisions made using a league table. Alternative types of league table have been suggested (Hutubessy *et al.*, 2001). Researchers have now turned their attention to improving the way the results of economic evaluations are presented to reflect the uncertainty surrounding ICERs. Approaches used include presenting confidence intervals around the ICER, the net benefit approach, and cost-effectiveness acceptability curves (see Chapter 10).

## How have economic evaluations been used?

There is a relatively recent trend for more economic evaluations being published in medical journals. There is now a requirement for economic evaluations to be an integral component of UK NHS R&D programme funded projects. UK decision-making bodies have started to incorporate the use of economic evaluations into their decision-making processes. One example is the National Institute for Clinical Excellence (NICE), which was established on 1 April 1999. It aims to supply national guidance on new and existing healthcare technologies, including medicines. This guidance takes the form of technology appraisals and clinical guidelines. The guidance is formed using a committee structure. Technology appraisals are developed using a committee that appraises submissions from manufacturers, sponsors and independent academic groups containing evidence on the clinical and economic impact of the particular technology in question.

A number of studies have started to explore whether economic evaluations are used by decision-makers, both centrally and locally, to inform resource allocation and whether the evaluations have an impact on decision-making and clinical practice. In 2003, a task force formed by the International Society of Pharmacoeconomics and Outcomes Research (ISPOR) produced a useful review of published empirical studies that explored decision-makers' attitudes to economic evaluations (Drummond *et al.* and the ISPOR Task Force, 2003). This review also presents a list of suggestions to improve the reporting of economic evaluations. The interested reader is directed towards this review for more detail, a summary of the studies included, and the recommendations for improving the reporting of economic studies for use by decision-makers.

The ISPOR Task Force concluded that there were a number of reasons why economic evaluations may not be used to inform decision-making. Decision-makers need to be sure that an economic evaluation is reliable and relevant. Reliable was defined as the presentation of accurate estimates that are free from bias. Decision-makers have expressed concern about the lack of transparency in economic studies, especially those using modelling. There was also concern over the extensive use of assumptions and the extrapolation of short-term health benefits observed in clinical studies to longer time periods for the purpose of economic evaluations. Decision-makers have also reported being uncomfortable with methods for calculating QALYs and willingness to pay, and prefer results to be presented as a cost–consequence analysis (see Chapter 5). A relevant evaluation would contain results that apply to the decision-maker's setting or local practice. A common problem is that economic evaluations do not generally explore the budgetary impact – the total cost – of the intervention on the NHS. Decision-makers also express concerns about studies performed in other locations and applying to those settings. Drummond and Pang (2001) present a good discussion about the issue of *transferability* of economic evaluations.

## Assessing the quality of economic evaluations

The overall design of an economic evaluation uses the same framework (see Chapters 5, 6, 7 and 8). This is discussed extensively by Drummond and BMJ Working Party (1996) and Gold *et al.* (1996). Ensuring good-quality economic evaluations and standardisation of their framework is one of the main approaches to encourage their application to inform decision-making in healthcare. In the early 1990s, the quality of published economic evaluations was reported to be below an acceptable standard (Bradley *et al.*, 1995; Mason and Drummond, 1995). A more recent review, published between 1990 and 2001, suggests that modest improvements in the quality of conducting and reporting economic evaluations seem to have taken place (Jefferson *et al.*, 2002). However, there are still improvements to be made in the clear description of methods, explanations of the approach used, and the quality of estimates of effectiveness.

## Using guidelines to improve the quality of economic evaluations

The use of guidelines may avoid bias in the reporting and conduct of economic evaluations and allow comparison between different evaluations. Guidelines have used different formats. Gold *et al.* (1996) describe a 'reference case' approach. A reference case is a 'standard set of methodological practices that an analyst would seek to follow in a cost-effectiveness study'. Researchers may decide to use other methods than those described in the reference case. However, using the reference case allows a meaningful comparison to be made between different studies. Drummond and the BMJ Economic Evaluation Working Party (1996), in the *British Medical Journal* guidelines, use a checklist approach. The researcher preparing a paper, or the reviewer assessing the quality of a paper, is advised to use this list to confirm that the relevant components of the economic evaluation are present.

A number of guidelines have been produced with the aim of standardising the conduct of economic evaluations used to inform decision-making. Hjelmgren *et al.* (2001) provide a useful review of the similarities and differences of available guidelines. These are not intended to be used as a 'cookbook', but rather to inform the use of correct methods. Health economists are continually working at improving the methods used in economic evaluation, and it is therefore necessary to continually update guidance in line with new methodological developments. Different countries have prepared different guidelines, and there is a sample list at the end of the chapter. Guidelines may be voluntary or mandatory. The UK Department of Health has opted to have voluntary guidelines. This means that the guidelines do not form part of a legally enforced evaluation process for the introduction of new health technologies such as medicines. However, guidance on the use of submissions to NICE does include detail on the design and conduct of economic evaluations. NICE has chosen to use a reference case approach similar to that described by Gold *et al.* (1996). In some countries, such as Australia, no new medicines may be made available under the Pharmaceutical Benefits Scheme unless the Pharmaceutical Benefits Advisory Committee (PBAC) recommends their use. This system of mandatory guidelines was the first to be put in place, in 1992. The decision of the PBAC is guided by submissions which include an economic evaluation of the new medicine compared to the current treatment for the condition under consideration.

## The BMJ Economic Evaluation Guidelines

In 1996, the *British Medical Journal* published explicit guidelines for the peer review process which aimed to improve the quality of submitted and published economic evaluations (Drummond and the BMJ Economic Evaluation Working Party, 1996). The authors suggest that these guidelines may be used to inform the review process of articles submitted to journals for publication, but may also be used by researchers designing economic evaluations to make sure the relevant components of the study are included. The basic components of a good economic evaluation are shown in Table 9.2, and are based on the recommendations described in the *British Medical Journal* guidelines (see Worked example 9.1).

**Table 9.2** Components of a good economic evaluation (adapted from Drummond and BMJ Economic Evaluation Working Party, 1996)

| *Section* | *Component* |
|---|---|
| Study design | 1. Study question:<br>• The economic importance of the question should be outlined<br>• The hypothesis being tested should be clearly stated<br>• The viewpoint(s) for the analysis should be clearly stated and justified<br>2. Selection of alternatives:<br>• The rationale for choice of the alternative programmes or interventions for comparison should be given<br>• The alternative interventions should be described in sufficient detail<br>3. Form of evaluation:<br>• The form(s) of evaluation used should be stated<br>• A clear justification should be given for the form(s) of evaluation chosen in relation to the question(s) being addressed |
| Data collection | 4. Effectiveness data:<br>• If the economic evaluation is based on a single study, the details of its design and results should be given<br>• If the economic evaluation is based on an overview of a number of effectiveness studies, details should be given of the method of synthesis<br>5. Outcome measurement and valuation:<br>• The primary outcome measure for the economic evaluation should be clearly stated<br>• If health benefits have been valued, details should be given of the methods used<br>• If changes in productivity (indirect benefits) are included, they should be reported separately and their relevance to the study question discussed<br>6. Costing:<br>• Quantities of resources should be reported separately from the prices (unit costs)<br>• Methods for the estimation of both quantities and prices (unit costs) should be given<br>• The currency and price date should be recorded and details of any adjustment for inflation, or currency conversion given<br>7. Modelling:<br>• Details should be given of any modelling used in the economic study<br>• Justification should be given of the choice of the model and key parameters |

**Table 9.2** (continued)

| | |
|---|---|
| Analysis and interpretation of results | 8. Adjustments for timing of costs and outcomes:<br>• The time horizon over which costs and outcomes are considered should be given<br>• The discount rate(s) should be given and the choice of rate(s) justified<br>• If costs and outcomes are not discounted an explanation should be given<br>9. Allowance for uncertainty:<br>• When stochastic data are reported, details should be given about which statistical tests were performed and the confidence intervals around the main variables<br>• When a sensitivity analysis (for deterministic data) is performed, details should be given and justification for the choice of variables for sensitivity analysis and the ranges over which they varied<br>10. Presentation of results:<br>• Incremental analysis should be reported, comparing the relevant alternatives<br>• Major outcomes should be presented in both disaggregated and aggregated forms<br>• Any comparisons with other healthcare interventions should be made only when a close similarity in study methods and settings can be demonstrated<br>• The answer to the original study question should be given; any conclusion should follow clearly from the data reported and should be accompanied by appropriate qualifications or reservations |

**WORKED EXAMPLE 9.1**    Using the BMJ Economic Evaluation Guidelines

Read the study by Elliott RA, Payne K, Moore JK, *et al.* (2003). Clinical and economic choices in anaesthesia for day surgery: a prospective randomized controlled trial. *Anaesthesia* 58: 412–416.

1.  **What is the study question being addressed? The aims and objectives of the economic evaluation, which define the research question, must be clearly described. The viewpoint and time horizon should be defined at the start of the evaluation.**

*Continued*

The aim of this study was to assess whether there were important differences in the relative costs and outcomes of general anaesthetic agents used in adult and paediatric day surgery. The study took the viewpoint of the NHS (direct costs) and the patient (outcomes and patient-related expenditure). The time horizon for the primary economic analysis was from patient admission to the day ward (or unit) until discharge. Patient resource use data were also collected until day 7 post discharge.

2.  **What are the relevant alternatives? At least two alternatives must be compared in the evaluation. Each should be described to explain who did what, to whom, where, and how often.**
    The four alternative anaesthetic regimens compared for adult day-case surgery were propofol induction and maintenance (P/P), propofol induction and isoflurane maintenance with nitrous oxide (P/I), propofol induction and sevoflurane maintenance with nitrous oxide (P/S), and sevoflurane induction and sevoflurane maintenance with nitrous oxide (S/S). The two alternative anaesthetic regimens compared for paediatric day-case surgery were propofol induction and halothane maintenance (P/H), and S/S.

    The authors reported that the interventions were chosen on the basis of a literature review and a survey of practice in the UK.

3.  **What was the form of the evaluation and effectiveness data? The type of economic evaluation (CMA, CEA, CUA or CBA) to be used should be described and the reason why that particular type was selected.**
    This study used cost-effectiveness analysis because the primary outcome measure was the number of postoperative nausea and vomiting events before discharge. Further details about why CEA was chosen were not given.

4.  **How were effectiveness data collected? For each type of economic evaluation there are two general approaches to collecting the effectiveness and cost data: retrospective and prospective. A retrospective study will use existing data sources from published studies. The effectiveness data would generally be obtained from a single clinical trial or the combined results of several studies, such as reported in a systematic review or meta-analysis. A prospective study will collect primary data ideally using a randomised controlled trial.**

*Continued*

This study derived effectiveness data from a single study, which was a randomised controlled trial.

5.   **What types of outcome measure were used? A vital step in the conduct of an economic evaluation is the identification and assessment of outcomes. The nature of the outcomes included in an analysis depends on the study viewpoint and the timeframe of the analysis, which are determined by the aims, objectives and research question. There are three main groups of outcome measure used in economic evaluations (see Chapter 4). These are measures of effectiveness, utility (which includes health-related quality of life), and monetary values. These each relate to types of economic evaluation: CEA, CUA and CBA, respectively.**
This study used an effectiveness measure, i.e. the number of postoperative nausea and vomiting (PONV) events before discharge.

6.   **How were costs identified and quantified? The costs included in an economic evaluation come under three main headings: direct, indirect and intangible. Direct costs are associated with the immediate consequences of a healthcare good or service. They are further subdivided into fixed, semifixed and variable costs (see Chapter 3).**
In this study, the effectiveness evidence and resource use data were collected between October 1999 and January 2001. The price year was 2000.

The cost of the alternative anaesthetic regimens was defined in terms of intraoperative resource use, postoperative resource use and post discharge (NHS contact). Intraoperative resource use covered induction and maintenance anaesthesia, other drugs, disposables, time in theatre, treatment of adverse events and staff time. Postoperative resource use covered PONV, pain, other drugs, other equipment, management of other adverse events, time to discharge, overnight admission and staff time. Variable costs were also reported, which were defined as the costs associated with the anaesthetic, drug, disposables, management of PONV and adverse events. Data on the length of stay (fixed costs) and staff time (semifixed costs) were also collected.

Neither the unit costs nor their source were reported. The quantities were estimated from actual data, which were collected by

*Continued*

trained research staff. The price year was 2000. The resources were collected during October 1999 and January 2001.

Indirect costs were not reported because they were not appropriate to the study perspective (NHS). All costs were reported in UK pounds sterling (£).

7.  **Were modelling approaches used in this study? Models are methods of representing the real world and can describe what is happening or suggest what should happen. Decision analysis is used to compare the alternative strategies by comparing all possible outcomes, probabilities, and, if available, utilities of each outcome (see Chapter 8).**
    This study was a prospective study and did not include any modelling approaches.

8.  **Were adjustments made for the timing of costs and outcomes? The number of years for which costs and outcomes are valued is guided by the study time horizon. If the timeframe for the analysis exceeds 1 year, future costs and outcomes should be discounted to the present value to account for individuals' positive time preferences.**
    Discounting was not carried out owing to the short timescale (less than 1 year) of the study.

9.  **Were allowances made for uncertainty? Sensitivity analysis is used to allow for uncertainty in economic evaluations. Economic studies that assimilate and analyse deterministic data must include a sensitivity analysis, and it is recommended that studies that use stochastic data will also need a sensitivity analysis for certain components of the data analysis (see Chapters 3 and 8).**
    This study collected stochastic data. A bootstrap estimation was used to identify the magnitude of uncertainty around the incremental cost-effectiveness ratios (ICERs) (see Chapter 10).

10.  **How were the results presented? The presentation of the results of an economic evaluation involves comparing the total costs and the total outcomes of one programme to another. The cost-effectiveness plane was developed to determine the relative significance of the incremental costs and outcomes of a programme. The recommended approach is to perform an incremental analysis, where**

*Continued*

**the additional costs and the additional benefits of a programme relevant to its alternative are calculated (see Chapter 5).**

**The method of statistical analysis for the cost–outcome ratio depends on whether the cost and outcome data are deterministic or stochastic. Standard statistical tests are not appropriate if the economic evaluation used retrospective data. Stochastic data allow more freedom in terms of potential statistical tests. It is possible to determine separate (pseudo) confidence intervals for the costs and effects using bootstrapping methods.**

**Provided the economic evaluation has been conducted according to accepted guidelines, the most important step is presenting the results to decision-makers. It is important to remember the identity of the key player, which is always the decision-maker for whom the study has been designed and performed.**

In this study, the ICERs were estimated on the principle of dominance and the interventions were ranked from highest to lowest effectiveness. Each intervention was compared with the comparator immediately below it in terms of cost.

In the adult study, the ICER was £296 per PONV case avoided for the P/P group compared to the P/S group, and £333 per PONV case avoided for the P/S group compared to the P/I group. The P/I group was both cheaper and more effective than the other anaesthetic agents, and therefore no ICER was calculated. The S/S group was dominated by the three other anaesthetic regimens in the adult study.

In the paediatric study, the P/H group was cheaper and more effective, and therefore dominated the S/S group. No ICER was calculated.

The authors reported the results of bootstrap estimations of sampling distributions of the ICERS. In the adult study, the results showed that the rank ordering was not stable and the differences between arms could be negative or positive in terms of net PONV and costs. In the paediatric study, the ICERs were all in the southeast quadrant, indicating that P/H is more effective and less costly than S/S, and the result is stable.

*Continued*

> The authors suggest that the important results from this study for decision-makers are that there are differences in variable costs between the study arms, indicating that the choice of anaesthetic agents will translate into secondary care budget differences. The main conclusions are that S/S is not a cost-effective regimen for day-case surgery in adults or children when pre-discharge PONV is used as the primary outcome measure.

## Interpreting economic evaluations

One aim of this book is to provide sufficient information for the reader to interpret the design, quality and relevance of published economic evaluations. However, it may not always be practical to collate and assimilate all the information necessary to do this. A number of resources are available that were designed to help busy decision-makers interpret and use the results of published economic evaluations. One such is the *NHS Economic Evaluation Database* (NHSEED). This is a structured database that contains abstracts of economic evaluations. The abstracts come in two formats, one for prospective economic evaluations (single study) and one for retrospective (modelling) economic evaluations that present a critical appraisal of the published study by an experienced health economist. Each abstract follows a set format agreed by a panel of senior health economists. The most useful part of the abstract for decision-makers is the section that sets out the NHS Centre for Reviews and Dissemination (CRD) Commentary. This provides a structured overview of the quality of the paper. Decision-makers have suggested that a useful development of the NHSEED abstracts would be a quality-scoring system, but this remains a methodological challenge for health economists (Hoffman *et al.*, 2002). A full description of the NHS Economic Evaluation Database is beyond the scope of this book and the interested reader should look at CRD Report 6 (CRD, 2001).

••••••••••••••••••••••••••••••••••••••••••••••••••••••••••••••••••

**SELF-DIRECTED STUDY EXERCISE** – Using the UK NHS Economic Evaluation Database

You are a member of the hospital Medicines Management Committee. A consultant anaesthetist has made an application to the committee to introduce a new method for anaesthetising his adult day-case patients. He wants to use a gas induction method rather than an intravenous induction method. You have found a reference to a paper: Elliott RA, Payne K, Moore JK, *et al.* (2003). Clinical and economic choices in anaesthesia for day surgery: a prospective randomized controlled trial. *Anaesthesia* 58: 412–416, which you think may help you critically appraise the anaesthetist's application.

1.  Obtain and read a copy of this paper. It contains a lot of information, and you may not be sure how to fully relate the clinical relevance of its findings to your local practice. You feel that you need further help to understand this paper.
2.  Locate and search the NHS Economic Evaluation Database for an abstract on the paper by Elliott *et al.* The NHS Economic Evaluation Database may be found at *http://www.york.ac.uk/inst/crd/nhsdhp.htm.* Using the following search strategy you will locate the abstract you require: anaesthesia (all fields) AND Elliott (author).
3.  What did the authors of this study conclude? Using the summary information from the abstract, you find that the authors concluded that sevoflurane induction and sevoflurane maintenance with nitrous oxide was more costly, with higher rates of postoperative nausea and vomiting (PONV) in both adult and paediatric day-surgery patients.
4.  Would you use this study to inform your decision-making process? Using the CRD Commentary section, you find information that seems to suggest that the study was of reasonable quality to inform decision-making. The reviewer noted that the authors did point out two limitations to their study, but it does appear relevant to your question regarding the use of sevoflurane in adult day-case patients in your hospital.
5.  What did you conclude? Given the findings from this study, you decide to ask the anaesthetist if he has further evidence supporting his application for the use of sevoflurane as an induction agent in adult day-case patients.

••••••••••••••••••••••••••••••••••••••••••••••••••••••••••••••••••••••••••

## References

Bradley CA, Iskedijan M, Lanctot KL, *et al.* (1995). Quality assessment of economic evaluations in selected pharmacy, medical and health economic journals. *Ann Pharmacother* 29: 681–689.

Drummond MF, Pang F (2001). Transferability of economic evaluation results. In: Drummond MF, McGuire AL, eds. *Economic Evaluation of Healthcare: Merging Theory with Practice.* Oxford: Oxford University Press.

Drummond MF and the BMJ Economic Evaluation Working Party (1996). Guidelines for authors and peer-reviewers of economic submissions to the BMJ. *Br Med J* 313: 275–283.

Drummond M, Brown R, Fendrick AM, *et al.* and the ISPOR Task Force (2003). Use of pharmacoeconomics information – report of the ISPOR Task Force on use of pharmacoeconomic/health economic information in health-care decision making. *Value in Health* 6: 407–416.

Elliott RA, Payne K, Moore JK, *et al.* (2003). Clinical and economic choices in anaesthesia for day surgery: a prospective randomized controlled trial. *Anaesthesia* 58: 412–416.

Gold MR, Siegel JE, Russell LB, Weinstein MC, eds. (1996) *Cost-Effectiveness in Health and Medicine.* New York: Oxford University Press.

Hjelmgren J, Berggren F, Andersson F (2001). Health economic guidelines similarities, differences and some implications. *Value in Health* 4: 225–250.

Hoffmann C, Stoykova BA, Nixon J, *et al.* (2002). Do healthcare decision-makers find economic evaluations useful? The findings of focus group research in UK health authorities. *Value in Health* 5: 71–78.

Hutubessy RCW, Baltussen R, Evans DB, *et al.* (2001). Stochastic league tables: communicating cost-effectiveness results to decision-makers. *Health Econ* 10: 473–477.

Jefferson T, Demicheli V, Vale L (2002). Quality of systematic reviews of economic evaluations in healthcare. *JAMA* 287: 2809–2812.

Mason J, Drummond M, Torrance G (1993). Some guidelines on the use of cost-effectiveness league tables. *Br Med J* 306: 507–502.

Mason J, Drummond M (1995). The DH register of cost-effectiveness studies: content and quality. *Health Trends* 27: 50–56.

Mauskopf J, Rutten F, Schofield W (2003). Cost-effectiveness league tables. Valuable guidance for decision makers? *PharmacoEconomics* 21: 991–1000.

NHS Centre for Reviews and Dissemination (2001). *Improving access to cost-effectiveness information for healthcare decision making: the NHS Economic Evaluation Database.* CRD Report 6, 2nd edn. York: University of York.

Sculpher M, Drummond M, Buxton M (1997). The iterative use of economic evaluation as part of a process of health technology assessment. *J Health Serv Res Policy* 2: 26–30.

## Further reading

Drummond MF, Pang F (2001). Transferability of economic evaluation results. In: Drummond MF, McGuire AL, eds. *Economic Evaluation of Healthcare: Merging Theory with Practice.* Oxford: Oxford University Press.

Gold MR, Siegel JE, Russell LB, Weinstein MC, eds. (1996). *Cost-Effectiveness in Health and Medicine.* New York: Oxford University Press.

Hjelmgren J, Berggren F, Andersson F (2001). Health economic guidelines similarities, differences and some implications. *Value in Health* 4: 225–250.

Mauskopf J, Rutten F, Schofield W (2003). Cost-effectiveness league tables. Valuable guidance for decision makers? *PharmacoEconomics* 21: 991–1000.

## Sample list of guidelines for the design and conduct of economic evaluations

Canadian Coordinating Office for Health Technology Assessment (CCOHTA) (1997). *Guidelines for Economic Evaluation of Pharmaceuticals*, 2nd edn. Ottawa: CCOHTA. Available from: *http://www.ccohta.ca/*

Commonwealth of Australia (1995). *Guidelines for the Pharmaceutical Industry on Preparation of Submissions to the Pharmaceutical Benefits Advisory Committee: including major submissions involving economic analyses.* Canberra, Australia: PBAC, 1995. Available from: *http://www.health.gov.au/pbs/general/ pubs/pharmpac/gusubpac.htm.*

Gricar JA, Langley PC, Luce B, *et al.* (2002). *AMCP's Format for Formulary Submissions: A Format for Submissions of Clinical and Economic Evaluation Data in Support of Formulary Consideration by Managed Healthcare Systems in the United States.* Alexandria (VA): Academy of Managed Care Pharmacy (AMCP). Available from: *http://www.amcp.org/* (accessed January 2004).

National Institute for Clinical Excellence (NICE) (2001). *Guidance for Manufacturers and Sponsors. Technology Appraisal Process Series No. 5* . London: National Institute for Clinical Excellence. Available from: *http://www.nice.org.uk*

Norwegian Medicines Control Authority (1999). *The Norwegian Guidelines for Pharmacoeconomic Analysis in Connection with Application for Reimbursement.* Oslo: Norwegian Medicines Control Authority Department of Pharmacoeconomics.

Ontario Ministry of Health (1994). *Ontario Guidelines for Economic Analysis of Pharmaceutical Products.* Ontario: Ministry of Health. Available from: *http://www.health.gov.on.ca/*

Ziekenfondraad (1999). *Dutch Guidelines for Pharmacoeconomic Research.* Amstelveen: Health Insurance Council (Ziekenfondraad).

# 10

## Statistical handling of data in economic analysis

### Introduction

This chapter examines the use of data in economic analysis. The first part describes the statistical analysis of cost data. Before beginning this section you will need to understand the concepts covered in Chapter 3, and you will also need a basic understanding of statistical distributions (such as normal distributions), descriptive statistics (mean, median standard deviation and confidence intervals), inferential statistics (parametric tests such as $t$-tests and ANOVA tests, and non-parametric tests such as $\chi^2$ tests).

The second part of the chapter describes the use of probabilistic sensitivity analysis to generate mean expected costs, outcomes and ICERs, and statistical measures of expected variance around the mean ICER. This method, also called *stochastic economic analysis*, or *probabilistic modelling*, allows estimation of the probability and extent to which uncertainty and variation in the data used affect the absolute and relative costs and outcomes. Before beginning this section, you will need to understand the concepts covered in Chapters 3, 4, 5 and 8. You will also need to understand the statistical concepts listed in the paragraph above.

### Statistical analysis of costs

#### The shape of cost data distribution

When carrying out economic analysis, it is important to find out by using statistical tests whether there are differences in costs between different treatment alternatives. The objective of the statistical analysis is to test whether there are statistically significant differences in resource use and costs between the treatment groups. Cost is a continuous variable, so it would seem that the costs of treatment can be compared between groups using standard independent samples $t$-tests.

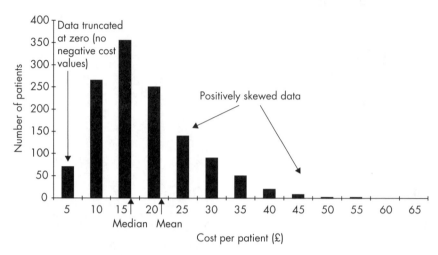

**Figure 10.1** Distribution of cost data.

However, the distribution of cost data is typically *truncated* and *positively skewed*. This is caused by the presence of a relatively small number of patients with high treatment costs (patients developing complications after surgery, for example) and the absence of negative costs (Barber and Thompson, 1998). This can create a long right-handed tail in the distribution. A theoretical example of the distribution of patient-based cost data is shown in Figure 10.1. This shows the truncated and skewed distribution. It also shows that the median is lower than the mean (arithmetic mean). This is an indication of positively skewed data.

The mean is £21. This, however, is sensitive to outliers. The median is often used with skewed or non-normal data and where there are outliers. It is also used in non-parametric tests. The median for this dataset is £16. The median is useful because we can use it to describe a 'typical cost' for a patient (Thompson and Barber, 2000). However, using the median will not allow policy-makers to determine the total cost of treatment for a group of patients. For this, the mean is required because total cost for a group is the mean cost multiplied by number of patients in the group.

Furthermore, summarising the distribution of costs can be problematic. Because of skewed data, standard deviation alone is not an ideal way to present the spread of costs between individuals. Use of the range may give a distorted picture of variability, and so it is considered more useful to present the interquartile range.

This is not the same type of data distribution as the normal distribution upon which standard parametric independent samples *t*-tests are based. Standard parametric statistical tests assume that observations are

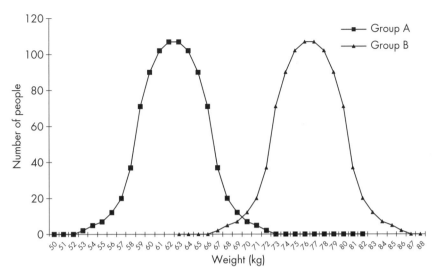

**Figure 10.2** Determining the difference between two normally distributed data sets.

random samples from a normal distribution with the same variance. An example of this is shown in Figure 10.2. The distribution of weights of two groups of people have been plotted, and we can see that these data have normal distributions. Therefore, a *t*-test can be used to test whether the difference in weight between groups A and B is statistically significant.

When comparing two sets of cost data, the distributions are more likely to look like those in Figure 10.3.

### When is a *t*-test the correct test to use?

We have said that the use of standard parametric statistical tests to look for differences between cost data may be inappropriate and the calculated means may be unreliable owing to the shape of distribution of cost data.

However, skewness may not be a problem for large samples, as the larger the sample size the more likely the central limit theorem will hold, and parametric assumptions will hold also. It has been reported that for samples larger than about 150, the *t*-test is generally robust (Barber and Thompson, 2000).

A published example of the appropriate use of *t*-tests for statistical analysis of cost data is an RCT of two different anaesthetic techniques in paediatric day surgery which obtained patient-based cost data (Elliott *et al.*, 2004). There were 159 and 163 patients, respectively, in each arm of the study. When sample distributions were examined, the skewness in

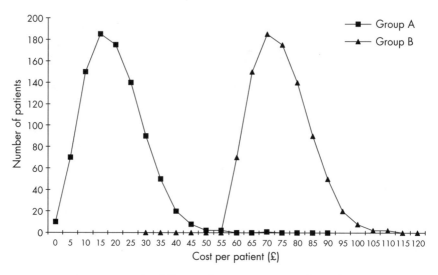

**Figure 10.3** Determining the difference between two sets of cost data.

the samples was found to be sufficiently low to indicate normality for the sampling distribution of the mean. The *t*-test was therefore used for cost variables and a statistically significant difference was found.

### Dealing with small sample sizes

Problems arise when analysing small samples. In summary, the *t*-test is robust for large samples but problems arise for small samples with skewness in the distribution. To judge whether skew in the data has important implications for the sampling of the mean, Briggs and Gray (1998) suggested that the skew in the sampling distribution of the mean ($S_m$) will be a factor:

$$S_m = S_s - \sqrt{n_s}$$

where $S_s$ is the skewness of the original sample and $n_s$ is the number of observations in the original sample.

There are three possible approaches to accommodate the problems of sample size and distribution in the analysis of cost data: non-parametric (rank sum) tests, transformation, and non-parametric bootstrapping. These methods are explained briefly here. For a more detailed handling of this subject, the reader is directed to Thompson and Barber (2000), Hart (2001), and Barber and Thompson (2000).

*Non-parametric tests*

For non-normal distributed data, non-parametric tests are recommended by conventional statistical guidelines. However, the non-parametric (rank sum) tests are better suited to hypothesis testing than to estimation. A *p* value is generated which shows the probabilities that the two samples are from the same distribution, and estimates of difference and confidence limits are based on assumptions that the shapes of the distributions are the same and only the location of the distribution is different (Hart, 2001). In addition, the estimates generated from rank sum tests effectively compare the difference in location between the two distributions, and thus compare medians. Therefore, these tests are inappropriate for cost data because economists are interested in the mean costs of treatment. The arithmetic mean is considered to be the most relevant measure for healthcare policy decisions, which should be based on information about the distribution of the costs of treating a patient group, as well as the average cost.

It is now generally accepted that using non-parametric tests may provide misleading conclusions (Thompson and Barber, 2000). However, many published studies of costs have 'revealed a lack of statistical awareness' by using these non-parametric tests (Barber and Thompson, 1998). It is important for the reader to examine statistical tests carefully in published studies.

*Transformation*

Data may be transformed to 'symmetrise' the distribution using natural log-transformation, square root transformations, or reciprocal transformation. This process reduces skewness and a normal distribution is approximated and similar size variances in the respective groups obtained. However, this means that geometric means are compared, and again arithmetic means cannot be compared. Positively skewed data such as costs will always produce a geometric mean that is lower than the arithmetic mean (Thompson and Barber, 2000). In addition, it is not possible to retransform cost differences to the original scale. This method has been recommended by some health economists (Rutten *et al.*, 1994) and used in some studies (Ellis *et al.*, 2000). However, it is now considered that these methods are inappropriate and are likely to produce misleading interpretation of results (Barber and Thompson, 1998, 2000; Thompson and Barber, 2000).

*Non-parametric bootstrapping (Barber and Thompson, 2000;*
*Briggs and Gray, 1998)*

Non-parametric bootstrapping is a data-based simulation method for assessing statistical precision. Bootstrap simulation allows a comparison of arithmetic means without making assumptions about the cost distribution. Bootstrapping compares arithmetic means while avoiding distributional assumptions.

In reality, one sample is available and statistics of interest are calculated from that sample. Bootstrapping is based on how values of that statistic would vary if the sampling process could be repeated many times.

The validity of the bootstrapping approach is based on two assumptions. First, as the original sample size approaches the population size so the sample distribution tends towards the population distribution. Second, as the number of bootstrap replications approaches infinity, so the bootstrap estimate of the sampling distribution of a statistic approaches the true sampling distribution. In a bootstrap analysis, the observed sample is treated as an empirical distribution, a sample is taken from that distribution, and the statistic of interest is calculated.

Random values are selected from the original sample (size $n_i$) with replacement to yield a bootstrap sample of size $n_i$, and the statistic of interest is calculated. 'Replacement' means that once a random value has been used for the bootstrap resample, it is put back into the original sample. Therefore, a bootstrap sample may include the costs for some patients more than once, while excluding the costs for other patients. The process is repeated many times. Between 50 and 200 replications are necessary to provide an estimate of standard error (Briggs *et al.*, 1997). Usually at least 1000 reiterations are carried out. This simulation process creates a sample of bootstrapped means with a distribution. The mean and other parametric statistics may be calculated for the bootstrap distribution. Most spreadsheet and database packages can carry out bootstrapping very easily. This method of testing cost differences is now being used regularly and there are many published examples (Grieve *et al.*, 2003; Lambert *et al.*, 1998).

Bootstrapping can be used either for primary analysis or as a check on the robustness for using parametric tests, such as the *t*-test with non-normal data. This check was carried out on cost data in the UK Prospective Diabetes Study (UK Prospective Diabetes Study Group, 1998). Here, the bootstrapped confidence intervals were compared with parametric confidence intervals and found to be robust. This is partly due to the large sample size of 1148 patients.

## Stochastic economic analysis

### Statistical problems with ICERs

The results of an economic evaluation can be used to make decisions about how to allocate resources. In Chapter 8 we showed how uncertainty about cost and outcome data can affect how decisions are made. Therefore, it is important that we present uncertainty about the results of our economic evaluations – that is, about incremental cost-effectiveness ratios (ICERs). Effect sizes and cost differences are associated with uncertainty, and we use confidence intervals (usually 95%) to represent this. Any uncertainty in these parameters will lead to uncertainty in the ICER derived from them. Although derived from sampled data for both outcome and costs, the ICER is a ratio. In fact, it is a ratio of differences, so there is a finite chance that the effect size may be zero. In this case it will not be possible for that ICER to be generated, because dividing a number by zero necessarily produces a result of infinity. This causes a problem in standard statistical analysis of ICERs. Generating a 95% confidence interval for an ICER is not appropriate to test its precision, as the ratio of the two distributions does not necessarily have a finite mean, or, therefore, a finite variance (Barber and Thompson, 2000).

### Methods for generating confidence intervals for ICERs

A number of approaches have been proposed for calculating confidence intervals, and Polsky et al. (1997) evaluated four methods: the Box method, the Taylor series method, the Fieller theorem method and the non-parametric bootstrap method. Confidence intervals for cost-effectiveness ratios resulting from the bootstrap method and the Fieller theorem method have been shown to be more dependably accurate than from the other two methods. It is beyond the scope of this book to describe all these methods in depth. For the interested reader, Briggs and Fenn (1998) also describe these four methods in more detail. For an example of the application of the Fieller theorem method in a published study see the UKPDS trial (UK Prospective Diabetes Study Group, 1998). Rather than bewilder the general reader and analyst, we confine ourselves to presenting the simplest, most appropriate method, which is the non-parametric bootstrap method. Therefore, the following section explains how this can be used for calculating quasi confidence intervals for ICERs.

### Generating quasi confidence intervals for ICERs using the non-parametric bootstrap method

The non-parametric bootstrap method does not generate true statistical confidence intervals for an ICER, and so we refer to the intervals generated as *quasi confidence intervals*.

Generating bootstrapped ICERs is similar to generating bootstrapped costs, as described above. In this situation, the ICERs are generated with replacement in the following way:

1.  Treatment group: sample with replacement $n_t$ cost/effect pairs, where $n_t$ is the sample size of the treatment group
2.  Control group: sample with replacement $n_c$ cost/effect pairs, where $n_c$ is the sample size of the control group
3.  Estimate the bootstrap ICER (Briggs *et al.*, 1997).

This method will produce a distribution of ICERs from which the mean can be generated. However, we cannot generate a true confidence interval.

### Graphical representation of bootstrapped ICERs

In Chapter 5 the cost-effectiveness plane was introduced and explained. In the cost-effectiveness plane, the horizontal axis represents the difference in effectiveness between two interventions and the vertical axis represents the corresponding difference in costs. We can plot our bootstrapped sample of ICERs on this plane, which allows us to visualise the variation within the bootstrapped sample of ICERs. This is shown in Figure 10.4.

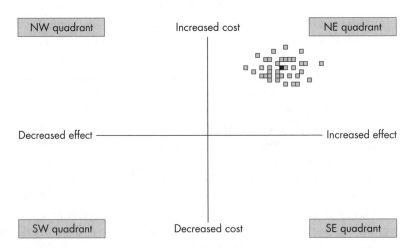

**Figure 10.4** Cost-effectiveness plane showing bootstrapped ICERs for a treatment that is more effective and more costly than the comparator.

We can draw an ellipse around the bootstrapped sample of ICERs to show the distribution of data. This is shown in Figure 10.5. This ellipse includes all the ICERs, including the outliers.

We can also draw an ellipse around 95% of the bootstrapped ICERs. Within this ellipse we have 95% of the possible ICERs. An approximation of the 95% confidence interval is given by the rays from the origin of the CE plane that are tangential to the ellipse (Briggs and Fenn, 1998). This is shown in Figure 10.6.

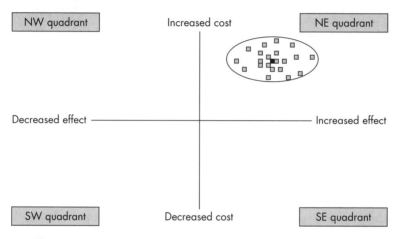

**Figure 10.5** Cost-effectiveness plane showing the elliptical shape of the distribution of bootstrapped ICERs for a treatment that is more effective and more costly than the comparator.

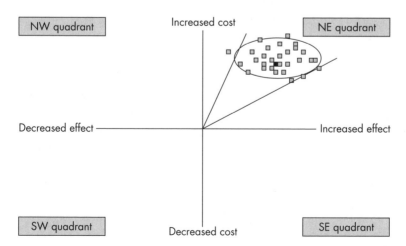

**Figure 10.6** Cost-effectiveness plane showing the elliptical shape of the distribution of 95% of bootstrapped ICERs for a treatment that is more effective and more costly than the comparator.

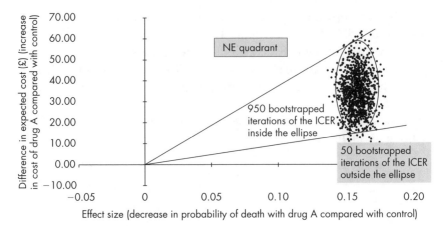

**Figure 10.7** Cost-effectiveness plane showing 1000 bootstrapped ICERs for an intervention that is more effective and more costly than the comparator, with quasi 95% confidence intervals for the ICER.

In reality we will have at least 1000 iterations of the bootstrapped ICER, producing a plot similar to the one in Figure 10.7. The ICER distribution shown in this graph suggests that it is highly likely that selecting the new treatment will be more effective and more costly.

Using this method, it is also possible to more easily interpret negative ICERs, which can result if either the cost or effect difference is negative. We may have a positive mean ICER, but once the bootstrapped distribution has been derived it may be clear that uncertainties in cost or effect mean that there are also uncertainties in the ICER.

### Uncertainties about difference in effect

We may have a situation where the mean effect size for an intervention is positive. However, if the 95% confidence interval around an effect size crosses zero, then we are not sure that the intervention is as effective as the mean effect size suggests. This uncertainty in effect size will lead to uncertainty in the ICER distribution. It may be that the mean ICER for the intervention suggests increased effect and increased costs. This is denoted by the dark square on the cost-effectiveness plane in Figure 10.8. However, once the bootstrapped distribution has been derived from the full range of effect and cost differences, it is clear that there are some instances where the ICER is negative (less effective and more costly). Figure 10.8 shows a typical bootstrap distribution for this type of ICER.

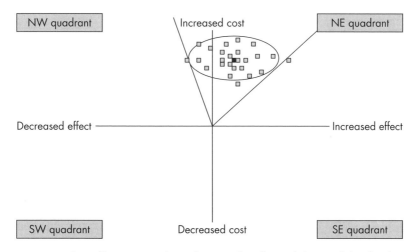

**Figure 10.8** Cost-effectiveness plane showing the elliptical shape of the distribution of 95% of bootstrapped ICERs for a treatment that is more costly than the comparator and where the difference in effectiveness is not significant at 5% level.

This is important because ICERs in the northwest quadrant suggest that we should not use that intervention because it is more costly and less effective (is dominated).

### Uncertainties about differences in cost

We may have a situation where the mean cost difference for an intervention is positive. However, if the 95% confidence interval around a cost difference crosses zero, then we are not sure that the intervention is more costly, as the mean effect size suggests. This uncertainty in cost difference will lead to uncertainty in the ICER distribution. It may be that the mean ICER for the intervention suggests increased effect and increased cost. This is denoted by the dark square on the cost-effectiveness plane in Figure 10.9. However, once the bootstrapped distribution has been derived from the full range of effect and cost differences, it is clear that there are some instances where the ICER is negative (more effective and less costly). Figure 10.9 shows a typical bootstrap distribution for this type of ICER.

This is important because ICERs in the southeast quadrant suggest that we should use that intervention because it is less costly and more effective (is dominant).

Graphical presentations of bootstrapped ICER distributions are very popular because they are straightforward to understand. Some published

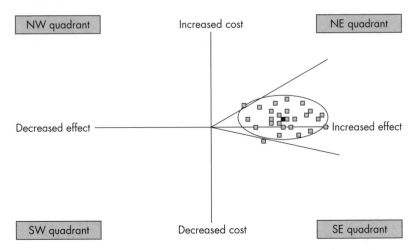

**Figure 10.9** Cost-effectiveness plane showing the elliptical shape of the distribution of 95% of bootstrapped ICERs for a treatment that is more costly than the comparator and where the difference in cost is not significant at 5% level.

examples are listed at the and of the chapter. Also, 2.5% and 97.5% percentiles can be extracted directly from the simulated data to give a quantitative measure of uncertainty for the ICER. This can only be done if there have been sufficient iterations.

### Estimating the probability of cost-effectiveness

We have seen that it is possible to represent the uncertainty concerning ICERs. Decision-makers often have problems with ICERs. We all agree that a lower ICER is more desirable than a high ICER because we are then paying less for a given improvement in effectiveness. However, we are not universally decided on what is the maximum size an ICER can be before we do not feel that we want to pay that amount for a given improvement in effectiveness. This means that there is no 'gold standard' cost per ICER above which we will not pay for a treatment. Therefore, if the ICER is below the decision-maker's own maximum willingness to pay for a given improvement in effectiveness, the treatment will be funded. However, if the ICER is above the decision-maker's own maximum willingness to pay for a given improvement in effectiveness, the treatment will not be funded. We call this maximum willingness to pay lambda ($\lambda$).

We can represent this graphically. In Figure 10.10 we have a cost-effectiveness plane showing a distribution of bootstrapped ICERs for a treatment that is more effective and more costly than the comparator.

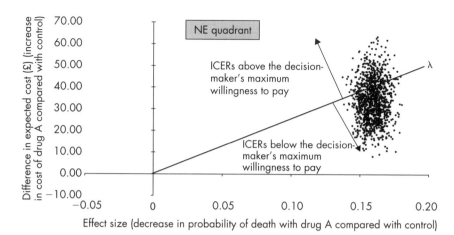

**Figure 10.10** Cost-effectiveness plane showing the distribution of bootstrapped ICERs for a treatment that is more effective and more costly than the comparator, and the decision-maker's maximum willingness to pay.

The ICER distribution shown in this graph suggests that it is highly likely that selecting the new treatment will be more effective and more costly.

The decision-maker's maximum willingness to pay for an extra unit of outcome is shown by the line from the origin, labelled λ. ICERs above or to the left of this line are above the decision-maker's maximum willingness to pay. If the true ICER is one of these points the treatment must be rejected, as the increased effect is not considered to be worth the increase in cost. ICERs below or to the right of this line are below the decision-maker's maximum willingness to pay. If the true ICER is one of these points, the treatment will be accepted.

In Figure 10.10, 65% of the ICERs are to the right of λ. This means that there is a 65% probability that the true cost-effectiveness of the intervention is below the decision-maker's maximum willingness to pay. On the basis of this information, the decision-maker may decide not to introduce the new treatment, as there is a 35% chance that the true ICER is above his/her maximum willingness to pay.

However, as was said earlier, we do not know the societal value for λ. The higher a decision-maker's maximum willingness to pay, the higher the probability that the treatment will be considered to be cost-effective. This is shown in Figure 10.11.

From this graph we can see that as λ increases, the more are ICERs below the decision-maker's maximum willingness to pay. This means that as λ increases, the higher becomes the probability that the treatment will be considered to be cost-effective. We can express this graphically,

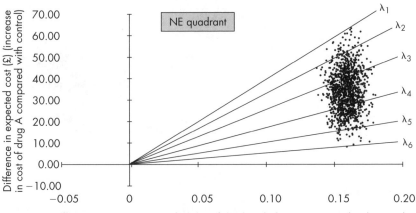

**Figure 10.11** Cost-effectiveness plane showing the distribution of bootstrapped ICERs for a treatment that is more effective and more costly than the comparator, and the decision-maker's maximum willingness to pay for a range of values of $\lambda$.

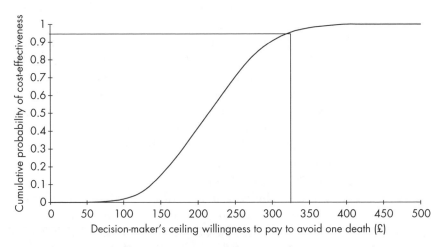

**Figure 10.12** Cost-effectiveness acceptability curve for a treatment that is more effective and more costly than the comparator.

using a cost-effectiveness acceptability curve (CEAcc) (Van Hout *et al.*, 1994; Fenwick *et al.*, 2001).

Figure 10.12 shows that if the decision-maker's maximum willingness to pay is £325 or more, there is a 95% probability that the intervention will be cost-effective.

One of the advantages of CEAccs is their ability to quantify the probability that an intervention is cost-effective in a simple manner that is understandable to decision-makers. It also takes away the traditional reliance on statistical rules about significance levels. Some published examples are given at the end of the chapter.

## More advanced topics

In this chapter we have looked at the statistical handling of costs and ICERs. Further subjects that are related to this area are *net benefit* and *expected value of information*. Reading on these more advanced subjects is provided in the Further reading list.

• • • • • • • • • • • • • • • • • • • • • • • • • • • • • • • • • • • • • • • • • • • • • • • • • • • •

**SELF-DIRECTED STUDY EXERCISES**

**EXERCISE 1**: Explaining bootstrapped ICERs

Read Grieve R, Thompson S, Normand C, *et al.* (2003). A cost effectiveness analysis of rhDNase in children with cystic fibrosis. *Int J Technol Assessment Healthcare* 19: 71–79. In this paper, the authors present the use of bootstrapped ICERs for choice of treatment in children with cystic fibrosis. Figures 1a to 1c present the results of the incremental economic analysis for three comparisons. For each analysis represented in these figures, answer the following questions:

1. **What is the mean ICER for the analysis, and what does this tell you about the two treatments under comparison? (Hint: is one dominant?)**
2. **What is the level of uncertainty around this ICER, and will it affect the decision about which treatment to choose? (Hint: is the uncertainty large or small, and does the distribution of ICERs cover more than one quadrant on the cost-effectiveness plane?)**
3. **What is the added value of expressing the uncertainty here using bootstrapping, and do you think this will affect the decision making process?**
4. **What are the limitations associated with the outcome measure used?**

This exercise can be repeated with other published studies that present bootstrapped ICER distributions. Suggested examples are Griffiths *et al.* (2001), Korthals-de Bos *et al.* (2003) and Goodacre *et al.* (2004) (see Further reading).

**EXERCISE 2**: Explaining cost-effectiveness acceptability curves

Read Delaney BC, Wilson S, Roalfe A, *et al.* (2000). Cost effectiveness of initial endoscopy for dyspepsia in patients over age 50 years: a randomised controlled trial in primary care. *Lancet* 356: 1965–1969. In this paper, the authors present the use of cost-effectiveness acceptability curves for choice of treatment in patients over 50 years of age with dyspepsia. Table 4 and Figure 3 present the results of the incremental economic analysis and cost-effectiveness acceptability analysis for initial endoscopy versus usual management. For the analysis represented in this figure answer the following questions:

1.   What is the mean ICER for the analysis, and what does this tell you about the two treatments under comparison? (Hint: is one dominant?)
2.   How robust is this ICER, and will this affect the decision about which treatment to choose? (Hint: look at the results in Table 4.)
3.   What do the cost-effectiveness acceptability curves in Figure 3 tell you about the two treatments under comparison? (Hint: what happens to the probability that one treatment is cost-effective as the ceiling willingness to pay is increased?)
4.   What does it mean when a cost-effectiveness acceptability curve crosses the y-axis?
5.   Can you explain the difference between the four cost-effectiveness acceptability curves in Figure 3?
6.   What is the added value of expressing the uncertainty here using cost-effectiveness acceptability analysis, and do you think this will affect the decision-making process?
7.   What are the limitations associated with the outcome measure used?

This exercise can be repeated with other published studies that present cost-effectiveness acceptability analysis. Suggested examples are Sculpher *et al.* (2004) (see below).

......................................................................

## References

Barber JA, Thompson SG (1998). Analysis and interpretation of cost data in randomised controlled trials: a review of published studies. *Br Med J* 317: 1195–1200.

Barber JA, Thompson SG (2000). Analysis of cost data in randomised controlled trials: an application of the non-parametric bootstrap. *Statistics Med* 19: 3219–3236.

Briggs A, Fenn P (1998). Confidence intervals or surfaces? Uncertainty on the cost effectiveness plane. *Health Econ* 7: 723–740.

Briggs A, Gray A (1998). The distribution of healthcare costs and their statistical analysis for economic evaluation. *J Health Serv Res Policy* 3: 233–245.

Briggs AH, Wonderling DE, Mooney CZ (1997). Pulling cost-effectiveness analysis up by its bootstraps: a non-parametric approach to confidence interval estimation. *Health Econ* 6: 327–340.

Elliott RA, Davies LM, Payne K, Moore JK, Harper NJN (2004). Costing day case anaesthesia: obtaining accurate patient-based costs for adults and children. *Int J Technol Assessment Healthcare* (in press).

Ellis SL, Carter BL, Malone DC, *et al.* (2000). Clinical and economic impact of ambulatory care clinical pharmacists in the management of dyslipidemia in older adults: the IMPROVE study. *Pharmacotherapy* 20: 1508–1516.

Fenwick E, Claxton K, Sculpher M (2001). Representing uncertainty: the role of cost effectiveness acceptability curves. *Health Econ* 10: 779–787.

Grieve R, Thompson S, Normand C, *et al.* (2003). A cost effectiveness analysis of rhDNase in children with cystic fibrosis. *Int J Technol Assessment Healthcare* 19: 71–79.

Hart A (2001). Mann–Whitney test is not just a test of medians: differences in spread can be important. *Br Med J* 323: 391–393.

Lambert CM, Hurst NP, Forbes JF, *et al.* (1998). Is day care equivalent to inpatient care for active rheumatoid arthritis? Randomised controlled clinical and economic evaluation. *Br Med J* 316: 965–969.

Polsky D, Glick HA, Willke R, Schulman K (1997). Confidence intervals for cost-effectiveness ratios: a comparison of four methods. *Health Econ* 6: 243–252.

Rutten-van Molken M, van Doorslaer EK, van Vliet RC (1994). Statistical analysis of cost outcomes in a randomized controlled trial. *Health Econ* 3: 333–345.

Thompson SG, Barber JA (2000). How should cost data in pragmatic randomised trials be analysed? *Br Med J* 320: 1197–1200.

UK Prospective Diabetes Study Group (1998). Cost effectiveness analysis of improved blood pressure control in hypertensive patients with type 2 diabetes. *Br Med J* 317: 720–726.

Van Hout BA, Al MJ, Gordon GS, Rutten FF (1994). Costs, effects and C/E ratios alongside a clinical trial. *Health Econ* 3: 309–319.

## Further reading

Claxton K (1999). The irrelevance of inference: a decision-making approach to the stochastic evaluation of healthcare technologies. *J Health Econ* 18: 341–364.

Claxton K (1999). Bayesian approaches to the value of information: implications for the regulations of new pharmaceuticals. *Health Econ* 8: 269–274.

Claxton K, Neuman PJ, Araki SS, Weinstein MC (2001). The value of information: an application to a policy model of Alzheimer's disease. *Int J Health Technol Assessment Healthcare* 17: 38–55.

Grieve A (1998). Issues for statisticians in pharmaco-economic evaluations. *Statistics Med* 17: 1715–1723.

O'Brien BJ, Drummond MF, Labelle RJ, Willan A (1994). In search of power and significance: issues in the design and analysis of stochastic cost-effectiveness studies in healthcare. *Med Care* 32: 150–163.

## Examples of economic evaluations that present graphical bootstrapped ICERs

Elliott RA, Payne K, Moore JK, *et al.* (2003). Clinical and economic choices in anaesthesia for day surgery: a prospective randomized controlled trial. *Anaesthesia* 58: 412–416.

Goodacre S, Nicholl J, Dixon S, *et al*. (2004). Randomised controlled trial and economic evaluation of a chest pain observation unit compared with routine care. *Br Med J* 328: 1–6.

Grieve R, Thompson S, Normand C, *et al*. (2003). A cost effectiveness analysis of rhDNase in children with cystic fibrosis. *Int J Technol Assessment Healthcare* 19: 71–79.

Griffiths TL, Phillips CJ, Davies S, *et al*. (2001). Cost effectiveness of an outpatient multidisciplinary pulmonary rehabilitation programme. *Thorax* 56: 779–784.

Korthals-de Bos IB, Hoving JL, van Tulder MW, *et al*. (2003). Cost effectiveness of physiotherapy, manual therapy and general practitioner care for neck pain: economic evaluation alongside a randomised controlled trial. *Br Med J* 326: 911–916.

## Examples of economic evaluations that present cost-effectiveness acceptability curves

Delaney BC, Wilson S, Roalfe A, *et al*. (2000). Cost effectiveness of initial endoscopy for dyspepsia in patients over age 50 years: a randomised controlled trial in primary care. *Lancet* 356: 1965–1969.

Multi-centre Aneurysm Screening Study Group (2002). Multi-centre aneurysm screening study (MASS): cost effectiveness analysis of screening for abdominal aortic aneurysms based on four year results from randomised controlled trial. *Br Med J* 325: 1135–1138.

Sculpher M, Manca S, Abbott J, *et al*. (2004). Cost effectiveness analysis of laparoscopic hysterectomy compared with standard hysterectomy: results from a randomised trial. *Br Med J* 328: 134–137.

# 11

## Valuing preferences

### Introduction

The previous chapters in this book have mainly addressed the methods of economic evaluation, which provide a framework for valuing the efficiency of an intervention. Information about people's preferences for an intervention may also be used to inform decision-making. This chapter describes an approach to value preferences.

Preference is a global term. In the valuation of healthcare interventions it is used to refer to different types of preference, utilities and values, which differ in how they are measured (Bryan *et al.*, 2002). A full description of the difference between utilities and values is beyond the scope of this book. Drummond *et al.* (1997) provide a useful discussion about the key differences in terms of how utilities and values are measured. This chapter focuses on one approach that is increasingly being used to value preferences for healthcare interventions, the *stated preference discrete choice* method. In the past this approach was commonly called conjoint analysis, but is now more accurately called a *discrete choice experiment* (DCE). Before beginning this chapter, you will need to understand the concept of utility covered in Chapter 4.

### Stated preference or revealed preference?

Collecting information on *revealed preferences* may be considered the gold standard for valuing preferences for healthcare interventions. This involves measuring the actual number of units of a healthcare intervention or service used (a measure of what people actually do). The intervention may be a technology, such as a drug for the treatment of psychosis, or a service, such as a cholesterol screening service. The revealed preference approach is not generally a practical option for measuring preferences for healthcare and pharmacy services. It will often not be feasible to obtain the information on the actual number of consumers. Decision-makers often want information about the potential value of a new service, which may have unique characteristics of which consumers have no prior knowledge.

Opinion polls and satisfaction surveys provide information about what is important to consumers and their level of satisfaction with the current good or service as provided. Satisfaction surveys have been used to determine career and job satisfaction in pharmacists, doctors and nurses. The disadvantage with these approaches is that they only provide limited information. They can only indicate whether or not someone is satisfied with a current service: they cannot be used to identify the factors – and their relative degrees of importance – that are driving the observed level of satisfaction.

Researchers have developed a practical set of methods known as *stated preference* methods, designed to measure what people say they will do in terms of using a healthcare service. A common theme in these methods is that they ask respondents to make choices based on a hypothetical scenario that is a description of an imaginary intervention or service, based on published evidence for similar interventions. There are a number of stated preference methods based on economic theory. *Discrete choice experiments* are one of these.

See Worked example 11.1.

**WORKED EXAMPLE 11.1**  Difference between revealed preference and stated preference

Last year, a community pharmacist set up a cholesterol screening service. The practice nurse, based in the GP's surgery, also offered a cholesterol screening service.

The pharmacist wanted to find out what local people thought about his service and so decided to measure the number of people who used the cholesterol screening service in the last month. He also persuaded the practice nurse to measure the number of people who used the practice screening service.

These are the results:

|  | Pharmacy service | General practice service |
|---|---|---|
| Number of people who used the service | 30 | 60 |
| Total number of people in the area | 50 000 | 50 000 |

*Continued*

The pharmacist concluded that people preferred to use the service offered by the practice nurse. They had revealed a preference for the other service. He wanted to find out what characteristics of the service he provided he could, or should, change to encourage people to use his service. Instead of setting up a new service immediately, the pharmacist decided he would enlist the help of a researcher to find out what people said they would prefer.

The following sections describe how a *discrete choice experiment* could be designed to try and answer this question.

## Discrete choice experiments

Discrete choice experiments (DCEs) are a relatively new method used in the valuation of healthcare interventions. They were originally used widely by market researchers. Ryan and Gerard (2003) and Ryan *et al.* (2001) have published useful reviews of the approach and its application to healthcare, and the interested reader should refer to these for detailed information.

The DCE method is firmly rooted in economic theory, specifically random utility theory, which closely reflects how we make decisions about which products to choose and use every day (see Gold (1996) for a more detailed description of random utility theory). The theory assumes that the total value (utility) a consumer attaches to an intervention or service is described by the sum of individual attributes (factors or characteristics) of that intervention or service. These attributes can relate to the clinical outcome of the service (e.g. number of people with raised cholesterol detected) or the process of providing the service (e.g. who provides it). The ability to incorporate both outcome and process attributes is one of the key advantages of this method. The attributes are then described by levels, which indicate the different values the attribute can take. DCEs estimate the individual effect these attributes have on consumers' preferences for a service. The theoretical basis of DCE assumes that consumers make trade-offs between the attributes.

Conjoint analysis is the wider term for a DCE. Conjoint analysis involves a survey that presents a series of hypothetical scenarios, and respondents are asked to rank them in order of preference or to rate each with a score. DCEs are a particular type of conjoint analysis. Respondents are asked to make a clear choice between two (or more) scenarios. In theory, the consumer has a stronger preference for, and will choose,

**Table 11.1** Possible attributes and levels

| Attribute | Levels |
| --- | --- |
| **Process attributes** | |
| Who conducts the medication review | Pharmacist |
| | General practitioner |
| Frequency of medication review | Monthly |
| | 3-monthly |
| | 6-monthly |
| | 12-monthly |
| Cost to you in terms of travel | £0 |
| | £5 |
| | £10 |
| | £20 |
| **Health outcome** | |
| Chance of improving your health by | 5% |
| reducing risk of an adverse event | 10% |
| | 25% |
| | 35% |
| **Non-health outcomes** | |
| Follow-up support | No |
| | Yes |

the scenario describing a service that reflects a higher value to them. DCEs may therefore be referred to as a *choice-based stated preference* method.

Table 11.1 shows an example of the attributes and levels that could be used to describe a medication review for the elderly service. This example has five attributes.

## Whose preferences count?

Before describing the DCE method in detail it is useful to have a brief discussion about the nature of preferences that should, or could, be valued. DCE uses a collective approach to elicit individuals' preferences, which are measured from their responses to the DCE. The preferences for this defined population are then estimated. The individuals may be members of the public, patients, pharmacists, doctors, or other health-care professionals. It is important to establish the views of current and future users of a service. Future users may be members of the public with no prior experience of using the service under evaluation. It may also be interesting to compare the preferences of service users (patients) with the preferences of those who provide the service (e.g. pharmacists).

## How do you do a discrete choice experiment?

The first step in a DCE is to decide which attributes and levels adequately describe the service to be evaluated. Systematically organised searches of the published literature are often supplemented by qualitative techniques, such as face-to-face interviews (semistructured or in depth) or focus groups, to define the individual attributes and levels that are important with respect to the service in question. A detailed discussion of these approaches is beyond the scope of this book. The interested reader should look at *CRD Report 4* (NHS Centre for Reviews and Dissemination, 2001) for information on conducting systematic literature reviews. A useful text about qualitative approaches is Arksey and Knight (1999). Britten (1995) and Kitzinger (1995) also provide useful insights into carrying out interviews and focus groups, respectively.

There is no formal guidance about the maximum number of attributes allowed in a DCE. However, respondents will find the task of completing the DCE more difficult with larger numbers of attributes. The more attributes, the more cognitively demanding the choices become. A general rule is to limit the number of attributes to a maximum of seven. The attributes and levels can be qualitative (such as who conducts the medication review) or quantitative (such as frequency of the medication review). Ideally, the DCE should be designed with a minimum number of qualitative compared to quantitative attributes. It may be useful to include a variable that represents the potential cost to the patient (for example travel). This provides a method of indirectly estimating the amount of money they are willing to trade off against changes in the other attributes. This valuation of 'willingness to pay' provides an indirect method of estimating the monetary value that consumers or patients attach to certain attributes in the service.

### Identify hypothetical scenarios and pairwise choices

The next step is to develop the choice question for each respondent to answer. The question must be phrased in a way that clearly expresses the choice each respondent is being asked to make regarding the service. The respondent must be informed exactly what they are expected to do (see Worked example 11.2).

**WORKED EXAMPLE 11.2** A choice question

Consider the example of the medication review service for the elderly.

1.  **How would you introduce the purpose of this questionnaire to the respondent?**
    The respondent must first be clear that that the DCE is trying to find out about people's views and preferences. It is not a survey that has correct answers. It is useful to include a section in the survey that explains this, for example:

    'I am interested in your views about a medication review service for older people. In particular, I would like to know about the good and bad aspects of the service that you think are important. The purpose of this questionnaire is to find out about your experiences and opinions about this service. Please try and answer each of the following questions. I want you to tell me what you think. There are no right or wrong answers. I am interested in your views.'

2.  **How would you phrase the question for respondents in each choice? The DCE is asking people to make a choice between two services based on defined attributes and levels. You want the respondent to consider only the attributes and levels described for them. There are two possible ways of phrasing the question.**

    • Please read the characteristics of each service. Which service, A or B, would you choose? Please tick the relevant box.

    • Please read the characteristics of each service. Which would you choose? You may choose service A, service B, or neither. Please tick the relevant box.

    The first approach does not allow the respondent to 'opt out' of making a decision. They are expected to select A or B.

    This approach assumes that they will use the service in question. It may be more reasonable to assume that the respondent decides they do not want to use either of the hypothetical services on offer. To accommodate this possibility you must phrase the question to include a 'neither' option.

## Designing the DCE

The design of a DCE is vital to the quality of the information obtained about people's preferences: a poorly designed experiment will be of limited or no value. Design is a skilled task and a number of researchers are working continuously to perfect the design of DCEs. Each DCE contains a number of separate choices. A general rule is that respondents can generally manage between 9 and 16 pairwise choices before they get tired or bored with the experiment (Hanley *et al.*, 2002).

The number of attributes and levels partly informs how many choices will be in the DCE. This is a key part of the design. The gold standard DCE design involves including the total number of possible scenarios to incorporate the total number of combinations of attributes and levels. This is called a 'full factorial design' (see Worked example 11.3).

---

**WORKED EXAMPLE 11.3** Calculating the total number of possible scenarios

Consider the example of the medication review service for the elderly (see Table 11.1).

1. **How many attributes are there in this design?**
   There are five.

2. **How many levels are associated with each attribute?**
   Two attributes have two levels. Three attributes have four levels.

3. **What is the total number of combinations of attributes and levels?**
   The total number of combinations is calculated by (number of levels)$^{\text{number of attributes with this level}}$.

The example of the DCE of a medication review service would generate $2^2 \times 4^3 = 256$ possible scenarios.

---

Using our rule of thumb, a maximum of 16 scenarios, this results in an unmanageable number of choices for each respondent to consider. To design a practical DCE it is necessary to reduce the number of scenarios in the final design. DCE designers use an approach called the fractional factorial design, which uses the principle of maintaining orthogonality. The orthogonal design means that each attribute can be assumed to have an independent effect on the overall utility of the service. This is important because it means that the individual effect of each attribute on respondents' preferences can be completely isolated. Software packages (SPEED or SPSS

Orthoplan) or design catalogues have been used by DCE designers to reduce the total number of scenarios to a number that respondents can feasibly cope with answering while maintaining an orthogonal design. These techniques generate a list of scenarios each describing the level to assign to each of the included attributes.

It is then necessary to create choices from these scenarios. A number of different approaches to this may be used, such as the constant comparison, or 'random' pairing of the 16 scenarios. In the constant comparison approach one scenario (often designed to describe an existing service) is paired against each of the 16 scenarios. Alternatively, the scenarios can be randomly paired such that 16 scenarios provide eight choices. The approach used affects the efficiency of the final design. A detailed description of the approaches available is beyond the scope of this book. Phillips *et al.* (2002) describe four criteria that have been used to maximise the efficiency of design and illustrate the use of these criteria with a DCE valuing preferences for a HIV service. The advanced reader would benefit from reading Louviere *et al.* (2000).

Table 11.2 shows an example of one choice question. This is a binary (two options) choice. It is also possible to design discrete choices with more than two options.

One criticism of DCEs is that respondents find making choices too demanding and may not understand the nature of the task. It is generally a good idea to include questions to assess internal validity. There are two possible approaches: include a choice in which one service would obviously be preferred over another, given the observed levels (a dominant choice); include the same choice on two occasions in the same DCE (a repeat choice). These two checks, for dominance and consistency, may then be used as a test for internal validity as a measure of whether the respondent understands the nature of the experiment being conducted.

**Table 11.2** Example of a pairwise choice

| Choice 1 | Service A | Service B |
| --- | --- | --- |
| Who conducts the medication review | GP | Pharmacist |
| Frequency of medication review | 6-monthly | 6-monthly |
| Cost to you in terms of travel | £10 | £5 |
| Chance of improving your health by reducing risk of an adverse event | 5% | 25% |
| Follow-up support | No | Yes |
| Which service would you prefer? Please tick one box only | ☐ | ☐ |

## Administer the DCE

The approaches used to administer the DCE are similar to that used by standard surveys. DCEs may be administered by post for self-completion or as part of a face-to-face interview. Similarly, the pitfalls in administering standard surveys also apply to DCEs. The key problem is achieving a reasonable response rate (Ryan and Gerard, 2003). This problem may be amplified with DCEs because they are cognitively demanding of the respondent, which may effectively reduce the observed response rate. To try to overcome this problem some DCEs have been administered using face-to-face interviews (Bryan *et al.*, 2002), which also provides an opportunity to explore qualitatively some of the reasons behind the respondents' stated preferences. It is also important to think about the target population and the correct sampling frame for the DCE. Related to this is the issue of the ideal sample size. It is not easy to run sample size calculations for DCEs. The sample size is normally guided by a balance between the number of possible respondents, the cost of conducting the DCE, and obtaining enough responses to analyse. Louviere *et al.* describe a possible approach to estimate sample size.

## Analyse the results

Before analysing DCE data the results from the questionnaire must be coded and entered into a suitable statistical software package. Practically, the questionnaire will be coded at the design stage. Phillips *et al.* (2002) provide a useful explanation of how to code and enter DCE data.

In most surveys, each respondent produces one response. DCEs are unusual in that each respondent produces more than one set of responses. This affects the way the data are analysed. DCE data are analysed using regression techniques. The analysis of a DCE is based on a number of assumptions, a full description of which is beyond the scope of this book. The two key assumptions are that each attribute has an independent effect on preferences, and that a linear additive model will describe the overall strength of preference for a service (utility). A basic linear additive model may be described using the example of a medication review service with five attributes. The probability of each respondent in the sample choosing A or B for each choice is dependent on these five attributes.

$$\text{Choose A or B} = \beta_1 \text{ who} + \beta_2 \text{ frequency} + \beta_3 \text{ cost} + \beta_4 \text{ chance} + \beta_5 \text{ support} + e + u$$

where $\Delta_1 \dots \Delta_5$ are the $\beta$ coefficients that describe the effect of each attribute.

The five attributes (who; frequency; cost; chance; support) are represented as the five main parameters in the equation. $\beta_1 \ldots \beta_5$ are the coefficients that describe the effect of each attribute. $e$ is the error term due to differences among observations. $u$ is the error term due to differences among respondents. The analysis method of choice for this model is the random effects probit procedure. This is because the dependent variable (choose A or B) in this model is binary. The random effects estimation is used because each respondent provides more than one observation when they answer each of the choices in the experiment.

## Interpretation of the results

The outputs of a DCE analysis describe the significance of each attribute and the relative importance of each attribute. The significance of each attribute is measured using the $p$ value attached to the estimated coefficient and indicates whether each attribute contributes to the overall model (see Worked example 11.4).

---

**WORKED EXAMPLE 11.4** Interpretation of the results

Imagine we have collected and analysed data from the DCE for the medication review for the elderly. Please remember that these are not actual data and are used for illustration purposes only.

The data look like this:

| Variable | Levels (code) | | $\beta$ | p value |
|---|---|---|---|---|
| Who | General practitioner (0) Pharmacist (1) | | 0.039 | 0.001 |
| Frequency | Monthly (12) 12-monthly (1) | 3-monthly (4) 6-monthly (2) | 0.010 | 0.000 |
| Cost | £0 (0) £10 (10) | £5 (5) £20 (20) | −0.003 | 0.002 |
| Chance | 5% (5) 25% (25) | 10% (10) 35% (35) | 0.049 | 0.000 |
| Support | No (0) Yes (1) | | 0.580 | 0.300 |

*Continued*

1.  **How many of the attributes affect preferences for this service?**
    Four of the attributes have β coefficients with $p < 0.005$. The support variable, which is a measure of whether follow-up support is provided, is not significant. This means it does not have a significant effect on preferences for this service.

2.  **What is the direction of the influence of each attribute?**
    The sign of β indicates the direction of the influence of each attribute. This is easy to interpret for quantitative variables (cost). A negative sign means that as cost increases people are less likely to choose the service. Cost has a negative impact on preferences. A positive sign on chance of improving health outcome indicates that people value improving health outcome from a medication review. These results are intuitively logical. More care is needed to interpret the sign of qualitative variables, which are coded using dummy variables. It is important to note the level coded as zero. The positive sign on the 'who' variable indicates that this population would prefer a pharmacist to conduct the review.

3.  **What is the relative order of importance of the remaining significant attributes?**
    This is indicated by the absolute size of the coefficient for each variable. Only significant variables should be included. The order of importance of these attributes is:

    * Chance
    * Frequency
    * Who
    * Cost.

4.  **How much is the population willing to pay for a pharmacist to provide a medication review service rather than a doctor?**
    DCEs allow estimation of the marginal rate of substitution (MRS) for each attribute. This is a measure of the amount of one attribute an individual is prepared to trade off against another. If we use the estimate of the β coefficient from the cost attribute we can estimate (indirectly) the willingness to pay (WTP) for a one-unit increase in each of the other attributes.

    WTP for a pharmacist providing a medication review
    $= 0.039/0.003 = £13$.

....................................................................

### SELF-DIRECTED STUDY EXERCISE

Obtain a copy of the paper Ubach C, Bate A, Ryan M, *et al.* (2002). Using discrete choice experiments to evaluate alternative electronic prescribing systems. *Int J Pharmacy Pract* 10: 191–200. You are going to use the results of this paper to inform the future development of an electronic prescribing system.

1.   **Whose preferences were elicited in this study?**

     This study explored the preferences of two groups, pharmacists and general practitioners.

2.   **How were the attributes and levels for this DCE identified?**

     The authors reported that they used a variety of methods to identify the attributes. This included a survey of attitudes to electronic prescribing, interviews and focus groups.

**Table 11.3** Attributes and levels included in DCE. Adapted from Urbach *et al.* (2002)

| Variable (name) | Levels | Coding for data entry |
|---|---|---|
| Typical response time | 1 second | 1 |
| (resp) | 5 seconds | 5 |
| | 10 seconds | 10 |
| Frequency of slow responses | Once a month | 12 |
| ($f_{slow}$) | Once every 6 months | 2 |
| | Once a year | 1 |
| Frequency of unscheduled downtime | Once a month | 24 |
| ($f_{unsch}$) | Once a year | 2 |
| | Once every two years | 1 |
| Length of unscheduled downtime | One hour | 1 |
| ($l_{unsch}$) | Five hours | 5 |
| | 12 hours | 12 |
| Frequency of scheduled downtime | Once a week | 52 |
| ($f_{sche}$) | Once a month | 12 |
| | Once a year | 1 |
| Frequency of lost/corrupt data | 1 in 1000 prescriptions | 100 |
| ($f_{lost}$) | 1 in 10 000 prescriptions | 10 |
| | 1 in 100 000 prescriptions | 1 |

**3.    What are the attributes and levels included in this DCE?**

Six important attributes were identified. These are described in Table 11.3.

**4.    What is the maximum possible number of scenarios that could be generated from this combination of attributes and levels?**

The DCE has six attributes. Each attribute has three levels. This means that $3^6 = 729$ possible electronic prescribing systems can be described.

**5.    How many scenarios were presented to the respondents?**

SPEED was used to identify a fractional factorial design from the full factorial design. This identified 27 scenarios to include in the final DCE. A total of 14 choices was presented to respondents. One scenario was repeated to make the 14 choices.

**6.    Which attributes should you consider in the design of an electronic prescribing system?**

Table 5 in the paper reports the results of the final progression model.

All attributes were highly significant when the preferences for pharmacists and GPs were analysed as a group ($p < 0.001$). This may be interpreted to mean that all these factors are important in the provision of an electronic prescribing system. The signs on the coefficients were all negative. The negative sign accords with what would be expected for these attributes. In general, you would expect people to prefer a faster response time and a low frequency of slow responses from the system.

Analysing the model in two groups revealed that pharmacists and GPs had slightly different preferences. The frequency of slow responses was not an important attribute for GPs.

- Length of unscheduled downtime is the most important factor for pharmacists.
- Typical response time is the most important factor for GPs.
- Frequency of lost/corrupt data is the least important factor for pharmacists and GPs.

This implies that pharmacists involved with preparing prescriptions would want a system that minimised the duration of crashes when the system cannot be used. GPs want a system that quickly downloads the details about a prescription on to the computer.

7. **How much are pharmacists and GPs willing to trade between the duration of unscheduled downtime to reduce the typical response time of the system?**

This can be answered by calculating the marginal rate of substitution (MRS) between duration of unscheduled downtime and the typical response time of the system.

For pharmacists:

- $-0.042$ is the estimated coefficient on typical response time.
- $-0.059$ is the estimated coefficient on length of unscheduled downtime.

The MRS is calculated as $-0.042/-0.059 = 0.7$. This means that pharmacists are willing to increase the length of unscheduled downtime by 0.7 hours (42 minutes) to reduce the typical response time by 1 second.

For GPs:

- $-0.042$ is the estimated coefficient on typical response time.
- $-0.033$ is the estimated coefficient on length of unscheduled downtime.

The MRS is calculated as $-0.042/-0.033 = 1.3$. This means that GPs are willing to increase the length of unscheduled downtime by 1.3 hours (78 minutes) to reduce the typical response time by 1 second.

. . . . . . . . . . . . . . . . . . . . . . . . . . . . . . . . . . . . . . . . . . . . . . . . . . . . . . . . . . . . . . . . . . . . . . .

## References

Arksey H, Knight P (1999). *Interviewing for Social Scientists.* London: Sage.

Britten N (1995). Qualitative interviews in medical research. *Br Med J* 311: 251–253.

Bryan S, Roberts T, Heginbotham C, McCallum A (2002). QALY-maximisation and public preferences: results from a general population survey. *Health Econ* 11: 679–693.

Drummond MF, O'Brien B, Stoddart GL, Torrance GW (1997). *Methods for the Economic Evaluation of Health Care Programmes,* 2nd edn. Oxford: Oxford University Press.

Gold ME, Siegel JE, Russell LB, Weinstein MC (1996). *Cost-Effectiveness in Health and Medicine.* Oxford: Oxford University Press.

Hanley N, Wright R, Koop G (2002). Modelling recreation demand using choice experiments: rock climbing in Scotland. *Environ Res Econ* 22: 449–466.

Kitzinger J (1995). Qualitative research. Introducing focus groups. *Br Med J* 311: 299–302.

NHS Centre for Reviews and Dissemination (2001). *Undertaking Systematic Reviews of Research on Effectiveness.* CRD Report 4, 2nd edn. York: University of York.

Ryan M, Bate A, Eastmond CJ, Ludbrook A (2001). Use of discrete choice experiments to elicit preferences. *Quality Healthcare* 10 (Suppl. 1): i55–60.

Ryan M, Gerard K (2003). Using discrete choice experiments to value healthcare programmes: current practice and future research reflections. *Appl Health Econ Health Policy* 2: 55–64.

Ryan M, Scott DA, Reeves C, *et al.* (2001). Eliciting public preferences for healthcare: a systematic review of techniques. *Health Technol Assessment* 5(5): 1–186.

Ubach C, Bate A, Ryan M, *et al.* (2002). Using discrete choice experiments to evaluate alternative electronic prescribing systems. *Int J Pharmacy Pract* 10: 191–200.

## Further reading

Arksey H, Knight P (1999). *Interviewing for Social Scientists*. London: Sage.

Britten N (1995). Qualitative interviews in medical research. *Br Med J* 311: 251–253.

Kitzinger J (1995). Qualitative research. Introducing focus groups. *Br Med J* 311: 299–302.

Louviere JJ, Hensher DA, Swait JD (2000). *Stated Choice Methods*. Cambridge: Cambridge University Press.

NHS Centre for Reviews and Dissemination (2001). *Undertaking Systematic Reviews of Research on Effectiveness*. CRD Report 4, 2nd edn. York: University of York.

Phillips KA, Maddala T, Johnson FR (2002). Measuring preferences for healthcare interventions using conjoint analysis: an application to HIV testing. *Health Serv Res* 37: 1681–1705.

Ryan M, Bate A, Eastmond CJ, Ludbrook A (2001). Use of discrete choice experiments to elicit preferences. *Quality Healthcare* 10 (Suppl. 1): i55–60.

Ryan M, Gerard K (2003). Using discrete choice experiments to value healthcare programmes: current practice and future research reflections. *Appl Health Econ Health Policy* 2: 55–64.

# 12

## Useful resources in health economics and economic evaluation

### Further key texts in health economics

This book is designed to be an introduction to economic techniques in evaluating healthcare for readers with no background in economics or health economics. In each chapter we have provided extensive lists of further reading and key texts in all areas. The following are recognised as central reference sources in health economics and economic evaluation. They provide authoritative and detailed discussions of economic theory applied to healthcare, international comparisons of healthcare systems, and more detailed descriptions of economic evaluation methodology. Readers wishing to expand their knowledge and skills in health economics beyond this introductory book are recommended to read these texts.

Drummond MF, O'Brien B, Stoddart GL, Torrance GW (1997). *Methods for the Economic Evaluation of Healthcare Programmes*, 2nd edn. Oxford: Oxford University Press.

Folland S, Goodman AC, Stano M (1997). *The Economics of Health and Healthcare*. New Jersey: Prentice Hall.

Gold MR, Siegel JE, Russell LB, Weinstein MC, eds. (1996). *Cost-Effectiveness in Health and Medicine*. New York: Oxford University Press.

Jefferson T, Demicheli V, Mugford M (1996). *Elementary Economic Evaluation in Healthcare*. London: BMJ Books.

McGuire A, Henderson J, Mooney G (1992). *The Economics of Healthcare*, 2nd edn. London: Routledge.

## Special interest groups and useful contacts for health economists

This list can be used as a starting point for contacting health economists and useful organisations.

Canadian Coordinating Office for Health Technology Assessment (CCOHTA).
http://www.ccohta.ca/entry_e.html

Database of Abstracts of Reviews of Effects (DARE)
http://www.york.ac.uk/inst/crd/darehp.htm

Health Economic Evaluation Database
http://www.ohe-heed.com/

Health Economists' Study Group (HESG)
http://www.city.ac.uk/economics/research/HESG.htm

Health Equity Network
http://www.ukhen.org/

Health Technology Assessment (HTA) Database
http://www.york.ac.uk/inst/crd/htahp.htm

Health Technology Assessment International
http://www.htai.org/

Health Technology Assessment (HTA) Programme
http://www.hta.nhsweb.nhs.uk/

International Health Economics Association (iHEA)
http://www.healtheconomics.org/

International Society for Pharmacoeconomic and Outcomes Research (ISPOR)
http://www.ispor.org/

NHS Economic Evaluation Database (NHS EED)
http://www.york.ac.uk/inst/crd/nhsdhp.htm

National Institute for Clinical Excellence (NICE)
http://www.nice.org.uk/

Office of Health Economics
http://www.ohe.org

Preference Elicitation Group (contact: a.j.oliver@lse.ac.uk).
http://www.lse.ac.uk/collections/LSEHealthAndSocialCare/eventsAnd
Seminars/Networkpage.htm

Society for Medical Decision Making
http://www.smdm.org/

# Glossary

**Agency relationship:** When someone is acting on behalf of another person, they are the agent involved in demanding goods or services for the other person

**Agent:** A person who is involved in the production or consumption of goods or services

**Allocative efficiency:** A measure of whether an intervention is worthwhile compared to other available interventions in society in terms of the costs and benefits

**Asymmetry of information:** An imbalance of knowledge, which generally occurs when the person supplying the good or service has more extensive knowledge about its potential benefits than the person demanding the good or service. The reverse may also be true

**Average cost:** Total costs divided by units of production (such as patients or hospital-bed days)

**Conjoint analysis:** A stated preference measure that uses a survey to elicit people's preferences for a hypothetical good or service based on a set of scenarios described in terms of attributes or levels. Respondents are asked to rate or rank between the series of hypothetical services described

**Consumers:** People who use (demand) goods or services

**Contingent valuation (see willingness to pay):** The use of a survey to find the monetary value (willingness to pay) people attach to a good or service that has been described using a hypothetical (imaginary) scenario

**Cost-effectiveness analysis:** A type of economic evaluation that measures the difference in costs and benefits of at least two interventions with measures of effectiveness that use single natural units to value health gain

**Cost-minimisation analysis:** A type of economic evaluation that measures the difference in costs of at least two interventions and assumes that the difference in effectiveness is the same

**Deterministic data:** Data from existing sources, represented by a point estimate. The data are not random

**Direct cost:** Cost borne by the healthcare system (medical direct costs), community and families (non-medical direct costs) in addressing the illness

**Discounting:** A calculation that estimates the present value of future costs and benefits

**Discrete choice experiment:** A stated preference measure that uses a survey to elicit people's preferences for a hypothetical good or service based on a set of scenarios presented as a series of direct choices between at least two services (or goods) described in terms of attributes and levels

**Dominance:** The state when an intervention is preferred because it is cheaper and more effective than the next relevant alternative

**Downstream medical costs:** Costs associated with providing a healthcare intervention that occurs in the future further down the clinical treatment pathway

**Economic evaluation:** The comparative analysis of the costs (resources) and benefits (health gain) of alternative interventions

**Effectiveness:** A measure of the influence (effect) of a healthcare intervention on patients' health. Ideally this should relate to when the intervention is used in practice (as opposed to a clinical trial setting)

**Efficiency:** Achieving the maximum benefit from a good or service for a given cost (available resources)

**Equity:** A concept related to fairness which addresses interpersonal comparisons between interventions

**Equity weights:** A method of incorporating a measure of people's preferences for equality (fairness) in economic evaluations

**External validity:** The generalisability of the results of a study to other settings or patient populations

**Externalities:** The situation when the (external) actions of a person (or firm) can affect the wellbeing of another person (or firm) in a good (or bad) way

**Fixed cost:** A cost that remains the same for a given period of time no matter how many units of a good or service are produced

**Healthy year equivalents:** A measure of the number of years in perfect health that has the same utility to the length of life in a health state (representing less than perfect health)

**Imperfect information:** When information on some aspect of the price or quality of a good or service is missing

**Incremental cost-effectiveness (utility) ratio:** The main summary measure used in economic evaluations, which is calculated by dividing the difference in costs between two services by the difference in effectiveness (utility) that represents the change in health gain

**Indirect cost:** Considered to be productivity losses caused by the problem or illness, borne by society as a whole

**Intangible cost:** Considered to be the costs of pain, grief and suffering and the loss of leisure time. The cost of a life is usually included in case of death

**Intermediate outcome:** A measure of benefit (effectiveness) that does not directly affect people's health status

**Internal validity:** The robustness of a study in terms of its design and freedom from bias

**Macroeconomics:** Using economic theories to study entire economies

**Marginal cost:** Costs associated with producing an extra unit of service, which in the short term are usually made up of variable costs

**Microeconomics:** Using economic theories to study the behaviour of individual consumers or firms

**Moral hazard:** When insurance cover for a good or service makes you less careful about how you use that good or service

**Opportunity cost:** The cost associated with a forgone benefit or lost opportunity

**Orthogonal:** A term used in the design of a discrete choice experiment that means the attributes contained in the experiment can be assumed to have an independent effect on the overall preference for the good or service being valued

**Perspective:** The viewpoint taken for an evaluation or study

**Positive time preference:** A state where people tend to prefer to receive benefits now rather than in the future

**Primary care:** Patients' first point of contact with the healthcare system, which may include services offered by general practitioners

**Producers:** People who make or manufacture (produce) goods or services

**Quality adjusted life year:** A measure of outcome that gives the weighted value of a year of life in terms of the quality of health or social wellbeing. It is the product of quality of life (measured in utility) times the remaining length of life following treatment (measured in years)

**Quality of life:** A measure of the overall level of satisfaction with life that may be affected by health (physical and mental) and social wellbeing

**Randomised controlled trial:** A type of study that randomly allocates people enrolled into the study to one of at least two interventions and measures the outcomes (good and bad) of using these interventions in a controlled setting

**Reference case:** A type of guideline for economic evaluations that describes the 'gold' standard for the individual components of the evaluation

**Resource:** The inputs used in the production of goods or services

**Revealed preference:** A measure of what goods or services people use based on actual data

**Secondary care:** Care offered by general hospitals

**Semifixed cost:** A cost that remains the same for a given unit of good or service produce but which then jumps to a higher fixed cost at a certain change in the amount of good or service produced

**Sensitivity analysis:** A series of methods that examine the robustness of the results of an evaluation by changing the value of individual or multiple variables used in the base-case analysis

**Shadow price:** Actual market prices for healthcare do not reflect social benefits and social costs. Shadow prices indicate the intrinsic or true value of a factor or product. They may deviate from market prices

**Societal cost:** The cost represented by a societal viewpoint that takes into account all potential costs

**Stated preference:** A measure of what goods or services people say (state) they prefer based on a hypothetical (imaginary) description of those services (goods)

**Stochastic data:** Data that have been collected and may be interpreted using standard statistical methods of comparison. There is some element of randomness in the data collected, which may be described by a point estimate with a distribution around them

**Supplier induced demand:** When people providing (supplying) a good or service have more extensive knowledge and are in a position to influence the level of service use

**Technical efficiency:** The decision has already been made that an intervention is worthwhile, but the best way of providing the good or service must be informed by the costs and benefits relative to other ways of providing that good or service

**Tertiary care:** Care offered by specialist or teaching hospitals

**Theory of the consumer:** An economic theory used to explain the behaviour of consumers involved in making decisions about which goods or services to use (buy) by aiming to maximise utility

**Theory of the firm:** An economic theory used to explain the behaviour of companies involved in the production of goods or services (firms) that aim to maximise profits

**Time horizon:** The length of time relating to the start and endpoint of an evaluation or study

**Utility:** A measure of the extent of satisfaction with a good or service

**Variable cost:** A cost that changes in proportion to the amount of a good or service produced

**Willingness to pay (see Contingent valuation):** A measure of the monetary benefit attached to a good or service. The use of a survey to find the maximum a person is prepared to pay for a good or service that has been described using a hypothetical (imaginary) scenario

# Index

Italicised entries refer to figures, tables or worked examples.